180 DAYS™ of Reading for Eighth Grade

Unit 4
WEEK 3
DAY
4–5

Name: ______________________ Date: ______________

As You Read

Circle the reasons rainforests are important to Earth. Then, underline the evidence provided to support those reasons.

Why Rainforests Matter

Rainforests are diverse forests that conjure up awe for most visitors. While they are beautiful and inspiring, rainforests also serve a vital purpose in taking care of our well-being and our planet. Keeping rainforests whole and healthy is crucial.

Rainforests may only cover a small percent of Earth's surface, but they produce about 20 percent of our planet's oxygen. These forests can also take in and store large amounts of carbon dioxide due to the large number of green plants in rainforests. They absorb carbon dioxide and produce oxygen through photosynthesis. Some people have called rainforests Earth's "thermostat" or "lungs."

Earth's water cycle also relies on rainforests. Rainforests generate a huge amount of moisture. Much of this water is added back to the atmosphere. This rain then falls across the planet. Moisture that builds in the Amazon Rainforest might later turn into rainfall over Texas. In fact, more than half of the rain that falls on rainforests returns to the atmosphere. Rainforests have a far-ranging impact when it comes to our planet's water cycle.

Humans also depend on rainforests for many products. These products help healthier lives. Some rainforest plants produce medicines that treat diseases. ... of our medicines come from tropical forest plants! For instance, more tha... ...nts that treat cancer only grow in rainforests. From asthma to malaria, ...eat many illnesses.

Rainforests also provide many people and animals with food needed for su... Different fruits and nuts all come from rainforests. Some Indigenous commun... built their homes within rainforests, too. They rely on the forests for food, sh... medicine.

Rainforests around the world are being cut down so the land can be used ... Around 14 percent of Earth's surface was once covered in rainfore... has shrunk to just 6 percent. Humans cut down rainforests to make... This has led to the extinction of many rainforest species. ... is a pressing topic that was discussed at a climate change conf... ...tries pledged to stop deforestation by 2030. Leaders from th... value of keeping rainforests safe.

...em of a rainforest is diverse, but all living things there are interconn... ...d animals rely on one another to survive. As we have seen, humans ...ainforests. Rainforests make a difference and help sustain our glob...

Authors

Monika Davies

Michelle Wertman, M.S.Ed.

Program Credits

Corinne Burton, M.A.Ed., *President* and *Publisher*
Emily R. Smith, M.A.Ed., *SVP of Content Development*
Véronique Bos, *VP of Creative*
Lynette Ordoñez, *Content Manager*
Melissa Laughlin, *Editor*
David Slayton, *Assistant Editor*
Jill Malcolm, *Series Graphic Designer*

Image Credits: p.32 (top) Alamy/Alpha Historical; p.32 (bottom) Alamy/Album (bottom); p.47 iStock/hocus-focus; p. 74 Library of Congress [LC-GLB23-0287 DLC; p.76 Associated Press; p.95 (top) Getty Images/Chris Farina/Corbis; p.95 (middle) Getty Images/Malcolm Clark / Stringe; p.113 Library of Congress Master Music Encyclopedia 200033481; p.114 iStock/traveler1116; p.120 Shutterstock/Shahjehan; p.121 Shutterstock/Aija Lehtonen; p.122 Shutterstock/Snehal Jeevan Pailkar; p.131 Shutterstock/ComposedPix; p.132 Shutterstock/ComposedPix; p.158 iStock/Tirthankar Das; p.167 (bottom left) iStock/Roberto Galan; p.176 Associated Press; all other images from Shutterstock and/or iStock.

Standards

A division of Teacher Created Materials
5482 Argosy Avenue
Huntington Beach, CA 92649
www.tcmpub.com/shell-education
ISBN 979-8-7659-2263-7

Printed by: **418**
Printed in: **USA**
PO#: **PO13886**

Table of Contents

Introduction

The Need for Practice

To be successful in today's reading classroom, students must deeply understand both concepts and procedures so that they can discuss and demonstrate their understanding. Demonstrating understanding is a process that must be continually practiced for students to be successful. According to Robert Marzano, "Practice has always been, and always will be, a necessary ingredient to learning procedural knowledge at a level at which students execute it independently" (2010, 83). Practice is especially important to help students apply reading comprehension strategies and word-study skills. *180 Days of Reading* offers teachers and parents a full page of reading comprehension and word recognition practice activities for each day of the school year.

The Science of Reading

For some people, reading comes easily. They barely remember how it happened. For others, learning to read takes more effort.

The goal of reading research is to understand the differences in how people learn to read and find the best ways to help all students learn. The term *Science of Reading* is commonly used to refer to this body of research. It helps people understand how to provide instruction in learning the code of the English language, how to develop fluency, and how to navigate challenging text and make sense of it.

Much of this research has been around for decades. In fact, in the late 1990s, Congress commissioned a review of the reading research. In 2000, the National Reading Panel (NRP) published a report that became the backbone of the Science of Reading. The NRP report highlights five components of effective reading instruction. These include the following:

- **Phonemic Awareness:** understanding and manipulating individual speech sounds
- **Phonics:** matching sounds to letters for use in reading and spelling
- **Fluency:** reading connected text accurately and smoothly
- **Vocabulary:** knowing the meanings of words in speech and in print
- **Reading Comprehension:** understanding what is read

There are two commonly referenced frameworks that build on reading research and provide a visual way for people to understand what is needed to learn to read. In the mid-1980s, a framework called the Simple View of Reading was introduced (Gough and Tunmer 1986). It shows that reading comprehension is possible when students are able to decode (or read) the words and have the language to understand the words.

The Simple View of Reading

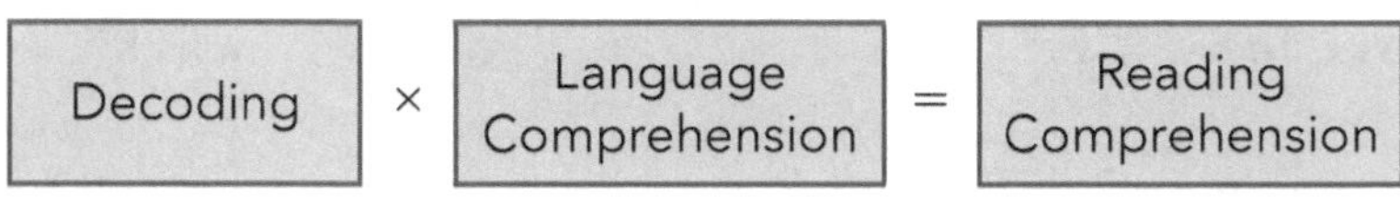

Another framework that builds on the research behind the Science of Reading is Scarborough's Reading Rope (Scarborough 2001). It shows specific skills needed for both language comprehension and word recognition. The "strands" of the rope for language comprehension include having background content knowledge, knowing vocabulary, understanding language structure, having verbal reasoning, and understanding literacy. Word recognition includes phonological awareness, decoding skills, and sight recognition of familiar words (Scarborough 2001). As individual skills are strengthened and practiced, they become increasingly strategic and automatic to promote reading comprehension.

The Science of Reading *(cont.)*

Many parts of our understanding of how people learn to read stand the test of time and have been confirmed by more recent studies. However, new research continues to add to the understanding of reading. Some of this research shows the importance of wide reading (reading about a variety of topics), motivation, and self-regulation. The conversation will never be over, as new research will continue to refine the understanding of how people learn to read. There is always more to learn!

180 Days of Reading has been informed by this reading research. This series provides opportunities for students to practice the skills that years of research indicate contribute to reading growth. There are several features in this book that are supported by the Science of Reading.

Text Selection

- Carefully chosen texts offer experiences in a **wide range of text types**. Each unit includes nonfiction, fiction, and a nontraditional text type or genre (e.g., letters, newspaper articles, advertisements, menus).
- Texts intentionally build upon one another to help students **build background knowledge** from day to day.
- Engaging with texts on the same topic for a thematic unit enables students to become familiar with related **vocabulary**, **language structure**, and **literacy knowledge**. This allows reading to become increasingly strategic and automatic, leading to better **fluency** and **comprehension**.

Activity Design

- Specific **language comprehension** and **word-recognition skills** are reinforced throughout the activities.
- Each text includes a purpose for reading and an opportunity to practice various reading strategies through annotation. This promotes **Close-Reading** of the text.
- Paired fiction and nonfiction texts are used to promote **comparison** and encourage students to **make connections** between texts within a unit.
- Students **write to demonstrate understanding** of the texts. Students provide written responses in a variety of forms, including short answers, open-ended responses, and creating their own versions of nontraditional texts.

This book provides the regular practice of reading skills that students need as they develop into excellent readers.

How to Use This Resource

Unit Structure Overview

This resource is organized into twelve units. Each three-week unit follows a consistent format for ease of use.

Week 1: Nonfiction

Day 1	Students read nonfiction and answer multiple-choice questions.
Day 2	Students read nonfiction and answer multiple-choice questions.
Day 3	Students read nonfiction and answer multiple-choice, short-answer, and open-response questions.
Day 4	Students read a longer nonfictional text, answer multiple-choice questions, and complete graphic organizers.
Day 5	Students reread the text from Day 4 and answer reading-response questions.

Week 2: Fiction

Day 1	Students read fiction and answer multiple-choice questions.
Day 2	Students read fiction and answer multiple-choice questions.
Day 3	Students read fiction and answer multiple-choice, short-answer, and open-response questions.
Day 4	Students read a longer fictional text, answer multiple-choice questions, and complete graphic organizers.
Day 5	Students reread the text from Day 4 and answer reading-response questions.

Week 3: Nontraditional Text

Day 1	Students read nontraditional text and answer multiple-choice and open-response questions.
Day 2	Students complete close-reading activities with paired texts from the unit.
Day 3	Students complete close-reading activities with paired texts from the unit.
Day 4	Students create their own nontraditional texts.
Day 5	Students write their own versions of the nontraditional text from Day 1.

How to Use This Resource *(cont.)*

Unit Structure Overview *(cont.)*

Paired Texts

State standards have brought into focus the importance of preparing students for college and career success by expanding their critical-thinking and analytical skills. It is no longer enough for students to read and comprehend a single text on a topic. Rather, the integration of ideas across texts is crucial for a more comprehensive understanding of themes presented by authors.

Literacy specialist Jennifer Soalt has written that paired texts are "uniquely suited to scaffolding and extending students' comprehension" (2005, 680). She identifies three ways in which paired fiction and nonfiction are particularly effective in increasing comprehension: the building of background knowledge, the development of vocabulary, and the increase in student motivation (Soalt 2005).

Each three-week unit in *180 Days of Reading* is connected by a common theme or topic. Packets of each week's or each unit's practice pages can be prepared for students.

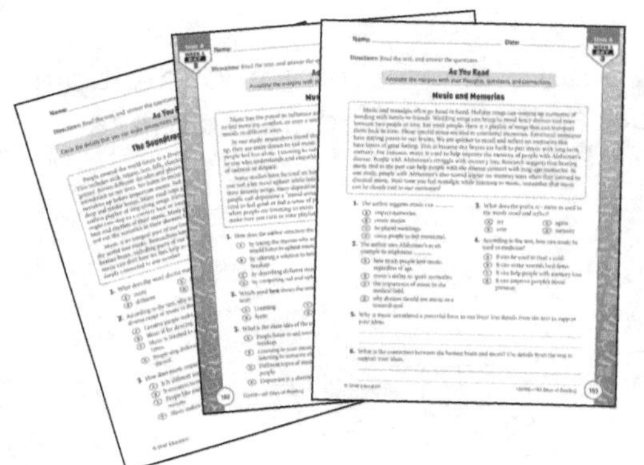

During Week 1, students read nonfictional texts and answer questions.

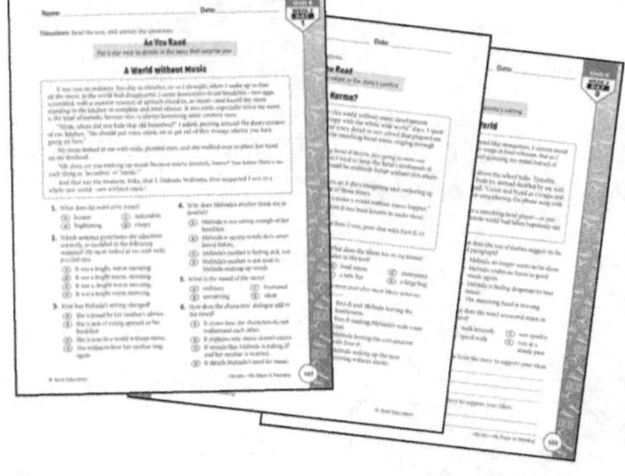

During Week 2, students read fictional texts and answer questions.

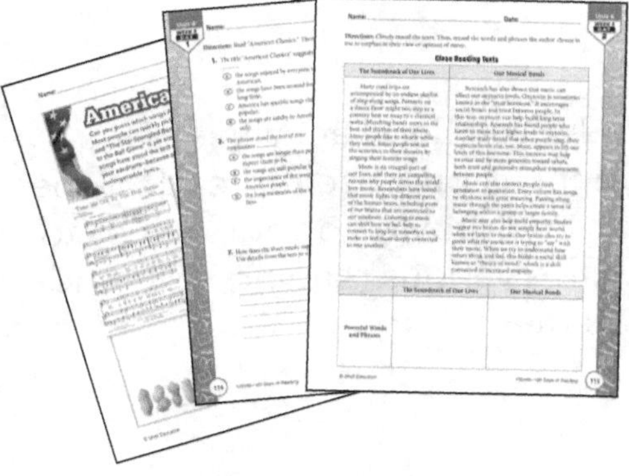

During Week 3, students read nontraditional texts (advertisements, poems, letters, etc.), answer questions, and complete close-reading and writing activities.

How to Use This Resource *(cont.)*

Student Practice Pages

Practice pages reinforce grade-level skills across a variety of reading concepts for each day of the school year. Each day's reading activity is provided as a full practice page, making them easy to prepare and implement as part of a morning routine, at the beginning of each reading lesson, or as homework.

Practice Pages for Weeks 1 and 2

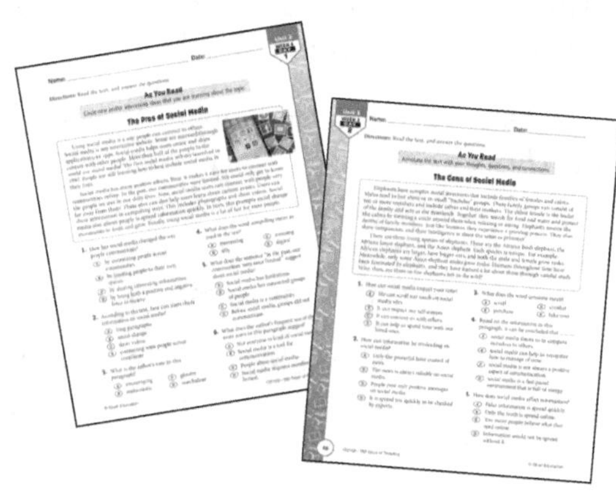

Days 1 and 2 of each week follow a consistent format, with a short text passage and multiple-choice questions.

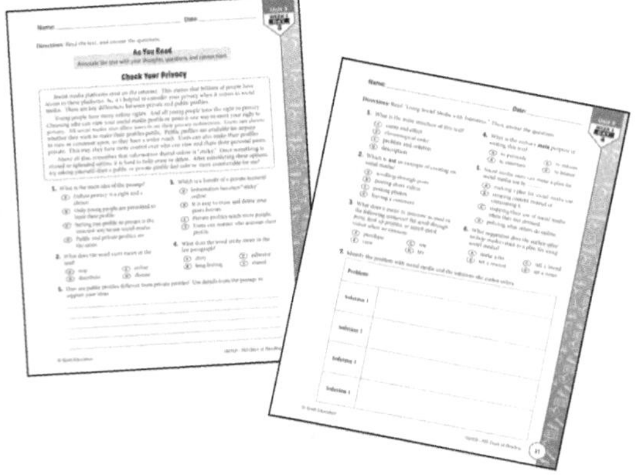

Days 3 and 4 have a combination of multiple-choice, short-answer, and open-response questions.

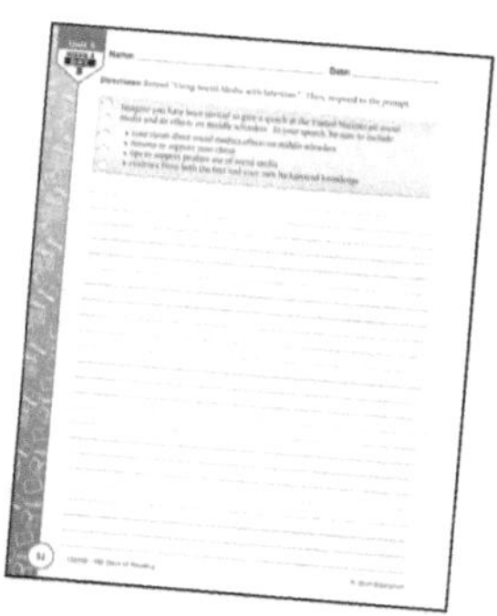

On day 5, students complete text-based writing prompts.

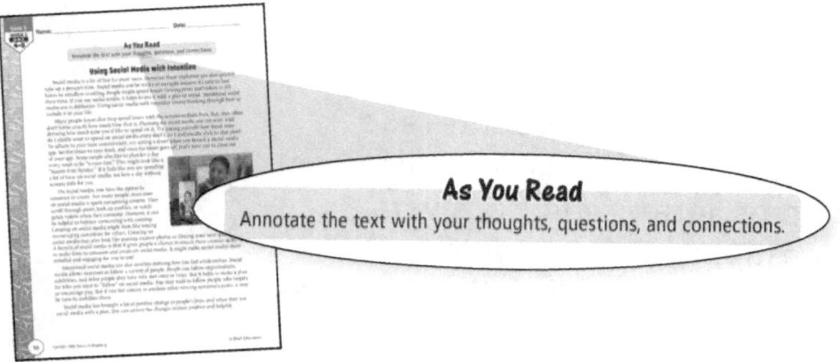

The As You Read activities give students a purpose for reading the texts and provide opportunities to practice various reading skills and strategies.

How to Use This Resource *(cont.)*

Student Practice Pages *(cont.)*

Practice Pages for Week 3

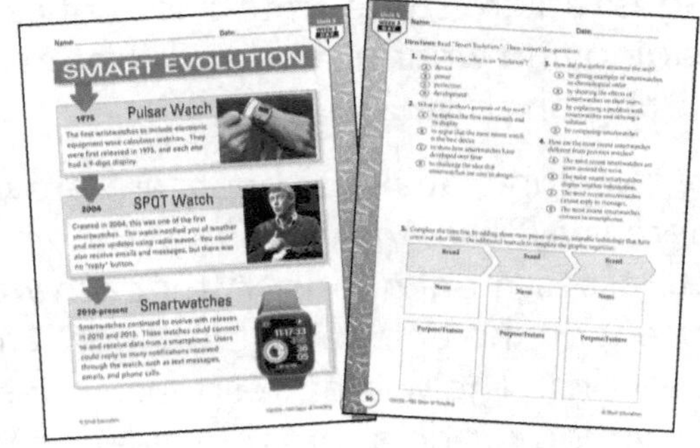

Day 1 of this week follows a consistent format, with a nontraditional text and multiple-choice and open-response questions.

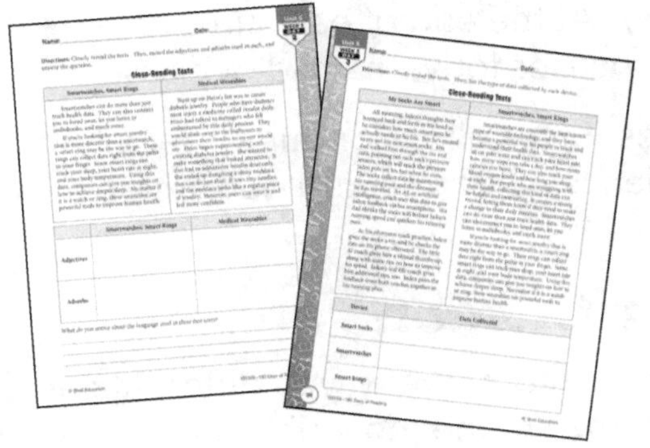

On days 2 and 3, students engage in close-reading activities of paired texts. Students are encouraged to compare and contrast different aspects of the texts they read throughout the unit.

On days 4 and 5, students think about the texts in the unit, respond to a writing prompt, and construct their own versions of diverse texts. Students are encouraged to use information from texts throughout the unit to inspire and support their writing.

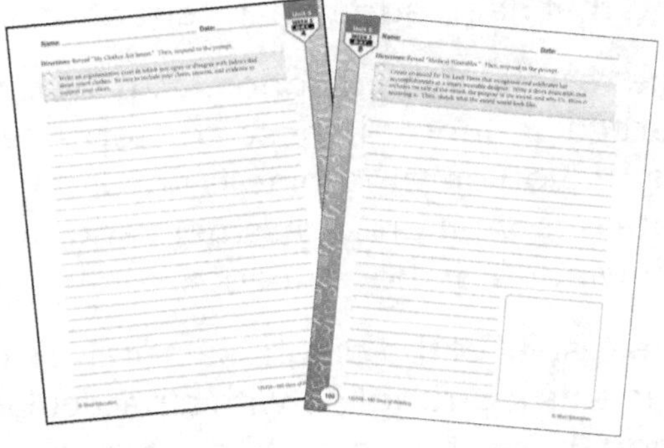

Instructional Options

180 Days of Reading is a flexible resource that can be used in various instructional settings for different purposes.

- Use these student pages as daily warm-up activities or as review.
- Work with students in small groups, allowing them to focus on specific skills. This setting also lends itself to partner and group discussions about the texts.
- Student pages in this resource can be completed independently during center times and as activities for early finishers.

How to Use This Resource *(cont.)*

Diagnostic Assessment

The practice pages in this book can be used as diagnostic assessments. These activity pages require students to think critically, respond to text-dependent questions, and utilize reading and writing skills and strategies. (An answer key for the practice pages is provided starting on page 230.)

For each unit, analysis sheets are provided as *Microsoft Word®* files in the digital resources. There is a *Class Analysis Sheet* and an *Individual Analysis Sheet*. Use the file that matches your assessment needs. After each week, record how many answers each student got correct on the unit's analysis sheet. Only record the answers for the multiple-choice questions. The written-response questions and graphic organizers can be evaluated using the writing rubric or other evaluation tools (see below). At the end of each unit, analyze the data on the analysis sheet to determine instructional focuses for your child or class.

The diagnostic analysis tools included in the digital resources allow for quick evaluation and ongoing monitoring of student work. See at a glance which reading genre students may need to focus on further to develop proficiency.

Using the Results to Differentiate Instruction

Once results are gathered and analyzed, use the data to inform the way to differentiate instruction. The data can help determine which concepts are the most difficult for students and that need additional instructional support and continued practice.

The results of the diagnostic analysis may show that an entire class is struggling with a particular genre. If these concepts have been taught in the past, this indicates that further instruction or reteaching is necessary. If these concepts have not been taught yet, this data is a great preassessment and demonstrates that students do not have a working knowledge of the concepts.

The results of the diagnostic analysis may also show that an individual or small group of students is struggling with a particular concept or group of concepts. Consider pulling aside these students while others are working independently to instruct further on the concept(s). You can also use the results to help identify individuals or groups of proficient students who are ready for enrichment or above-grade-level instruction. These students may benefit from independent learning contracts or more challenging activities.

Writing Rubric

A rubric for written responses is provided on page 229. Display the rubric for students to reference as they write. Score students' written responses, and provide them with feedback on their writing.

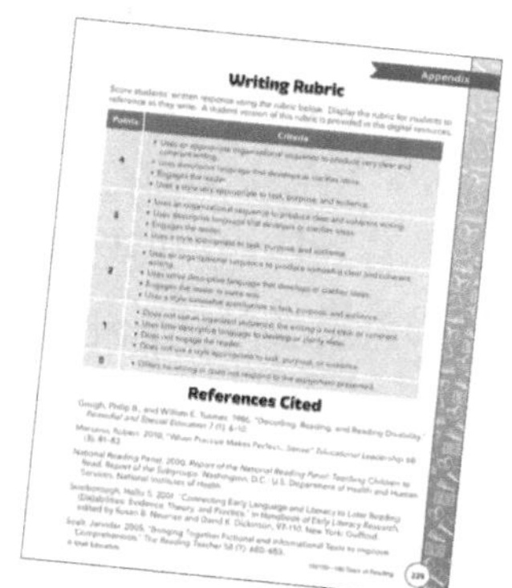

Name: ______________________________ Date: ________________

Directions: Read the text, and answer the questions.

As You Read

Underline information that is new or interesting to you. Take notes in the margins to show your thinking.

The History of Pizza

For many Americans, pizza ranks as one of their favorite meals. Pizza has a history that stretches far back in time. The first pizzas were simple flatbreads with toppings. Ancient Egyptians, Romans, and Greeks all ate similar kinds of pizzas. However, pizza as we now know and love it was first baked in Naples, Italy.

In the early 1800s, Naples was a bustling waterfront city. Many people had little money to spend on food. So, they needed cheap meals that were quick to eat. Pizza became a go-to meal for the people of Naples when street vendors started selling flatbreads with toppings. These first pizzas had toppings including tomatoes, oil, and cheese.

Some legends say that in 1889, Italy's Queen Margherita came through Naples. She was tired of eating French food everywhere she traveled, which was popular at the time. So, she opted to switch her daily menu to include pizzas. Her favorite pizza had a distinct color scheme: white cheese, red tomatoes, and green basil. Legends say from that point on, it was called the *pizza margherita*. This type of pizza remains popular today!

1. What is the central idea of this passage?

- (A) Pizza has been loved by all types of people throughout history.
- (B) Pizza first started in Naples to feed diverse population.
- (C) The margherita pizza was named after a queen who was fond of it.
- (D) There are many types of pizzas to enjoy.

2. Which detail **best** supports the central idea of this text?

- (A) Pizza was a cheap meal for the people of Naples.
- (B) Queen Margherita of Italy loved the pizza of Naples.
- (C) In the 1800s, Naples was a bustling waterfront city.
- (D) Pizza recipes have not changed over time.

3. What does the word *bustling* mean in the text?

- (A) tranquil
- (B) active
- (C) coastal
- (D) lifting

4. What role does the second paragraph play in this passage?

- (A) It describes the different types of pizza that can be found in Italy.
- (B) It describes a legend of how pizza margherita go its name.
- (C) It explains how pizza first became popular in Naples, Italy.
- (D) It introduces pizza as a food eaten long ago, in some form or another.

5. What does the word *distinct* mean in the text?

- (A) colorful
- (B) favorite
- (C) bright
- (D) noticeable

Name: ______________________________ Date: ______________

Directions: Read the text, and answer the questions.

As You Read

Underline information that is new or interesting to you. Take notes in the margins to show your thinking.

Arrival in America

Picture this: it was the turn of the 20th century. Millions of people immigrated to the United States. A huge number of people came from Italy. Many people hailed from the city of Naples. Lots of these people brought recipes for pizza. For years, pizza stayed in Italian communities in the United States. Pizza was first served as a snack for Italians. However, after World War II, pizza's popularity began to soar.

During the war, some American troops spent time in Naples. There, they sampled delicious Italian foods. This included pizza! After returning home, soldiers wanted to keep eating their favorite Italian meals. The idea of pizza spread rapidly after that. Soon, people across the country loved it.

After the war, the American fast-food industry began to grow. Pizza quickly became a classic fast-food item because it was cheap and quick to make. Around this time, the frozen pizza was also invented. People wanted meals they could pop in the oven and quickly bake. Frozen pizzas fit that need. Throughout time, pizza has remained a top meal choice in the United States for many people.

1. What does the word *hailed* mean in the first paragraph?

- (A) lived
- (B) came
- (C) rained
- (D) changed

2. What does the phrase *began to soar* tell readers about pizza's popularity?

- (A) More Italian Americans ate pizza.
- (B) Fewer Italian Americans loved pizza.
- (C) It changed the way people saw pizza.
- (D) It stretched beyond Italian culture.

3. Which line from the passage best supports the central idea?

- (A) Many people hailed from the city of Naples.
- (B) However, after World War II, pizza's popularity began to soar.
- (C) There, they sampled delicious Italian foods.
- (D) The frozen pizza was also invented.

4. Pizza first became popular in the United States because _______.

- (A) Italian Americans started sharing their recipes and opening pizzerias
- (B) American soldiers started eating it after returning from Naples
- (C) Americans wanted something cheap and easy to make
- (D) Businesses could make frozen pizzas easily

5. Which detail **best** reflects the author's point of view of pizza in America?

- (A) Italian Americans brought pizza recipes from Italy.
- (B) Pizza was loved by many American soldiers.
- (C) Pizza quickly became a popular fast-food item.
- (D) They sampled delicious Italian foods.

Name: ______________________ Date: ______________

Directions: Read the text, and answer the questions.

As You Read

Underline information that is new or interesting to you. Take notes in the margins to show your thinking.

Pepperoni Power

A medley of toppings can be put onto a pizza. Pineapple can be added for a hint of sweetness. Some people prefer meat-only toppings. Other people like to add vegetables, including bell peppers or mushrooms. But one topping that you may encounter the most is pepperoni. Pepperoni is an iconic pizza topping. In fact, it is the most popular pizza topping in the United States. But what exactly is it?

Pepperoni can be made from ground pork or ground beef. Sometimes, the pork and beef are combined. Pepperoni makers take the meat and add a few more ingredients to spice things up. Paprika is the first addition. This red spice colors the meat and gives it a spicy flavor. Garlic and fennel seeds are often mixed into the meat, too. These seasonings give pepperoni its warm, complex flavor.

Pepperoni was first made in the United States. Some early Italian American butchers wanted to make a dried salami with dried chilies. However, ingredients in the United States differed from those in Italy. Historians think that butchers used paprika instead of chilies. And with that change, pepperoni was born!

1. What does the word *medley* mean as used in the following sentence? *A medley of toppings can be put onto a pizza.*
   - (A) layers
   - (B) interference
   - (C) variety
   - (D) song

2. How is pepperoni different from other Italian meats?
   - (A) Italian butchers wanted to make a mild, spicy meat.
   - (B) Pork and beef are combined.
   - (C) Pepperoni is made with chiles.
   - (D) Pepperoni is made with paprika.

3. Where does the spicy flavor of pepperoni come from?
   - (A) mushrooms
   - (B) paprika
   - (C) salt
   - (D) fennel seeds

4. Which detail supports the author's claim that pepperoni is an iconic pizza topping?
   - (A) Pepperoni is a different type of Italian meat.
   - (B) Pepperoni is the most popular pizza topping in the United States.
   - (C) Pepperoni is made with paprika.
   - (D) Pepperoni is not actually from Italy.

5. How did American ingredients affect the pepperoni we enjoy today? Use details from the passage to support your ideas.

____

____

____

____

Name: ______________________________ Date: ______________

As You Read

Underline information that is new or interesting to you.
Take notes in the margins to show your thinking.

Pizza Styles in the United States

There are countless ways to make pizza. Certain toppings and flavors are staples across the United States, such as pepperoni. But pizza looks (and tastes!) different across the country. Many cities or regions have their own styles of pizza.

New York-style pizza

In New York City, pizza lovers are likely looking for their New York–style pies. These pizza slices have a thin crust. Mozzarella cheese forms a thick layer on top. New York–style pizzas are massive in size, usually covering a pan that's 18 inches (46 centimeters) or more. Most of the time, one can grab the whole pie or simply a slice. People often eat these giant slices by folding them in half.

deep-dish pizza

In Chicago, two styles of pizza top the charts. The deep-dish pizza is perhaps the best-known outside the city. Deep-dish pizza looks like a pie, and it has a thick, pastry-like crust. Cheese coats the bottom, while toppings are generously added on top. Crushed tomato is the final layer on this distinct pie. It takes about 30 minutes for a deep-dish pizza to emerge from the oven fully cooked! Chicago's pizza spots also serve a tavern-style pizza. This pizza is prepared with dough that has been rolled out. Once baked, the crust is crispy and wafer-thin. Sauce and cheese are spread over top. Most distinctly, tavern-style pizza is cut into a grid. Some of the pieces are rectangular, while some of the crust pieces end up looking like triangles!

California-style pizza

In the early 1980s, a few California chefs reimagined pizza. Their creativity led to California-style pizza, which is rooted in fresh, healthy ingredients. This style of thin-crust pizza is known for its untraditional nature. California-style pizza usually features toppings that are in season, such as fresh vegetables and other unconventional ingredients, such as goat cheese and peanut sauce.

Detroit-style pizza

Detroit-style pizza has a unique backstory. It emerged when a Detroit cook used steel trays from an auto factory to bake his pizzas. Detroit-style involves a deep-dish pizza with a thick crust. Huge amounts of cheese are layered on top. In the oven, the cheese crisps and burns slightly around the edges. This gives it a charred flavor. A Detroit-style pizza must be baked in an oily steel pan, or it's not "Detroit-style."

Across the United States, chefs have reimagined what makes a pizza. The styles of pizza are as varied as the cities that love this comfort food. Pizza might taste and look different from city to city, but there's one thing most people can agree upon: pizza is delicious!

Name: ______________________________ Date: ______________

Directions: Read "Pizza Styles in the United States." Then, answer the questions.

1. Which sentence best summarizes the author's perspective on American pizza?

Ⓐ Certain toppings and flavors are staples across the United States, such as pepperoni.

Ⓑ Their creativity led to California-style pizza, which is rooted in fresh, healthy ingredients.

Ⓒ Detroit-style pizza has a unique backstory.

Ⓓ The styles of pizza are as varied as the cities that love this comfort food.

2. What does the word *distinctly* mean in the following sentence? *Most distinctly, tavern-style pizza is cut into a grid.*

Ⓐ likely
Ⓑ noticeably
Ⓒ deliciously
Ⓓ crispy

3. What does the phrase *in season* mean in the fourth paragraph?

Ⓐ creative
Ⓑ popular
Ⓒ fashionable
Ⓓ freshly grown

4. Which style of pizza is most similar to Detroit-style pizza?

Ⓐ California-style pizza
Ⓑ deep-dish pizza
Ⓒ tavern-style pizza
Ⓓ New York-style pizza

5. How does the author organize the paragraphs?

Ⓐ by describing different types of American pizza styles

Ⓑ by comparing American pizza to other pizzas in the world

Ⓒ by detailing the problem with pizza and offering a solution

Ⓓ by explaining the effects of pizza on different American cities

6. Compare and contrast the different pizza styles discussed in the passage.

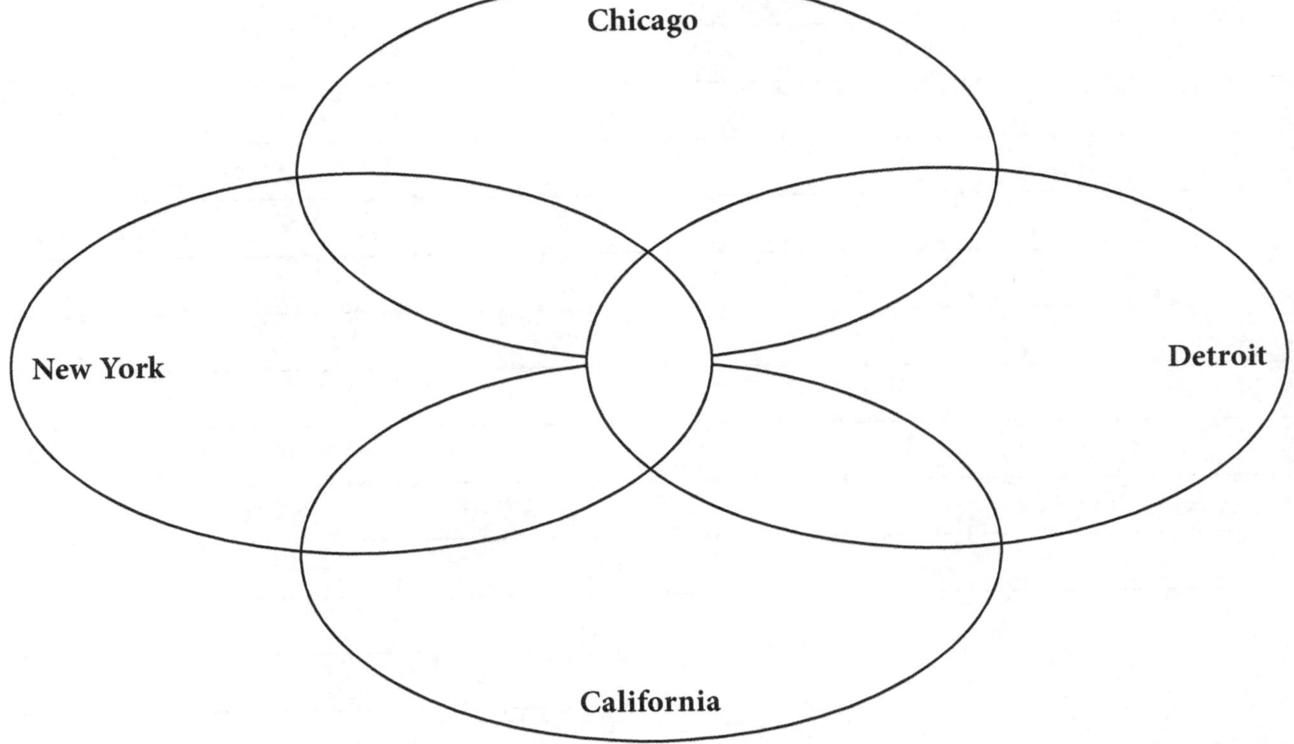

Name: ______________________ Date: ______________

Directions: Reread "Pizza Styles in the United States." Then, respond to the prompt.

Choose your favorite pizza style from the passage. Write a letter to a friend explaining why this style is so perfect. Include a claim and at least two reasons to support your claim. Include details from the text to support why the style you chose sounds the best.

Name: ______________________________ Date: ____________________

Directions: Read the text, and answer the questions.

As You Read

Pay close attention to what characters think, say, and do. Annotate their thoughts, words, and actions.

Cooking: A Family History

Ever since I was little, I've been terrified of my family's kitchen. I ought to admit that our family kitchen is not a scary place. In fact, it's the prettiest room of our house! Our kitchen has blue walls and white diamond tiles lining the backsplash. My grandmother, Nonna, always says that our kitchen is the beating heart of our home. And, my grandfather, Ojiisan, is always there, measuring and mixing ingredients.

For as long as I can remember, I've steered clear of cooking in our kitchen. My family thinks it's because I hate cooking. But it's actually because everyone in my family is an incredible cook. Nonna makes the best spaghetti on the west side of town. Ojiisan is a master at cooking *okonomiyaki*, a savory pancake. My brother makes a delicious grilled cheese. But I can't even toast bread without burning it!

Every generation of my family loves cooking in the kitchen—except me. But then Nonna corners me on a Friday afternoon after my basketball practice, and everything changes.

1. Why does the narrator say she's *steered clear of cooking* in the family kitchen?

- (A) She loves her Nonna's cooking.
- (B) Her grandmother told her she is a bad cook.
- (C) She cannot cook as well as her family.
- (D) She burnt a piece of toast.

2. What does the word *cornered* mean in the text?

- (A) yelled at
- (B) angled
- (C) pushed
- (D) confronted

3. What does the phrase the *beating heart of our home* reveal about the kitchen?

- (A) It is where the family comes together.
- (B) It is seldom used.
- (C) It is the place that makes the narrator sad.
- (D) It is the place with the loudest sounds.

4. The description of the narrator's grandfather as "always measuring and mixing ingredients" suggests ______.

- (A) he loves to cook
- (B) he is not a good cook
- (C) he wants to learn Italian recipes
- (D) is too busy to cook

5. Which detail would be most important to include in a summary of the story?

- (A) The narrator is afraid of her family kitchen.
- (B) The kitchen is a pretty room.
- (C) The narrator cannot even cook toast.
- (D) The narrator's grandfather cooks delicious pancakes.

Name: ______________________________ Date: ________________

Directions: Read the text, and answer the questions.

As You Read

Pay close attention to what characters think, say, and do. Annotate their thoughts, words, and actions.

Ready to Cook?

Nonna has always tried to coax me into the kitchen, and every year or so, she attempts to get me to chop, mix, or experiment with a recipe. But I know I will never be a talented cook like her, so I have always found a way to dodge kitchen duty. My personal policy is that I will happily set the table and delightfully eat the food in front of me. But I need to be kept far, far away from the stove and any measuring spoon.

However, Nonna is having none of my excuses today. She pulls me into the kitchen while I am still wiping sweat from my forehead from practice.

"Today, we are baking a pizza!" she says.

I try to refuse, telling her that I will just make a mess and create something inedible.

"Giulia," Nonna says, "it is okay to make mistakes in the kitchen. Our mistakes help us cook better next time. And you will have me, your very dear Nonna, beside you. Trust me, pizza is easy!"

Nonna points to the kitchen counter, and I can see she's already laid out measuring bowls and cups. She's ready for us to cook—and there is no turning back.

1. Which word is a good synonym for *delightfully*?

- (A) stubbornly
- (B) unfortunately
- (C) cheerfully
- (D) nearly

2. What is Nonna's opinion of Giulia?

- (A) Giulia just needs the opportunity to practice and make mistakes in the kitchen.
- (B) Giulia will only be a good cook if Nonna teaches her.
- (C) Giulia cares too much about basketball and needs to learn to take care of her family.
- (D) Giulia is a great cook and is pretending so she doesn't have to do chores.

3. How do Nonna's actions and words affect Giulia?

- (A) Giulia appreciates her grandmother's attention.
- (B) Giulia feels angry at her grandmother for forcing her to cook.
- (C) Giulia is able to go back to playing basketball.
- (D) Giulia learns she cannot avoid cooking with Nonna.

4. What is the theme of this passage?

- (A) Family will always be there for you.
- (B) Listen to your elders—they know best.
- (C) It is important to not give up.
- (D) Excuses will not prevent you from being responsible.

Name: ______________________ Date: ______________

Directions: Read the text, and answer the questions.

As You Read

Pay close attention to what characters think, say, and do. Annotate when a character is beginning to change.

Crust, Sauce, Cheese

"I'm going to let you know a small secret," Nonna says. "You only need three things for a good pizza: crust, sauce, and cheese."

She pauses for a brief moment, her brow furrowing. "Well, and yes, adding lots of toppings helps, too."

"You also need a good chef to start with," I say, doubting myself. Nonna shakes her head at me and rubs my cheek with a firm hand.

"Giulia, I know how much you love eating pizza, and I promise you, when you make this food you love, you will feel more connected to your Italian roots!"

I look at Nonna, and I notice that her hands are growing more wrinkled and that her shoulders stoop a bit more than they used to. But even though she's getting older, Nonna has a confidence and ease in the kitchen that I've always deeply admired. I remember something my mom told me long ago: My grandparents would not be here forever, and I should always make time for them. Nonna wants to share her family's pizza recipe with me, and I can feel how important this is for her. I think to myself, *I can try cooking a pizza—for Nonna.*

1. Why does Giulia make pizza with Nonna?

- (A) Giulia knows that Nonna is not asking her but demanding.
- (B) Giulia feels that playing basketball is making Nonna jealous.
- (C) Giulia has been missing her grandmother's company.
- (D) Giulia realizes this is an opportunity she may not always have.

2. Why does the author italicize some words in the last sentence?

- (A) to show the narrator is speaking out loud to Nonna
- (B) to show that the narrator is speaking inside her head
- (C) to show the narrator's actions
- (D) to emphasize how much the narrator has changed

3. What is a theme revealed in this passage? Use details from the story to support your ideas.

____

____

4. How has Giulia changed since the beginning of the story? Use details from the story to support your ideas.

____

____

____

Name: ______________________________ Date: ____________________

As You Read

Pay close attention to what characters think, say, and do. Annotate when a character is beginning to change.

Cooking with Nonna

Nonna nudges me and points to a picture of me playing basketball on the fridge.

"See that bold and brave Guilia on the court?" Nonna asks me. "I know she can tackle anything—including this margherita pizza."

I smile back at Nonna, and I am grateful she picked the margherita pizza as our first pizza to cook together. This pizza has always reminded me of the Italian flag with its white, green, and red colors.

First, we begin making our crust together. Nonna coaches me through the process, getting me to slowly add warm water, yeast, and sugar together. The first step is over, and I haven't made a mistake yet, which boosts my confidence. We add a few more ingredients. After letting the dough rest, Nonna places a rolling pin my hand. I shake my head, trying to give it back to her, but she firmly pushes the pin back to me. So, I slowly begin rolling out the dough, but I can't seem to get the dough into a perfect circle. Instead, the dough rolls into an oblong shape, and my stomach starts to coil into knots. My shoulders start tensing up, too, because I want this pizza to be perfect! Just as I'm about to give up in frustration, Nonna claps her hands in delight.

"I love this shape for our margherita pizza," she says. "It gives our pizza such character and pizzazz."

Next, in a large, steel mixing bowl, we pour in canned tomatoes to make the sauce. Nonna shows me how to squish the red pulp of the tomatoes between our fingers, creating a chunky sauce. Then, we spread our tomato sauce along our dough, leaving an inch around the edges of the pie. Nonna places a massive ball of mozzarella cheese into my hands, and she instructs me to tear it into smaller bits. I place the mozzarella chunks onto our pizza, and Nonna coaches me to place more in the center, so the cheese can "spread its wings."

Nonna places our pizza into the oven, and the smell as it cooks is so delightful that it makes my eyes and mouth water. Nonna pulls out the pizza just as the crust starts to turn a darker shade of brown, and Nonna places fresh basil leaves in my hands. I gleefully sprinkle them all over the pizza, and Nonna finishes it off with a smooth swirl of olive oil and a dash of sea salt flakes.

We serve our pizza to our family, and everyone tells me how delicious the pizza is and how happy their stomachs are. As I bite into the first slice of pizza I have ever made, I think of how connected I am to my Italian roots—and how connected I am to my Nonna.

Name: ____________________ Date: ____________

Directions: Read "Cooking with Nonna." Then, answer the questions.

1. Which line from the story best reveals how Nonna views Guilia's cooking?

- Ⓐ "I love this shape for our Margherita pizza," she says. "It gives our pizza such character and pizzazz."
- Ⓑ Nonna shows me how to squish the red pulp of the tomatoes between our fingers.
- Ⓒ Nonna places a massive ball of mozzarella cheese into my hands, and she instructs me to tear it into smaller bits.
- Ⓓ We serve our pizza to our family, and everyone tells me how delicious the pizza is and how happy their stomachs are.

2. Which detail best shows how Giulia's perspective on cooking has changed?

- Ⓐ Margherita pizza reminds Giulia of the Italian flag.
- Ⓑ Nonna wants Giulia to be as confident in the kitchen as she is on the basketball court.
- Ⓒ Giulia feels connected to her Italian roots.
- Ⓓ Giulia's pizza is enjoyed by her whole family.

3. What mood does the phrase *my stomach starts to coil into knots* create in the story?

- Ⓐ exhausted
- Ⓑ optimistic
- Ⓒ gloomy
- Ⓓ uneasy

4. How does the author's use of descriptive details affect the theme?

- Ⓐ They show the differences between different types of pizzas.
- Ⓑ They symbolize the love between Nonna and her granddaughter.
- Ⓒ They describe the step-by-step process of baking a pizza from scratch.
- Ⓓ They highlight the amount of help Giulia needs in the kitchen.

5. What do Guilia and Nonna do right after Guilia rolls out the dough?

- Ⓐ They let the dough rest.
- Ⓑ They put chunks of mozzarella cheese on the pizza.
- Ⓒ They mix ingredients together for the crust.
- Ⓓ They mix ingredients together for the tomato sauce.

6. Compare Giulia playing basketball to Giulia cooking with her Nonna. Use details from the story to support your ideas.

____

____

____

____

____

____

____

____

Name: ______________________________ Date: ______________

Directions: Reread "Cooking with Nonna." Then, respond to the prompt.

Think of a time you had to try something you felt you would not succeed at, but you gave it a try and you *did* succeed. Write a short essay comparing your experience to Giulia's experience. Include how your experience was similar and different. Use details from your own story and from the passages this week.

Name: ______________________________ Date: ________________

SEARCH RECIPES BEVERAGES BREAKFAST DESSERTS MAIN DISHES SIDE DISHES

A Pizza Lover's Guide to the Globe

How is everything in your world this week, fellow pizza lovers? Welcome back to a new weekly installment in my pizza recipe series! This week, I'm tossing you a recipe for the most mouthwatering, chewy, and crispy pizza crust you've ever tasted. It's a hand-me-down from the Italian side of my family. Apparently, we (meaning me, my mom, my grandma, and my ancestors) have been making it for the past century. Pro tip: Shake some Italian seasoning into the dough before you roll it out for an extra kick of flavor!

Iconic Pizza Crust Recipe

All you need are five ingredients to make a chewy, crispy crust for your next pizza!

EQUIPMENT

round pizza pan
large bowl
measuring cups
stand mixer or wooden spoon

INGREDIENTS

- ☐ 1 cup of warm water
- ☐ 1 package of yeast
- ☐ 1 teaspoon of white sugar
- ☐ 2 ½ cups bread flour
- ☐ 2 tablespoons of olive oil
- ☐ 1 teaspoon of salt

DIRECTIONS

1. Preheat your oven to 450 degrees Fahrenheit, and use an oil spray to grease your round pizza pan.
2. Add the warm water to your large bowl. Sprinkle in the yeast and sugar, and mix it all together. Let the mixture sit for about 10 minutes.
3. Next, add the flour, oil, and salt to the yeast mixture. Use a stand mixer or wooden spoon to mix it all together until the texture is smooth.
4. Let the dough rest for about five minutes.
5. Lightly add flour to your countertop. Roll the dough out in a big circle that will fit your pizza pan.
6. Add pizza sauce, cheese, and your favorite toppings to your crust.
7. Bake in the oven for about 15-20 minutes, or until the crust turns brown.
8. Allow your pizza to cool, and then dig in!

REVIEWS

Name: ______________________________ Date: ______________

Directions: Read "Iconic Pizza Crust Recipe." Then, answer the questions.

1. What is the purpose of this recipe?
   - (A) to inform readers of how to prepare a pizza
   - (B) to convince readers to try baking a pizza
   - (C) to persuade readers that pizza is easy to make
   - (D) to entertain readers with a fun story about homemade pizza

2. How is this recipe organized?
   - (A) by showing the effects of quality ingredients
   - (B) by providing a solution for a chewy pizza dough
   - (C) by sequencing the step-by-step directions of baking a pizza
   - (D) by comparing how to create dough to how to assemble a pizza

3. What is **most likely** the author's perspective of this recipe?
   - (A) It is important to spend time cooking at home with family.
   - (B) Everyone should make their own pizza.
   - (C) Pizza should be served with a salad.
   - (D) Pizza dough is easy to prepare at home.

4. Which detail best supports the author's perspective of this recipe?
   - (A) You can roll the dough on your countertop.
   - (B) There are only five ingredients, so it is an easy recipe.
   - (C) A wooden spoon can be used if you do not have a stand mixer.
   - (D) Bake the pizza for 15–20 minutes.

5. What other information could be added to this recipe? Why would these additions be an improvement?

____

____

____

____

____

Name: ______________________________ Date: ________________

Directions: Closely read these excerpts. Study the recipe on page 23. Then, record the structure of each text (e.g., chronological, cause and effect) and evidence that supports your assessment.

Close-Reading Texts

Arrival in America	Pepperoni Power
Picture this: it was the turn of the 20th century. Millions of people immigrated to the United States. A huge number of people came from Italy. Many people hailed from the city of Naples. Lots of these people brought recipes for pizza. For years, pizza stayed in Italian communities in the United States. Pizza was first served as a snack for Italians. However, after World War II, pizza's popularity began to soar. During the war, some American troops spent time in Naples. There, they sampled delicious Italian foods. This included pizza! After returning home, soldiers wanted to keep eating their favorite Italian meals. The idea of pizza spread rapidly after that. Soon, people across the country loved it. After the war, the American fast-food industry began to grow. Pizza quickly became a classic fast-food item because it was cheap and quick to make.	A medley of toppings can be put onto a pizza. Pineapple can be added for a hint of sweetness. Some people prefer meat-only toppings. Other people like to add vegetables, including bell peppers or mushrooms. But one topping that you may encounter the most is pepperoni. Pepperoni is an iconic pizza topping. But what exactly is it? Pepperoni can be made from ground pork or ground beef. Sometimes, the pork and beef are combined. Pepperoni makers take the meat and add a few more ingredients to spice things up. Paprika is the first addition. This red spice colors the meat and gives it a spicy flavor. Garlic and fennel seeds are often mixed into the meat, too. These seasonings give pepperoni its warm, complex flavor.

	Arrival in America	Pepperoni Power	Iconic Pizza Crust Recipe
Text Structure			
Evidence			

Name: ________________________________ Date: ________________

Directions: Closely read the excerpts. Then, explain how each text supports the claim in the chart.

Close-Reading Texts

The History of Pizza	Cooking with Nonna
In the early 1800s, Naples was a bustling waterfront city. Many people had little money to spend on food. So, they needed cheap meals that were quick to eat. Pizza became a go-to meal for the people of Naples when street vendors started selling flatbreads with toppings. These first pizzas had toppings including tomatoes, oil, and cheese. Some legends say that in 1889, Italy's Queen Margherita came through Naples. She was tired of eating French food everywhere she traveled, which was popular at the time. So, she opted to switch her daily menu to include pizzas. Her favorite pizza had a distinct color scheme: white cheese, red tomatoes, and green basil. Legends say from that point on, it was called the *pizza margherita*. This type of pizza remains popular today!	I smile back at Nonna, and I am grateful she picked the Margherita pizza as our first pizza to cook together. This pizza has always reminded me of the Italian flag with its white, green, and red colors. First, we begin making our crust together. Nonna coaches me through the process, getting me to slowly add warm water, yeast, and sugar together. The first step is over, and I haven't made a mistake yet, which boosts my confidence. We add a few more ingredients. After letting the dough rest, Nonna places a rolling pin my hand. I shake my head, trying to give it back to her, but she firmly pushes the pin back to me. So, I slowly begin rolling out the dough, but I can't seem to get the dough into a perfect circle. Instead, the dough rolls into an oblong shape, and my stomach starts to coil into knots. My shoulders start tensing up, too, because I want this pizza to be perfect! Just as I'm about to give up in frustration, Nonna claps her hands in delight.

Claim: Margherita pizza is a simple but delicious pie loved by many.

The History of Pizza	Cooking with Nonna

Name: ______________________________ Date: ______________

Directions: Think about the texts from this unit. Then, respond to the prompt.

Imagine you are being interviewed on a podcast about American food. Write an argument explaining why pizza is an important part of American culture. Include evidence from at least three different texts in the unit.

Name: ______________________________ Date: ______________

Directions: Think about the texts from this unit. Then, respond to the prompt.

Imagine you are creating a new pizza recipe. Your local pizzeria is going to bake and sell your pizza and post about it on their website. Write a description and recipe for your pizza. Make sure to include:

- a paragraph describing your recipe and topping choices
- ingredients
- steps to layering the toppings

Name: ______________________________ Date: ____________________

Directions: Read the text. Then, answer the questions.

As You Read

Annotate important ideas about friendship.

Taylor Swift and Selena Gomez

Life is easier—and a lot more fun—with a friend or two by your side! Taylor Swift and Selena Gomez know this; they have been friends for many years. The two singer-songwriters met in 2008 because of who they were dating at the time. Although both of their relationships did not last, their friendship did! Swift and Gomez became fast friends because they both work in the entertainment industry.

Both Taylor Swift and Selena Gomez are very busy due to their jobs, but over the years, they have always made time for one another. They have celebrated each other's birthdays and attended award shows and industry parties together. Gomez has even put in surprise appearances at a few of Swift's concerts when she is on tour. They both like to lift each other up and celebrate their career successes together.

1. What is the meaning of the phrase *lift each other up* in the last sentence?

- (A) Each person holds the other one in the air.
- (B) Each person makes the other feel more confident.
- (C) Each person says negative things about the other.
- (D) Each person tries to do the same thing as the other.

2. Which detail best captures the central idea of the passage?

- (A) Gomez and Swift met many years ago.
- (B) Both friends work in the entertainment industry.
- (C) Both friends are very busy.
- (D) Gomez and Swift support each other's careers.

3. How does the author develop the idea of Gomez and Swift's friendship?

- (A) by giving examples of how the friends treat each other
- (B) by detailing how the friends met
- (C) by comparing the artists' careers to their friendship
- (D) by describing how the friends feel about their friendship

4. What is the author's perspective of the artists' friendship?

- (A) It is as strong as the average friendship.
- (B) It is hard to make new friends.
- (C) Jealousy harms a friendship.
- (D) Having a similar career creates a strong bond.

5. What is the main purpose of the dashes in the first sentence?

- (A) to clarify the information before it
- (B) to reveal the definition of a phrase
- (C) to show an abrupt change in thought
- (D) to show a change in the narrator

Name: ______________________________ Date: ____________________

Directions: Read the text, and answer the questions.

As You Read

Annotate important ideas about friendship. Circle the similarities between Taylor Swift and Selena Gomez.

Competition and Success

Being in the public spotlight can put a lot of pressure on someone to succeed. In such a competitive industry, it would be easy for either Swift or Gomez to feel jealous or fall out of touch with each other. But the two friends have always had each other's backs. Swift and Gomez stay in regular contact. They have gone through life's ups and downs together. Both of them have weathered public criticism and judgment. Through it all, the two singer-songwriters are endlessly supportive of each other. They publicly state their support and make an effort to promote their friend's work. Long-term friendships that last a lifetime take time, effort, and commitment. Swift once said, "Longevity is something you really can find very precious and rare in friendships." Their friendship indicates a strong connection and close bond that the two will likely share for more years to come.

1. What does the word *indicates* mean in the text?

- (A) points to
- (B) contributes to
- (C) jokes about
- (D) closeness

2. What does the word *criticism* mean in the phrase *public criticism*?

- (A) advice
- (B) ideas
- (C) creativity
- (D) feedback

3. How is the paragraph organized?

- (A) by comparing and contrasting Swift's and Gomez's careers
- (B) by explaining the effects a bad friendship
- (C) by listing detailed steps in chronological order
- (D) by giving examples of the friendship between Swift and Gomez

4. What does the word *weathered* mean as used in the following sentence? *Both have weathered public criticism and judgment.*

- (A) understood
- (B) been through
- (C) cheered up
- (D) stormed

5. Based on the information in this passage, what do you think Taylor Swift's perspective of friendships might be?

- (A) Having common interests is the only way to build a strong friendship.
- (B) True friends always brag about each other.
- (C) It is rare and special when friendships last a long time.
- (D) You can have more than one best friend.

6. Why does the author use quotation marks around the following sentence? *Longevity is something you really can find very precious and rare in friendships.*

- (A) to show that it has informal words or phrases
- (B) to show another character is speaking
- (C) to show it is a direct quote from another person
- (D) to show that something has multiple meanings

Name: ______________________________ Date: ________________

Directions: Read the text, and answer the questions.

As You Read

Make connections to the text, and record your thoughts and ideas in the margins.

C. S. Lewis and J. R. R. Tolkien

What connects two people together in friendship? Sometimes it's common interests. Other times, it's a mutual understanding that comes from overcoming similar challenges. A good friend can often make you laugh, and they are always in your corner. However, they probably will not shy away from giving you tough feedback you might need to hear. There are many famous friendships throughout history, but C. S. Lewis and J. R. R. Tolkien had a friendship that is less well-known.

The two authors shared a lot in common. Both of them wrote series of books that captured the imaginations of people across the world. Lewis wrote the Narnia series, while Tolkien wrote the Lord of the Rings series. The two men also both grew up in England. They taught at Oxford University, which is where they met.

1. What is the purpose of the second paragraph?

- (A) to introduce the idea of and reasons for friendship
- (B) to show examples of Lewis's and Tolkien's common experiences
- (C) to show examples of Lewis's and Tolkien's friendship
- (D) to explain the effects of a strong friendship

2. Which of the following lines from the passage is a compound sentence?

- (A) Both of them wrote series of books that captured the imaginations of people across the world.
- (B) Other times, it's a mutual understanding that comes from overcoming similar challenges.
- (C) They taught at Oxford University, which is where they met.
- (D) A good friend can often make you laugh, and they are always in your corner.

3. What did Tolkien and Lewis have in common? Do you think this was enough to ignite a friendship? Why or why not?

____

____

4. Why do you think the author chose to start the passage with a question? How would you answer that question?

____

____

____

Name: ______________________ Date: ____________

As You Read

Underline reasons why Lewis and Tolkien are friends.

Friendship through the Years

Lewis and Tolkien first met while on the job at Oxford University. The two of them became friends over their interest in Norse mythology. They also bonded over their service in World War I. Lewis and Tolkien found that they could relate to each other's struggles after serving in the war. Their experiences in the war connected them on an emotional level, too. Together, they also enjoyed intellectual debates. Their friendship was built on layers of understanding.

After a few years of friendship, the two of them launched their own literary club. The club was known as "The Inklings." During club hours, the two men lamented how the fantasy genre lacked engaging narratives. The seeds for both Lewis's and Tolkien's future books were planted in these conversations. Both men began writing their first books shortly thereafter. Neither Lewis or Tolkien were confident readers would enjoy—or even read—their books. But the two authors were quick to encourage each other. It's possible the creative worlds of Narnia and Middle-earth would not exist without this friendship between writers.

C. S. Lewis

Although they were once fierce friends, the two men eventually turned into rivals. Lewis initially had more success as a writer. And Tolkien disagreed with some of Lewis's choices in his personal life. Their connection became more about their differences than their similarities. Over time, the two close friends became divided and were living separate lives.

When Lewis died, Tolkien grieved the loss of his friend. He wrote to his daughter, "So far I have felt the normal feelings of a man of my age—like an old tree that is losing all its leaves one by one: this feels like an axe-blow near the roots." His words convey the deep impact that Lewis had on his life.

J. R. R. Tolkien

The story of Lewis and Tolkien's friendship has a bittersweet ending. But while they were friends, the two authors had a profound influence on each other's lives and literary works. While their friendship was complicated, it left its mark on both men.

Name: ______________________________ Date: ____________

Directions: Read "Friendship through the Years." Then, answer the questions.

1. How does the author structure the passage?

- Ⓐ by detailing the writers' childhoods
- Ⓑ by outlining a solution to a difficult friendship
- Ⓒ by explaining the causes and effects of the writers' friendship
- Ⓓ by comparing Tolkien's writing to Lewis's writing

2. Why did World War I affect the men's relationship?

- Ⓐ They had similar experiences as soldiers.
- Ⓑ They debated about writing.
- Ⓒ They read books about the war.
- Ⓓ They taught about the war at Oxford.

3. How does this simile show Tolkien's feelings about the death of his friend? *...like an old tree that is losing all its leaves one by one: this feels like an axe-blow near the roots.*

- Ⓐ It explains how Tolkien felt the loss of his friend slowly.
- Ⓑ It describes Tolkien's own death.
- Ⓒ It illustrates how intensely painful the loss was.
- Ⓓ It shows how much Tolkien regretted their fighting.

4. What **most likely** caused conflict in Tolkien and Lewis's friendship?

- Ⓐ differences in writing styles
- Ⓑ judging each other's life choices
- Ⓒ their experiences in World War I
- Ⓓ the death of Lewis

5. Why does the author use a dash in the following sentence? *Neither Lewis or Tolkien were confident readers would enjoy—or even read—their books.*

- Ⓐ to explain why readers wouldn't enjoy the books
- Ⓑ to emphasize the writers' concerns
- Ⓒ to separate the writers' worries in a list
- Ⓓ to show the opposite of the word *enjoy*

6. How did the writers' friendship affect their writing?

- Ⓐ They were both interested in Norse mythology.
- Ⓑ Tolkien grew jealous of Lewis's success.
- Ⓒ They shared stories of the war together.
- Ⓓ They discussed ideas for their books.

7. Complete a sequence to show the development of Tolkien and Lewis's friendship.

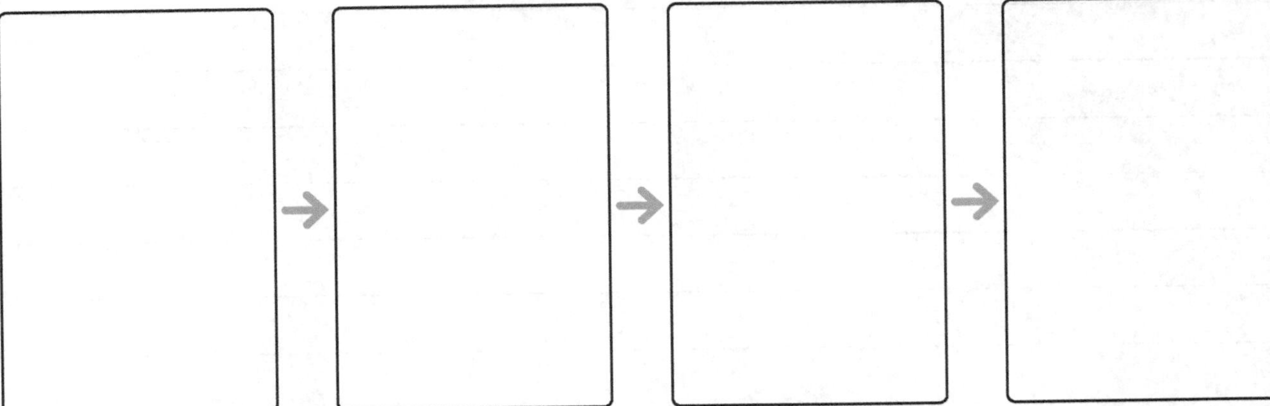

Unit 2
WEEK 1
DAY
5

Name: ____________________ Date: ____________

Directions: Reread "Friendship through the Years." Then, respond to the prompt.

Imagine you are a reporter interviewing C. S. Lewis and J. R. R. Tolkien together. Based on the text, create a list of questions to ask the two authors about their friendship and careers. Under each question, write their respones.

Name: ______________________________ Date: ________________

Directions: Read the text, and answer the questions.

As You Read

Underline Kendall description of her friendship with Bethany. Record any connections you have to the story in the margins.

A Gray Monday

It was a gray Monday afternoon when Kendall realized it was official: she was drifting apart from Bethany. Kendall felt this realization sock her in the gut. She looked down at her gray pants and the gray seat beneath her. Everything felt gray—including her mood. For the last three years, Bethany had been the ketchup to Kendall's mustard, the moon to her stars. But lately, something had gone topsy-turvy in their friendship.

Bethany met Kendall only three years ago, but it felt like they had known each other for a decade at least. They loved the same movie (*Back to the Future*), ordered the same thing at the burger shop (cheeseburger, extra relish), and never ran out of things to talk about. They also had similar families, with each girl having two parents and an annoying younger brother.

Kendall always felt a bit smug when people talked about getting into fights with their friends. Kendall and Bethany never fought, and this was a clear sign they were great at the whole friendship game, right? But Bethany wasn't replying to her text messages, and it had been at least two weeks since they had even had a one-on-one catch-up. Something was up—but what?

1. What is the central idea of this text?

- (A) A friend is being ignored.
- (B) A change in friendship is positive.
- (C) A once-strong friendship feels like it is weakening.
- (D) Commonalities strengthen a friendship.

2. What does the phrase *sock her in the gut* show about Kendall's feelings?

- (A) She realizes that Bethany is her best friend.
- (B) She is scared to lose Bethany as a friend.
- (C) Kendall hurt Bethany's feelings.
- (D) Kendall got hit in the stomach.

3. Why does Kendall feel like everything is "gray"?

- (A) She is bored.
- (B) She is wearing gray clothing.
- (C) It is winter.
- (D) She is sad without her friend.

4. Why does the author use parentheses in the second paragraph?

- (A) to set off important facts
- (B) to add dialogue
- (C) to list the opposite idea
- (D) to give examples

5. What does the word *smug* mean as used in the text?

- (A) humored
- (B) arrogant
- (C) joyous
- (D) anxious

Name: ____________________ Date: ____________

Directions: Read the text, and answer the questions.

As You Read

Underline Bethany's perspective of Kendall.

Gossip and Secrets

It was a gray Monday afternoon when Bethany realized she could not avoid Kendall forever. Bethany knew her best friend was starting to grow suspicious. She also knew that avoiding Kendall's texts was not the best way to deal with everything going on between them. Kendall was a loyal and close friend. But Bethany also knew Kendall loved to gossip, and that was the root cause of their current predicament.

Kendall never knew how to hold a secret safe in her hands. For a long time, that did not bother Bethany because Bethany was not a secretive kind of person. Bethany was someone who people could rely on, and she never faced down any big issues of her own. She liked to think of herself as "drama-free." Bethany loved staying out of the spotlight, while Kendall loved to hold court under any light.

Things had started to change in Bethany's life, and she knew a big storm was headed her way. She wanted to share her troubles with Kendall and hoped she could trust her. So, on that gray Monday, Bethany finally went to find her best friend.

1. What is Bethany's perspective of Kendall?

- (A) Kendall never pays attention to drama.
- (B) Kendall is a good listener to all her friends.
- (C) Kendall is popular at school.
- (D) Kendall does not always think before talking.

2. How does the author structure the passage?

- (A) by showing the effects of the friendship on Bethany
- (B) by sequencing the beginning to the end of the friendship
- (C) by comparing the two friends' personalities
- (D) by introducing a solution to Bethany's problem

3. What is the theme of the passage?

- (A) It is not easy to lose a friend.
- (B) Bethany is going through a difficult time alone.
- (C) Friends can help you get through anything.
- (D) Sometimes friends can be opposites of each other.

4. How does the structure help convey the theme?

- (A) by detailing how different the characters are from each other
- (B) by explaining why Bethany needs to end her friendship with Kendall
- (C) by detailing how Bethany will solve her problem
- (D) by showing that Kendall is good at keeping secrets

Name: ______________________ Date: ____________

Directions: Read the text, and answer the questions.

As You Read

Underline the characters' actions. Write what it reveals about their points of view.

The Fight

Kendall saw Bethany first as she was crossing the wide park by their school. Kendall could tell by the way Bethany's shoulders were squarely set, like a tin soldier, that this was not going to be a fun conversation.

"You've been avoiding my texts," Kendall said as soon as Bethany was within hearing distance. "I've sent you dozens of messages about Jenni's boyfriend problems, and you haven't even bothered to send a 'hi' back!"

Bethany flinched and narrowed her eyes. "I'm sorry, Kendall, but I just don't care about what's going on with Jenni. We barely talk to her and barely know her, so why should I reply to your random texts about her?"

Kendall's mouth dropped open a little. "You should reply because that's what we do: I send you texts about what's going on at school, and you listen and tell me that I'm way too interested in other people! Talking to each other every day is, like, a basic rule of friendship."

"How can we be friends when there is no room for me to tell you what's going on in my life?" Bethany replied, tears forming in her eyes. She saw Kendall grow worried, but before she could say anything, Bethany walked away.

1. How does the author's use of dialogue affect the story?

- Ⓐ It explains how the characters met.
- Ⓑ It shows how the characters respond to each other.
- Ⓒ It details what the characters are doing.
- Ⓓ It emphasizes the characters' feelings.

2. What is Kendall's perspective of the situation in this passage?

- Ⓐ She does not understand why the friendship has changed.
- Ⓑ She wants Bethany to care about gossip.
- Ⓒ She thinks Bethany is jealous of her friendship with Jenni.
- Ⓓ She cares about other people's problems too much.

3. Why do you think Bethany walks away from Kendall at the end of the text? Use details from the story to support your ideas.

____

____

4. Why do you think the conversation between Kendall and Bethany unfolded the way that it did? Use details from the story to support your ideas.

____

____

Name: ______________________ Date: ______________

As You Read

Underline how the characters are feeling. Mark where the characters begin to change.

The Trust between Friends

Bethany thought back to her fight with Kendall and felt a tender weight in her stomach. The two of them had never fought before, and Bethany had never cried in front of Kendall before. Bethany had seen Kendall cry numerous times, though, because Kendall was never embarrassed by it and always said it felt so cathartic to have a release of emotions. But Bethany had spent years learning to hold her feelings back, pushing them deep inside. And after the fight yesterday, Bethany now felt like a gushing waterfall kept falling from her eyes, no matter how much she tried to hold it back.

A knock sounded on her bedroom door, and her mom peeked her head around the corner. Bethany looked up, wiping at her eyes, and saw Kendall standing in the doorway with a plate of peanut butter cookies in her hands. Bethany's mom quietly clicked the bedroom door shut, and Kendall folded up her legs and sat across from Bethany.

"I'm so sorry, Bethany," Kendall whispered. "Are you crying because I'm a total jerk?"

Bethany sighed, shaking her head, feeling her braids brush from side to side. Kendall nudged Bethany's shoulder, waiting for her friend to open up.

Bethany sighed again and continued, "Long story short, my parents are officially getting divorced, and they're moving into separate homes across the city. I wanted to tell you—of course I did—but I was also so afraid because you tell everyone everything. And I thought…I don't trust you to not tell everyone what's going on with me, even if we're best friends."

Kendall stared down at the cookies in her lap, feeling very small. She had never thought about how her gossiping might make Bethany think that she couldn't keep a secret.

"Bethany, first of all, I am so, so sorry, and I don't want you to be alone in figuring this out. I am your best friend, and I always want to be there for you. And I get it, I am usually not great at keeping secrets, but this one is safe with me, I promise."

Tears kept leaking out of Bethany's eyes, and Kendall pulled her friend into a giant hug. "Oh man, I hate fighting with you," Kendall muttered.

Bethany gave a watery laugh and leaned back to look her friend in the eye. "It's okay for us to fight, you know. I think it helps us get to know each other better—as long as we spend time figuring out what's going on and how to solve it."

The two friends smiled at each other and, at the same time, picked up a peanut butter cookie so they could eat together.

Name: ______________________ Date: ______________

Directions: Read "The Trust between Friends." Then, answer the questions.

1. What does the phrase *a tender weight* show in the following sentence? *Bethany thought back to her fight with Kendall and felt a tender weight in her stomach.*

- (A) Bethany has stomach pain from her fight with Kendall.
- (B) Bethany is feeling sick to her stomach.
- (C) Bethany is too stubborn to reach out to Kendall.
- (D) Bethany is saddened by the situation with Kendall.

2. Which line from the passage best shows that Kendall has changed?

- (A) A knock sounded on her bedroom door, and her mom peeked her head around the corner.
- (B) Kendall nudged Bethany's shoulder, waiting for her friend to open up.
- (C) She had never thought about how her gossiping might make Bethany think that she couldn't keep a secret.
- (D) Tears kept leaking out of Bethany's eyes, and Kendall pulled her friend into a giant hug.

3. Which word best captures the mood of the story?

- (A) reflective
- (B) pessimistic
- (C) agitated
- (D) serene

4. What do the cookies symbolize in the story?

- (A) an apology
- (B) bitterness
- (C) the friends' fight
- (D) gossip

5. What does the word *cathartic* mean in the following sentence? *Bethany had seen Kendall cry numerous times...and always said it felt so cathartic to have a release of emotions.*

- (A) strength
- (B) relief
- (C) depression
- (D) brave

6. Which of the following sentences from the story is an example of a compound-complex sentence?

- (A) Kendall stared down at the cookies in her lap, feeling very small.
- (B) Tears kept leaking out of Bethany's eyes, and Kendall pulled her friend into a giant hug.
- (C) Bethany looked up, wiping at her eyes, and saw Kendall standing in the doorway with a plate of peanut butter cookies in her hands.
- (D) Kendall nudged Bethany's shoulder, waiting for her friend to open up.

7. How would you have apologized to your friend if you were Kendall? How does your plan compare with what happened in the story?

____

____

____

____

____

____

Name: ______________________________ Date: ______________

Directions: Reread "The Trust between Friends." Then, respond to the prompt.

Kendall is approached by a friend at school who is curious about why Kendall and Bethany seemed to be fighting. Write a narrative story about this exchange. Remember the promise Kendall made to Bethany. What will Kendall think, say, and do in this situation? Include a beginning, middle, and end to your story.

Name: ______________________________ Date: ____________________

1 **Winter 2008**

Bethany and Kendall are born.

2 **Summer 2018**

Bethany and Kendall meet for the first time. They are next-door neighbors.

3 **Fall 2018**

Bethany lends Kendall her favorite sweater, and they decide to be best friends for life.

4 **Winter 2018**

The two friends have a joint birthday party to celebrate turning 10!

5 **Spring 2019**

Bethany and Kendall join the same soccer team.

6 **Fall 2019**

Bethany and Kendall have their first sleepover together.

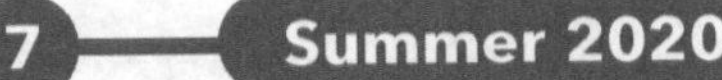

7 **Summer 2020**

Bethany and Kendall share video calls with each other and stay in touch from a distance.

8 **Spring 2021**

Bethany and Kendall have their first fight, and they learn how to navigate the conflict together.

9 **Winter 2021**

Bethany's parents officially divorce, and Kendall calls Bethany every day to see how she is doing.

10 **Spring 2025**

The two best friends graduate high school and look toward a hopeful future—one that they will share together.

Name: ______________________ Date: ______________

Directions: Read the time line on page 41. Then, answer the questions.

1. During which time does the biggest conflict in their friendship occur?
   - (A) Fall 2019
   - (B) Spring 2021
   - (C) Winter 2018
   - (D) Spring 2025

2. In what type of structure does the author organize the text?
   - (A) cause and effect
   - (B) chronological order
   - (C) problem and solution
   - (D) description

3. How do Bethany and Kendall meet?
   - (A) They are next-door neighbors.
   - (B) They are on the same soccer team.
   - (C) They attend the same birthday party.
   - (D) They go to high school together.

4. How does the time line help readers understand Bethany and Kendall's friendship?
   - (A) It shows major events in their friendship.
   - (B) It highlights why they fight and how they patch up their friendship.
   - (C) It details the importance of navigating a friendship from afar.
   - (D) It provides a solution to difficult situations in a friendship.

5. How do Bethany and Kendall remain friends?
   - (A) They play many sports together.
   - (B) They go to summer camp together.
   - (C) The two make the effort to talk as often as possible.
   - (D) They graduate high school together.

6. What could the author add to the time line to make it more interesting or informational for readers?

____

____

____

____

____

____

____

Name: ______________________ Date: ______________

Directions: Closely read these excerpts. Then, compare and contrast the relationships of the two pairs of friends.

Close-Reading Texts

Friendship through the Years	The Trust between Friends
Neither Lewis or Tolkien were confident readers would enjoy—or even read—their books. But the two authors were quick to encourage each other. It's possible the creative worlds of Narnia and Middle-earth would not exist without this friendship between writers. Although they were once fierce friends, the two men eventually turned into rivals. Lewis initially had more success as a writer. And Tolkien disagreed with some of Lewis's choices in his personal life. Their connection became more about their differences than their similarities. Over time, the two close friends became divided and were living separate lives. When Lewis died, Tolkien grieved the loss of his friend. He wrote to his daughter, "So far I have felt the normal feelings of a man of my age—like an old tree that is losing all its leaves one by one: this feels like an axe-blow near the roots." His words convey the deep impact that Lewis had on his life.	Kendall stared down at the cookies in her lap, feeling very small. She had never thought about how her gossiping might make Bethany think that she couldn't keep a secret. "Bethany, first of all, I am so, so sorry, and I don't want you to be alone in figuring this out. I am your best friend, and I always want to be there for you. And I get it, I am usually not great at keeping secrets, but this one is safe with me, I promise." Tears kept leaking out of Bethany's eyes, and Kendall pulled her friend into a giant hug. "Oh man, I hate fighting with you," Kendall muttered. Bethany gave a watery laugh and leaned back to look her friend in the eye. "It's okay for us to fight, you know. I think it helps us get to know each other better—as long as we spend time figuring out what's going on and how to solve it." The two friends smiled at each other and, at the same time, picked up a peanut butter cookie so they could eat together.

Lewis and Tolkien	Kendall and Bethany
Both	

Name: ______________________________ Date: ________________

Directions: Closely read the texts. Then, determine a common central idea or theme between the two. Support your answer with evidence from both texts.

Close-Reading Texts

Competition and Success	Time Line
Being in the public spotlight can put a lot of pressure on someone to succeed. In such a competitive industry, it would be easy for either Swift or Gomez to feel jealous or fall out of touch with each other. But the two friends have always had each other's backs. Swift and Gomez stay in regular contact. They have gone through life's ups and downs together. Both of them have weathered public criticism and judgment. Through it all, the two singer-songwriters are endlessly supportive of each other. They publicly state their support and make an effort to promote their friend's work. Long-term friendships that last a lifetime take time, effort, and commitment. Swift once said, "Longevity is something you really can find very precious and rare in friendships." Their friendship indicates a strong connection and close bond that the two will likely share for more years to come.	5. **Spring 2019:** Bethany and Kendall join the same soccer team. 6. **Fall 2019:** Bethany and Kendall have their first sleepover together. 7. **Summer 2020:** Bethany and Kendall share video calls with each other and stay in touch from a distance. 8. **Spring 2021:** Bethany and Kendall have their first fight, and they learn how to navigate the conflict together. 9. **Winter 2021:** Bethany's parents officially divorce, and Kendall calls Bethany every day to see how she is doing. 10. **Spring 2025:** The two best friends graduate high school and look toward a hopeful future—one that they will share together.

Central Idea:

Swift and Gomez	Bethany and Kendall

Name: ______________________________ Date: ______________

Directions: Think about the texts from this unit. Then, respond to the prompt.

Create a time line that chronicles the milestones—or important moments—shared by you and a good friend. Elaborate on each milestone by describing important details.

Name: ______________________________ Date: ________________

Directions: Think about the texts from this unit. Then, respond to the prompt.

Imagine you are writing a newspaper article about friendships. Create a list of the top 10 tips to be a supportive friend. Explain each tip and why it is important for maintaining a friendship.

Name: ______________________________ Date: ______________

Directions: Read the text, and answer the questions.

As You Read

Annotate the text with your thoughts, questions, and connections.

The Pros of Social Media

Using social media is a way people can connect to others. Social media are websites or apps through which people can communicate. Social media help users create and share content with other people. More than half of the people in the world use social media! The first social media website launched in 1997. People are still learning how to best include social media in their lives.

Social media have many positive effects. First, it's easy for users to connect with communities online. In the past, our communities were limited. We could only get to know the people we met in our daily lives. Now, social media users can connect with people very far away from them! These sites can also help users learn about current events. Users can share information in compelling ways. This includes photographs and short videos. Social media also allow people to spread information quickly. In turn, this prompts social change movements to form and grow. Finally, using social media is a lot of fun for many people.

1. How has social media changed the way people communicate?

- (A) by connecting people across communities
- (B) by limiting people to their own spaces
- (C) by limiting information
- (D) by introducing audio phone calls

2. According to the text, how can users share information on social media?

- (A) long paragraphs
- (B) voice messages
- (C) short videos
- (D) written requests

3. What is the author's tone in this passage?

- (A) ominous
- (B) enthusiastic
- (C) gloomy
- (D) nonchalant

4. What does the word *compelling* mean as used in the text?

- (A) interesting
- (B) silly
- (C) amusing
- (D) digital

5. What does this sentence suggest about social media? *In the past, our communities were limited.*

- (A) Social media has limitations.
- (B) Social media has connected groups of people.
- (C) Social media is a place where people live.
- (D) Before social media, people did not communicate.

Name: ______________________ Date: ______________

Directions: Read the text, and answer the questions.

As You Read

Annotate the text with your thoughts, questions, and connections.

The Cons of Social Media

Frequent social media use has some downsides. While it can be fun to use, it can easily take up too much time if you're not careful. For many people, it's easy to get caught up in scrolling through social media posts. This is because social media sites are built to capture a user's attention. This can come at a cost. School work or time with loved ones may get pushed to the side in favor of time spent online.

Another downside is that social media use can tap into our insecurities. We might see pictures of people at fun parties or traveling to interesting places. This may make our lives seem less exciting in comparison. And when we compare our lives to others, this can lead to us feeling unhappy.

Finally, people can learn incorrect information from social media. Because information spreads so quickly on social media, it can be hard to discern what is true and what's not. Keeping these social media issues in mind is important so you can make healthy and safe choices.

1. How can social media affect your time?

- (A) People can scroll too much on social media sites.
- (B) It can affect people's self-esteem.
- (C) It can connect us with others.
- (D) It can help people spend one-on-one time with loved ones.

2. How can information be misleading on social media?

- (A) Only powerful people have control of news.
- (B) The news is always reliable on social media.
- (C) People post only positive messages on social media.
- (D) It is spread quickly, making it hard to know what's true.

3. Which is a synonym for *cost* as it is used in this text?

- (A) scroll
- (B) purchase
- (C) money
- (D) sacrifice

4. Based on the information in this text, it can be concluded that ______.

- (A) social media use has many advantages
- (B) social media can help us recognize how to manage our time
- (C) social media use has many downsides
- (D) social media are fast-paced environments full of energy

5. How does social media affect information?

- (A) False information is spread quickly.
- (B) Only the truth is spread online.
- (C) Information is not spread on social media.
- (D) Information would not be spread without it.

Name: ______________________________ Date: ________________

Directions: Read the text, and answer the questions.

As You Read

Annotate the text with your thoughts, questions, and connections.

Check Your Privacy

Social media platforms exist on the internet. This means that billions of people have access to these platforms. So, it's helpful to consider your privacy when it comes to social media. There are key differences between private and public profiles.

Young people have many online rights. And all young people have the right to privacy. Choosing who can view your social media profile or posts is one way to exert your right to privacy. All social media sites allow users to set their privacy restrictions. Users can choose whether they want to make their profiles public. Public profiles are available for anyone to view or comment upon, so they have a wider reach. Users can also make their profiles private. This way, they have more control over who can view and share their personal posts.

Above all else, remember that information shared online is "sticky." Once something is shared or uploaded online, it is hard to fully erase or delete. After considering these options, try asking yourself: does a public or private profile feel safer or more comfortable for me?

1. What is the main idea of the passage?

Ⓐ Online privacy is a right and a choice.
Ⓑ Only young people are permitted to limit their profile.
Ⓒ Setting you profile to private is the smartest way to use social media.
Ⓓ Public and private profiles are the same.

2. What does the word *exert* mean in the text?

Ⓐ stop
Ⓑ distribute
Ⓒ utilize
Ⓓ choose

3. Which is a benefit of a private account?

Ⓐ Information becomes "sticky" online.
Ⓑ It is easy to erase and delete your posts forever.
Ⓒ Private profiles reach more people.
Ⓓ Users can restrict who accesses their profile.

4. What does the word *sticky* mean in the last paragraph?

Ⓐ dirty
Ⓑ long-lasting
Ⓒ adhesive
Ⓓ erased

5. How are public profiles different from private profiles? Use details from the passage to support your ideas.

____

____

____

____

____

Name: ______________________ Date: ______________

As You Read

Annotate the text with your thoughts, questions, and connections.

Using Social Media with Intention

Social media is a lot of fun for most users. However, these platforms can also quickly take up a person's time. Social media can be tricky to navigate because it's easy to lose hours to mindless scrolling. People might spend hours viewing posts and videos to fill their time. If you use social media, it helps to use it with a plan in mind. Intentional social media use is deliberate. Using social media with intention means thinking through how to include it in your life.

Many people know that they spend hours with screens. But, they often don't know *exactly* how much time that is. Planning for social media use can start with defining how much time you'd like to spend on it. Try asking yourself: how much time do I ideally want to spend on social media every day? Can I realistically stick to that plan? To adhere to your time commitment, try setting a timer when you launch a social media app. Set the timer to your limit, and once the timer goes off, that's your cue to close out of your app. Some people also like to plan for a day every week to be "screen-free." This might look like a "Screen-Free Sunday." If it feels like you are spending a lot of time on social media, see how a day without screens feels for you.

On social media, you have the option to consume or create. For many people, most time on social media is spent consuming content. They scroll through posts, look up profiles, or watch quick videos when they consume. However, it can be helpful to balance consuming with creating. Creating on social media might look like leaving encouraging comments for others. Creating on social media may also look like posting creative photos or filming your own quick videos. A benefit of social media is that they give people a chance to stretch their creative skills. Try to make time to consume *and* create on social media. It might make social media more mindful and engaging for you to use!

Intentional social media use also involves noticing how you feel while online. Social media allows everyone to follow a variety of people. People can follow friends, organizations, celebrities, and other people they have only met once or twice. But it helps to make a plan for who you want to follow on social media. You may want to follow people who inspire or encourage you. But if you feel uneasy or anxious when viewing someone's posts, it may be time to unfollow them.

Social media has brought a lot of positive change to people's lives, and when they use social media with a plan, this can ensure the changes remain positive and helpful.

Name: ______________________________ Date: ________________

Directions: Read "Using Social Media with Intention." Then, answer the questions.

1. What is the main structure of this text?

- (A) cause and effect
- (B) chronological order
- (C) problem and solution
- (D) description

2. Which is **not** an example of creating on social media?

- (A) scrolling through posts
- (B) posting short videos
- (C) posting photos
- (D) leaving a comment

3. What does it mean to *consume* as used in the following sentence? *They scroll through posts, look up profiles, or watch quick videos when they consume.*

- (A) purchase
- (B) view
- (C) use
- (D) try

4. What is the author's **main** purpose in writing this text?

- (A) to persuade
- (B) to entertain
- (C) to inform
- (D) to humor

5. Social media users can manage their time on social media ______.

- (A) using a timer
- (B) creating content instead of consuming it
- (C) stopping their use of social media when they feel stressed
- (D) policing what others do online

6. Identify the problem with social media and the solutions the author offers.

Problem:	
Solution 1	
Solution 2	
Solution 3	
Solution 4	

Name: ______________________ Date: ______________

Directions: Reread "Using Social Media with Intention." Then, respond to the prompt.

Imagine you have been invited to give a speech at the United Nations on social media and its effects on middle schoolers. In your speech, be sure to include:

- your claim about social media's effects on middle schoolers
- reasons to support your claim
- tips to support positive use of social media
- evidence from both the text and your own background knowledge

Name: ______________________________ Date: ______________

Directions: Read the text, and answer the questions.

As You Read

Make and record predictions about the characters and events in the story. Underline areas of the text that influenced your predictions.

Aisha, the Photographer

It took one year, four months, and ten days, but Aisha had *finally* convinced her parents to let her open a social media account. Aisha loved her parents, but she figured they worried too much.

"I think there are too many fake accounts on these social media sites," her mom had said. "And I do not want this to pull you away from your studies, Aisha."

But Aisha was too excited to fully hear what her mom had to say. Aisha loved taking photographs, and she had an endless stream of photos saved on her phone. She liked taking up-close pictures of things people don't typically look at closely. Her photographs included the undersides of leaves and the shiny, chrome edges of gumball machines. Aisha loved showing these photos to her friends, and she wanted to be able to share them instantaneously. Aisha had already thought in great detail about what exactly she wanted to include in her profile. She had no doubt that this social media app was the perfect place to stretch her creative muscles.

1. Why does Aisha want to use social media?
   - (A) She wants to socialize with her friends.
   - (B) She likes to take photos and share them.
   - (C) She wants her parents to be less controlling.
   - (D) She likes to see other people's photos.

2. What is Aisha's mother's view on social media?
   - (A) It will be a distraction from school.
   - (B) It will motivate Aisha.
   - (C) It will encourage her to take better pictures.
   - (D) It will cause bullying at school.

3. How could you best describe Aisha from this passage?
   - (A) determined
   - (B) worrisome
   - (C) disobedient
   - (D) kind

4. What does this line reveal about Aisha's mom? *I think there are too many fake accounts on these social media sites.*
   - (A) She is determined to catch frauds online.
   - (B) She is worried people won't like Aisha's photos.
   - (C) She is concerned people are not who they seem online.
   - (D) She wishes Aisha to be the honest one online.

5. What does the italicized word in the first sentence suggest?
   - (A) Aisha has been asking to use social media for a while.
   - (B) Aisha has been successful in convincing her parents for things in the past.
   - (C) Aisha gives up easily.
   - (D) Aisha's parents are strict and don't let Aisha be social.

Name: ______________________ Date: ______________

Directions: Read the text, and answer the questions.

As You Read

Make and record predictions about the characters and events in the story. Underline areas of the text that influenced your predictions.

The Highlight Reel

Aisha set up her profile with her mom, eagerly going through each step. Her mom helped her find the privacy settings, and the two of them made sure her profile was hidden from public view.

"You can only add friends, okay, Aisha?" her mom said sternly. "We will talk about who you are following on this app at least once a week, too, to make sure you are not following anyone you don't know."

Aisha nodded, excited to start finding her friends online. Once her mom left her alone, Aisha quickly scrolled through and looked up her friends, tapping the "follow" button on each of their profiles. Soon, the home page of her app was flooded with pictures and short videos.

Aisha scrolled through it all, catching brief glimpses of her friends' lives. There was a photo of Harry at his parents' cabin in the Rocky Mountains. Jane posted a short video of a fancy meal at what appeared to be a pretty high-priced restaurant. Aisha smiled at the photos, but she also felt her heart speed up a little. Her parents did not have a cabin in the Rockies, and they could never afford to eat at such an expensive restaurant...was this what she was supposed to show on her profile?

1. How does Aisha's mom support Aisha's interest?

- (A) by worrying too much
- (B) by making Aisha's profile public
- (C) by helping her post her first picture
- (D) by letting her use the app with guidelines

2. What does the word *glimpses* mean in the text?

- (A) glares
- (B) lights
- (C) wealthy
- (D) looks

3. What does the use of ellipses (...) suggest?

- (A) Aisha is confused by the app's rules.
- (B) Aisha wants to be like her friends.
- (C) Aisha is second guessing herself.
- (D) Aisha does not like her friends' posts.

4. How does Aisha's perspective of the app begin to change?

- (A) She is unsure of how to use it.
- (B) She does not like her art anymore.
- (C) She begins to question her friendships.
- (D) She chooses no longer to use it.

5. By referring to the home page of the app as *flooded with pictures and short videos*, the narrator suggests ______.

- (A) Aisha is concerned about not posting as much as her friends
- (B) Aisha has already posted many photos
- (C) Aisha does not know how to use the app
- (D) Aisha's friends use the app frequently

Name: ____________________ Date: ____________

Directions: Read the text, and answer the questions.

As You Read

Make and record predictions about the characters and events in the story. Underline areas of the text that influenced your predictions.

The First Post

The last person Aisha followed on the app was her sister, Ghazal. Ghazal was about six years older than Aisha, and her profile only had three photos, which were different shots of her goldendoodle puppy, Simon.

Aisha went to her own profile and chewed her lip, trying to decide what her first post should be. Should she post a picture of her face, maybe with a goofy grin? Maybe she could post that nice picture of her with her parents, but would people think she had no friends and only spent time with her family? Aisha's brain went into overdrive, imagining every possible thought people could think when viewing her first post. Aisha wanted her first post to be perfect and for everyone she knew to "like" it.

But thoughts kept nagging at her: What if they didn't, and what if nobody even commented or liked the post? Aisha's brain kept serving up questions that she couldn't answer, and she felt her stomach knotting up. Wasn't her time on the app meant to be fun?

1. What do the questions that Aisha asks reveal about her?

- (A) Aisha knows she will make the right choice.
- (B) Aisha loves using social media.
- (C) Aisha is afraid she won't be popular anymore.
- (D) Aisha is feeling self-conscious.

2. What does the word *overdrive* mean in the text?

- (A) slowed down
- (B) route
- (C) hyperactive
- (D) halt

3. What does the fact that Ghazal only has three photos reveal about her?

- (A) Ghazal loves taking photos.
- (B) Posting on social media is not as important to her.
- (C) The app requires a certain number of posts.
- (D) Ghazal is an artist like Aisha.

4. Which word best describes Aisha's mood?

- (A) anxious
- (B) weary
- (C) excited
- (D) optimistic

5. How is social media affecting Aisha? Use details from the story to support your answer.

____

____

6. What advice would you give Aisha if you could? Use details from the story to support your answer.

____

____

Name: ______________________ Date: ______________

As You Read

Underline areas of the text that prove or disprove your predictions from this week.

What Matters Most

Aisha had spent an hour, five minutes, and about 32 seconds trying to figure out what to post before she called Ghazal. When Aisha was stuck in any shape or form, she liked to call Ghazal. Her older sister always had a few wise words to say, and Aisha knew she needed some perspective.

Ghazal picked up her phone after three rings and said, "Aisha?" Aisha immediately launched into a detailed description of every thought she'd had in the last hour. She told Ghazal about the cool things other people were posting, including Janet's expensive meal and Harry's drool-worthy cabin in the mountains. Ghazal just listened while Aisha got more and more worried about how her life compared to her friends.

"Aisha, what did you want to post before you saw other people's photos? I thought you wanted to post all those cool photos that you like to take."

Aisha slowed down, remembering why she first wanted to get on social media. "Yeah, I guess I didn't want to post pictures of myself...I just wanted to share my photographs with, like, you and my friends."

Aisha could almost hear Ghazal nodding over the phone. "Look, sis, social media can be tricky to figure out sometimes. We see what other people put online, and it is human nature to compare it to what we're doing, you know? But at the end of the day, people are just showing you a highlight reel of all the cool stuff in their life. People don't often post about the tough day they had or the things they're actually struggling with. Janet might have had a cool meal at a cool restaurant—but she might have also had a tough day at home. We just don't know when we're looking at someone's profile, so it's best not to compare ourselves too much."

Aisha listened intently to her sister's advice, nodding her head.

"You are such an amazing photographer, Aisha," Ghazal continued. "You see the world from a different viewpoint, and I like seeing our world through your eyes. I think your idea to share your photographs is a neat idea, and I think people will really like them. But even if they don't, what matters is what *you* think of your photographs."

Aisha took a deep breath, nodding, and she felt her shoulders lose their tension. "Ghazal, you're a great sister; have I ever told you that?"

"You can always tell me again," her sister replied, laughing.

The two sisters hung up, and Aisha looked down at her phone. She scrolled through her photographs, picking a photo she'd taken of her mom and sister. With a smile, she posted her first picture.

Name: ______________________________ Date: ________________

Directions: Read "What Matters Most." Then, answer the questions.

1. How does Ghazal help Aisha?

- (A) by comparing Aisha to her friends
- (B) by telling Aisha the benefits of social media
- (C) by warning Aisha never to use a public profile
- (D) by reminding Aisha of her intentions

2. Why does Aisha turn to Ghazal?

- (A) Ghazal shares their mother's worries.
- (B) Aisha looks up to Ghazal.
- (C) Ghazal is a social media expert.
- (D) Ghazal is friends with Aisha's friends, too.

3. What is the theme of the text?

- (A) Don't compare yourself to others.
- (B) Seek advice from your sibling.
- (C) Older siblings always have the answer.
- (D) Aisha is a great photographer.

4. How does the mood shift in the story?

- (A) from gloomy to surprised
- (B) from angry to calm
- (C) from anxious to relieved
- (D) from jealous to comforted

5. How does Ghazal affect Aisha?

- (A) She convinces to Aisha not use social media.
- (B) She reminds Aisha to be herself.
- (C) She makes Aisha feel anxious.
- (D) She stops Aisha from making a big mistake.

6. Which statement would be **most** important to include in a summary of the story?

- (A) Aisha is an artist with a great eye for detail.
- (B) Aisha's mother was determined to control her social media use.
- (C) Aisha's sister, Ghazal, only posts pictures of her dog.
- (D) Aisha's sister, Ghazal, tells her not to compare herself to others.

7. How are social media posts different from real life? Use details from the story to support your ideas.

Social Media Posts	**Real Life**
____________________	____________________
____________________	____________________
____________________	____________________
____________________	____________________
____________________	____________________
____________________	____________________

Name: ______________________ Date: ____________

Directions: Reread "What Matters Most." Then, respond to the prompt.

Imagine you are Aisha, and you are creating your first social media post. Draw a picture that captures Aisha's art. In the caption, make sure to include a description of the art and details about Aisha from the text.

Name: ______________________________ Date: ____________________

Online Bullying

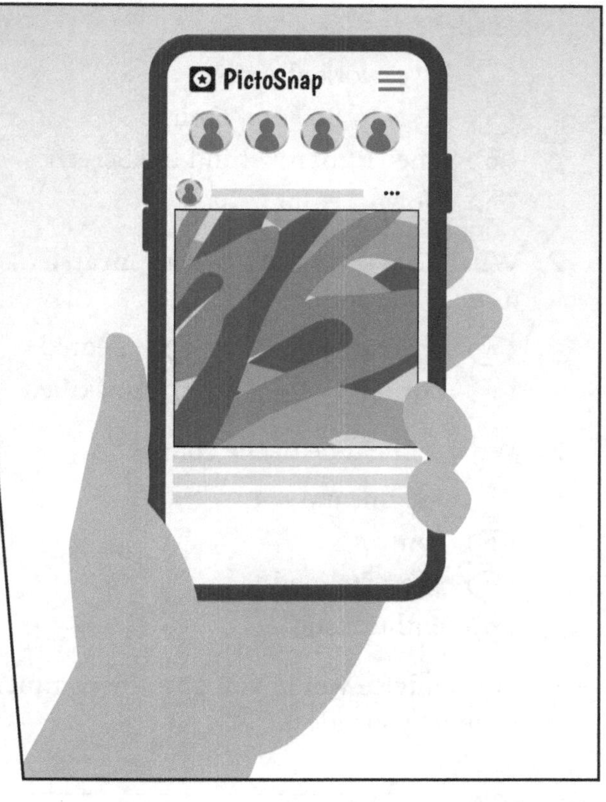

Name: ______________________________ Date: ____________________

Directions: Read "Online Bullying." Then, answer the questions.

1. Which is the best alternative title for this comic?

- (A) Overworked Artist
- (B) How to Be Kind Online
- (C) The Human Behind the Screen
- (D) How to Paint

2. What does the word *amateur* mean as used in the comic?

- (A) artistic
- (B) boring
- (C) talented
- (D) unskilled

3. What is the tone of the comic?

- (A) judgmental
- (B) control
- (C) overwhelmed
- (D) enthusiastic

4. How does the commenter seem to affect the artist?

- (A) The artist knows that online words don't matter.
- (B) The artist becomes more determined.
- (C) The artist is angry.
- (D) The artist feels hurt.

5. By calling the artist an amateur, the commenter suggests ______.

- (A) they are jealous of the artist's talent
- (B) the artist does not know how to select colors
- (C) they are angry at the artist
- (D) the artist should continue to try new things

6. What advice would you give the commenter in this comic? Use details from the comic to support your ideas.

____

____

____

____

____

____

Name: ______________________________ Date: ________________

Directions: Closely reread the texts. Then, break down the effects social media can have on its users by completing the cause-and-effect chart.

Close-Reading Texts

The Cons of Social Media	The Highlight Reel
Another downside is that social media use can tap into our insecurities. We might see pictures of people at fun parties or traveling to interesting places. This may make our lives seem less exciting in comparison. And when we compare our lives to others, this can lead to us feeling unhappy.	Once her mom left her alone, Aisha quickly scrolled through and looked up her friends, tapping the "follow" button on each of their profiles. Soon, the home page of her app was flooded with pictures and short videos. Aisha scrolled through it all, catching brief glimpses of her friends' lives. There was a photo of Harry at his parents' cabin in the Rocky Mountains. Jane posted a short video of a fancy meal at what appeared to be a pretty high-priced restaurant. Aisha smiled at the photos, but she also felt her heart speed up a little. Her parents did not have a cabin in the Rockies, and they could never afford to eat at such an expensive restaurant…was this what she was supposed to show on her profile?

Cause		

Effect	Effect	Effect

Name: ____________________ Date: ____________

Directions: Closely reread the texts. Then, find a common idea or theme between the texts. Include evidence from each text to support your idea.

Close-Reading Texts

What Matters Most	Using Social Media with Intention
"You are such an amazing photographer, Aisha," Ghazal continued. "You see the world from a different viewpoint, and I like seeing our world through your eyes. I think your idea to share your photographs is a neat idea, and I think people will really like them. But even if they don't, what matters is what *you* think of your photographs." Aisha took a deep breath, nodding, and she felt her shoulders lose their tension. "Ghazal, you're a great sister; have I ever told you that?" "You can always tell me again," her sister replied, laughing.	On social media, you have the option to consume or create. For many people, most time on social media is spent consuming content. They scroll through posts, look up profiles, or watch quick videos when they consume. However, it can be helpful to balance consuming with creating. Creating on social media might look like leaving encouraging comments for others. Creating on social media may also look like posting creative photos or filming your own quick videos. A benefit of social media is that they give people a chance to stretch their creative skills. Try to make time to consume *and* create on social media. It might make social media more mindful and engaging for you to use!

Common Idea or Theme:

What Matters Most	Using Social Media with Intention

Name: ______________________________ Date: ______________

Directions: Reread "Online Bullying." Then, respond to the prompt.

Imagine you saw the comment from the boy to the artist. Send a reply to the boy that teaches him how to be a better online consumer and creator. Be kind in your response, too.

Name: ______________________________ Date: ______________

Directions: Think about the texts from this unit. Then, respond to the prompt.

Imagine you have just created a new social media application, or app, that promotes positive interactions between its users. Create an advertisement that includes the name of the app, the logo for the app, the app's purpose, and any other special features you want to include.

Name: ______________________________ Date: ________________

Directions: Read the text, and answer the questions.

As You Read

Underline new or interesting ideas about the topic.

Who Are Volunteers?

Volunteers are people who help other people without being paid for it. Some volunteers give their time while others share their abilities or resources. People can volunteer in many different ways.

Volunteers work at many different places. This can include animal shelters, schools, churches, and more! Some people volunteer at food banks or soup kitchens. These are places that provide food to people who struggle to get enough to eat. Volunteers can also work in parks or cities and clean up trash. Volunteers may help "beautify" spaces by painting or restoring areas. There are endless opportunities for volunteering in the world.

Emergency situations can also create a need for volunteers. During the COVID-19 pandemic, thousands of people signed up to volunteer. Volunteers provided care and support to vulnerable groups of people, such as the elderly. They sent them cards or delivered groceries to them. People who used to work as nurses came out of retirement and volunteered their time to help take care of people. In times of crisis like this, volunteers are a huge source of help. But volunteering is not only something people can do in an emergency. People can volunteer in their communities year-round, too!

1. Why do people volunteer?

- (A) to earn extra money during an emergency
- (B) to show off their skills
- (C) to help those in need
- (D) because others made them do it

2. Which is **not** a way that volunteers can be helpful?

- (A) They keep goods for themselves.
- (B) They help people who are sick with medical care.
- (C) They send cards to people.
- (D) They collect food for others.

3. According to the text, when can people volunteer?

- (A) when they're in a pandemic
- (B) during a medical emergency
- (C) after people are in need
- (D) all of the above

4. What is the main idea of the text?

- (A) Volunteers are retired nurses who offer extra help.
- (B) Volunteers are important members of a community.
- (C) Volunteers can help at food banks.
- (D) COVID-19 was a difficult time for many around the world.

5. What is the text structure of the passage?

- (A) chronological order
- (B) descriptive
- (C) compare and contrast
- (D) question and answer

6. What is the author's tone?

- (A) appreciative
- (B) concerned
- (C) agitated
- (D) neutral

Name: ______________________ Date: ______________

Directions: Read the text, and answer the questions.

As You Read

Circle places in the text where you make connections.

Surprising Benefits for Volunteers

More than 1 billion people volunteer across the world. Around a third of Americans schedule time once a year to volunteer. Most people have busy schedules, so finding time to volunteer can be tricky. But for many people, it is worth the time and effort to support the common good.

There are many surprising benefits to volunteering. People who volunteer feel more connected to others. Volunteers meet people from different walks of life with different experiences. Volunteering is also an opportunity to make new friends. Volunteers get the chance to understand the world from different perspectives. Additionally, studies show that volunteering can help people mentally. Volunteering helps reduce stress and increase happiness levels. Researchers think these two benefits result from the connections volunteers make with others. Volunteering can also help people find a new direction in their lives. For example, some volunteers work in fields they are interested in. They often end up building skills for a future career. Finally, research suggests volunteers have increased self-esteem. Someone who volunteers might feel like they are stepping outside of their comfort zone. They may also need to learn new skills. Both tasks increase pride in oneself.

1. According to the text, what may prevent some people from volunteering?
   - (A) Some people may want to travel.
   - (B) Some people want to support the common good.
   - (C) Some people may be too busy.
   - (D) Some people are looking for different experiences.

2. How do volunteers understand the world from different perspectives?
   - (A) by connecting with others
   - (B) by having different experiences
   - (C) by meeting new people
   - (D) all of the above

3. What is the text structure of paragraph 2?
   - (A) problem and solution
   - (B) compare and contrast
   - (C) cause and effect
   - (D) description

4. Which word or phrase signals the text structure in paragraph 2?
   - (A) result
   - (B) often
   - (C) also
   - (D) finally

5. How can volunteering affect a volunteer's future?
   - (A) by gaining skills in a new field
   - (B) by having a busy schedule
   - (C) by feeling happier
   - (D) by seeing new places in the world

6. What is the author's purpose in this text?
   - (A) to tell a story
   - (B) to persuade
   - (C) to entertain
   - (D) to instruct

Name: ______________________________ Date: ________________

Directions: Read the text, and answer the questions.

As You Read

Star ideas that are interesting to you.

Discovering Volunteer Opportunities

There are thousands of groups looking for volunteers of all ages. But which opportunities are right for you? It can be useful to ask yourself some questions while researching. For starters, do you like to work with certain groups of people? Maybe you enjoy spending time with students your age, or perhaps you want to help seniors in your neighborhood. Knowing whom you want to work with gives you a starting point. Next, ask yourself if there are certain causes you feel passionately about. Do you care deeply about the environment? You can look for environmental groups nearby that need volunteers. Then, ask yourself how much time you have in your schedule and determine how much time you can commit to volunteering. Some volunteer opportunities ask for a specific time commitment. Lastly, reflect on your volunteering goals. Some people volunteer because they want to help their communities. Others volunteer because they want to try something new, meet people who share their interests, or build knowledge and experience in areas they hope to work one day. Answering these questions will help you know why you want to volunteer. And this will help you choose the right volunteer opportunity for you!

1. Why does the author ask the reader questions throughout the paragraph?

- (A) to show the reader how confusing volunteering can be
- (B) to explain that volunteering requires hard work
- (C) to help the reader reflect on their goals and values
- (D) to test the reader's abilities

2. What is the purpose of this passage?

- (A) to explain the pros and cons of being a volunteer
- (B) to describe a day in the life of a volunteer
- (C) to explain to readers the benefits of volunteering
- (D) to encourage readers to discover why and how they want to volunteer

3. Which tip do you find most helpful? Why? Use details from the passage to support your ideas.

____

____

____

4. Why do people volunteer? Use details from the passage to support your ideas.

____

____

____

Name: ______________________________ Date: ________________

As You Read

Star ideas that are interesting to you. Circle places where you makes connections. Record your connections in the margins.

Volunteer Variety

There are many ways to volunteer in your community. Your local library is likely on the lookout for volunteers, and community theaters and animal shelters also welcome volunteers. Sports teams, national parks, and senior centers often need assistance. Remember your volunteering goals, and look for groups that might be a good match for you.

One way to start volunteering is to simply help out in your neighborhood. Many of your neighbors would welcome a helping hand. You could offer to rake leaves for someone down the block. You could mow the lawn or shovel the driveway for someone a few doors down. If a family you know is having a tough time, maybe you can deliver meals to them. Consider dropping off notes just to make people smile. If you have a stack of old books, pick some to donate to a shelter, or read stories to younger students at your school library. Bake sales are also a popular way to volunteer. You can bake items to sell and donate your profits to your favorite charity. These are just a few ways you can help out people in your community.

Are you passionate about taking care of the environment? If you live near the ocean, beach clean-ups take place every year. You could even plan one of your own! Ocean Conservancy runs international beach clean-ups where volunteers gather to collect plastic and trash from the shorelines. If you don't live near a beach, another way to volunteer is to explore your closest national parks. The National Park Service offers the Volunteers-In-Parks (VIP) program where they welcome volunteers of all ages. But if you are far from a park or an ocean, you can take care of your environment in other ways, too. Help keep your community clean by picking up litter in public areas. (Make sure to wear gloves, though!) Throwing away discarded trash supports the beautification of your local neighborhood.

Finally, volunteering can involve gathering resources for others. Some students go to school without all the supplies they need. The Kids in Need Foundation is a group that supports teachers and students in under-resourced schools. They have lots of volunteer opportunities. You can organize a school-supply drive or start a fundraiser to lend them a helping hand.

There are many creative ways to volunteer! Giving back to your community helps others, and it also helps you feel more connected to others. How might you lend a hand today?

Name: ______________________ Date: ____________

Directions: Read "Volunteer Variety." Then, answer the questions.

1. What is the central idea of the text?

- (A) There is only one way to volunteer.
- (B) Everyone can find time to volunteer.
- (C) There are ways to volunteer for everyone.
- (D) Volunteers are essential parts of a community.

2. Which line from the text best supports the central idea of the text?

- (A) Remember your volunteering goals, and look for groups that might be a good match for you.
- (B) You could offer to rake leaves for someone down the block.
- (C) Ocean Conservancy runs international beach clean-ups where volunteers gather to collect plastic and trash from the shorelines.
- (D) Help keep your community clean by picking up litter in public areas.

3. What does the word *beautification* mean in the following sentence? *Throwing away discarded trash supports the beautification of your local neighborhood.*

- (A) cleaning up
- (B) helping out
- (C) ignoring
- (D) making attractive

4. What is the text structure of paragraph three?

- (A) problem and solution
- (B) cause and effect
- (C) compare and contrast
- (D) chronological

5. What does the term *under-resourced* mean in the following sentence? *The Kids in Need Foundation is a group that supports teachers and students in under-resourced schools.*

- (A) without water
- (B) too many items
- (C) lacking supplies
- (D) closed

6. Create your own graphic organizer showing the central idea of the text and the details that support it.

Unit 4
WEEK 1
DAY
5

Name: ____________________ Date: ____________

Directions: Reread "Surprising Benefits for Volunteers" on page 66 and "Volunteer Variety" on page 68. Then, respond to the prompt.

Write a letter to your best friend encouraging them to volunteer with you. In your letter, be sure to include:

- how you want to volunteer and why
- how volunteering will benefit others
- how volunteering will benefit both of you

Name: ______________________________ Date: ______________

Directions: Read the text, and answer the questions.

As You Read

Underline details about the character.

Meet Ella

Ella Fitzgerald stood on the side of the stage at the Apollo Theater, her stomach twisted in knots as she watched the Edwards Sisters dance up a storm in front of her. Ella looked down at her weary boots as she tugged at a strand of disheveled hair.

I look nothing like them, she thought to herself. *How can I possibly go onstage after them?*

Ella was here on Amateur Night at the Apollo, and she'd planned to dance for the talent competition. However, she was slotted to perform after the Edwards Sisters, and the sisters were incredibly talented dancers. Ella felt like she only had a tablespoon of their talent.

The Edwards Sisters exited the stage, and Ella's name was called. Hands pushed her forward. She stumbled onstage under a harsh spotlight. A crowd of people stared up at her. It felt like thousands of eyes were upon her, looking at her, waiting for her to do something.

"What's she going to do?" someone asked, the question drifting up to her from the crowd.

1. What does the idiom *stomach twisted in knots* from the text reveal about Ella Fitzgerald?
   - (A) She is surprised.
   - (B) She does not know where she is.
   - (C) She has a stomachache.
   - (D) She is nervous.

2. What figurative language is used in the following sentence? *Ella felt like she only had a tablespoon of their talent.*
   - (A) metaphor
   - (B) simile
   - (C) idiom
   - (D) personification

3. Why does Ella Fitzgerald not want to dance?
   - (A) She has already performed many.
   - (B) She thinks she is not as good as the other performers.
   - (C) She is too sick to dance and wants to go home.
   - (D) The crowd is too big.

4. Why does the author use short sentences in paragraph 3?
   - (A) to show how fast everything is happening
   - (B) to detail how prepared Ella is
   - (C) to contrast the crowd with the dancers
   - (D) to show how long and detailed the Edwards Sisters' dance is

5. Ella Fitzgerald was a real person, and this story is **narrative nonfiction**. What you can infer that means?
   - (A) Everything in the story is made-up.
   - (B) Some events are real, but the author took some creative liberties.
   - (C) Everything in the story is real.
   - (D) Most events are real, and the author took no creative liberties.

Name: ______________________________ Date: ______________

Directions: Read the text, and answer the questions.

As You Read

Write a ∞ wherever you make connections. Summarize the connections in the margins.

Ella's First Song

Ella could hear the echo of *boos* chanting from the crowd as they rocked back and forth on their feet. She could feel the impatience of the crowd who wanted to be entertained and transported. Ella took a deep breath, and she could feel her voice rising, begging her to sing. Ella quickly turned to the band behind her and asked, "Can you play Hoagy Carmichael's 'Judy' for me, fellas?"

The band members nodded and quickly began to play the opening chords of the song. "Judy" had been her mother's favorite tune, and Ella knew the lyrics of this song backward and forward.

Ella started to sing, and she immediately fell into the rhythms of the song, feeling the music soar through her soul. As she sang, she imagined her melodies weaving and tugging at the hearts throughout the crowd in front of her. When she looked out, the faces of so many beautiful people looked back at her. They all stood, quiet and rapt, as she sang to them—heart to heart. A feeling of acceptance and love enveloped Ella, and in that moment, she knew she wanted to sing before people for the rest of her life.

1. What is Ella Fitzgerald's talent?

- (A) She is a musician.
- (B) She does not have a talent.
- (C) She is a dancer.
- (D) She is a singer.

2. Why does Ella Fitzgerald choose the song "Judy"?

- (A) It was her mother's favorite song.
- (B) She knows it very well.
- (C) both A and B
- (D) none of the above

3. How does the mood shift in the text?

- (A) from grumpy to unappreciative
- (B) from agitated to awed
- (C) from lackadaisical to determined
- (D) from awkward to unimpressed

4. What figurative language is used in the following sentence? *As she sang, she imagined her melodies weaving and tugging at the hearts throughout the crowd in front of her.*

- (A) personification
- (B) metaphor
- (C) simile
- (D) hyperbole

5. How does this experience affect Ella Fitzgerald?

- (A) It teaches her how to sing.
- (B) It shows her what she is passionate about.
- (C) It encourages her to be a musician.
- (D) It stops her from pursuing her dream.

6. What is the theme of the passage?

- (A) Perform in front of a large crowd.
- (B) Be confident in your abilities.
- (C) Singing can change the world.
- (D) Everyone is talented in their own way.

Name: ______________________________ Date: ______________

Directions: Read the text, and answer the questions.

As You Read

Write a ∞ wherever you make connections. Summarize the connections in the margins.

Giving Back

A few months after that first Apollo appearance, Ella received a call letting her know that she had a tryout to be a band's lead female singer. But when Ella arrived at the audition, she could tell the band leader, Chick Webb, wanted nothing to do with her. He side-eyed her, muttering to his lead singer that she "just wouldn't do." Ella bristled at Chick's dismissal; although she didn't look like women in movies or television, she knew how to sing the lights out. She was determined to show them all the power of her voice. After her tryout, Chick reluctantly gave her a two-week trial with the band, and at the end of the two weeks, she was hired! Later, Ella smiled to herself as she pocketed her salary of $12.50 for her week's work.

When Ella was offstage, she'd feel her shy, reserved nature pull over her. But when she walked onstage, she felt herself come alive. More and more, Ella realized how music brought people together. She knew it was her job to reach out to her audience, help lift their spirits, and bring them all together through joyful song.

1. Why does Chick not want to hire Ella in the beginning?
   - Ⓐ He does not think she could sing.
   - Ⓑ He does not think she is attractive enough.
   - Ⓒ He cannot pay her enough.
   - Ⓓ She is too talented, so he feels jealous.

2. According to the text, how does the Apollo appearance affect Ella's life?
   - Ⓐ It leads to fewer opportunities.
   - Ⓑ It leads to her getting an audition.
   - Ⓒ It shakes her confidence.
   - Ⓓ all of the above

3. Why does Chick eventually hire Ella?
   - Ⓐ He sees how talented she is.
   - Ⓑ He teaches her how to sing.
   - Ⓒ She changes her style.
   - Ⓓ She learns how to dance.

4. What is a likely theme or message in this passage?
   - Ⓐ It is important to be generous with your money and possessions.
   - Ⓑ There is no excuse not to volunteer.
   - Ⓒ Appreciate people for their talent, not just their looks.
   - Ⓓ Take time to appreciate family and friends.

5. Describe a connection you made to the story.

____

____

____

Name: ______________________________ Date: ____________________

As You Read

Star the cause-and-effect relationships in the story.

A Heart Full of Happiness

At the end of our lives, do we look back and ask how we'd like to be remembered? Ella felt that question tug at her over the next decades as her singing career began to soar. She sang with Chick Webb's band until his death, and in time, the band became hers. With more time, she started to hear her voice on the radio, and her favorite tunes became her everyday companions.

When World War II struck, Ella knew she wanted to do her part, and the best way she knew how to help was to reach out with her voice. Ella decided to volunteer and sing for soldiers across the United States. When she put on her first performance for them, she looked out at a sea of young faces around her stage. Some of them would not return home, she knew, while others would return to their country with deep scars for memories. With her whole heart, Ella sang to the soldiers, reaching out with her melodies to boost their spirits and morale. She hoped she could bring even a small spoonful of comfort to them.

Nearly two decades later, when Ella was asked to sing for the March of Dimes, she didn't hesitate. The March of Dimes was a television broadcast that raised money for polio patients. Polio had been crisscrossing the nation, killing thousands. Ella knew if her voice could bring in any help at all, she'd lend her melodies—free of charge. For Ella, it was never about the money she made; it was about the people she helped.

The organization asked her to sing on their televised broadcast, and Ella chose her tune "Like Someone in Love" to sing. Wrapped in a starry, midnight dress, Ella held her hands together as she sang to the invisible audience watching her from their televisions. She imagined her voice reaching through their screens, reminding them they could help, too. When she closed her song, Ella stared into the camera, speaking directly to her audience. "I wanted to talk to you for a moment, friends, about a very important job that we have to do," she said. "And we've got to do it fast so we can bring a heart full of happiness to more than 100,000 polio patients lying in hospital beds. They're depending on us to get them out." Then, she asked her audience to donate money to the cause.

That day, Ella sang and spoke from her heart, and people listened and helped out in return. Ella's career would continue to soar, and she would continue to help others. *How do I want to be remembered?* Ella sometimes wondered. For all her days, she hoped she'd be remembered for bringing a heart full of happiness to others.

Name: ______________________ Date: ______________

Directions: Read "A Heart Full of Happiness." Then, answer the questions.

1. Why does Ella Fitzgerald volunteer during World War II and the polio epidemic?

- (A) She knows she needs to help her country.
- (B) She feels pressured to volunteer.
- (C) She is angry about the war.
- (D) She is worried polio will spread.

2. How does Ella choose to volunteer?

- (A) fashion
- (B) traveling
- (C) collecting food
- (D) singing

3. How does Ella decide how to help?

- (A) She wishes to end the war.
- (B) She hears from soldiers who need her.
- (C) She is encouraged by other people.
- (D) She reflects on her talents.

4. What is likely the author's perspective of Ella's volunteer work?

- (A) Ella shared her talent to help others.
- (B) Ella only cared about her music career.
- (C) Ella tried to become more popular by volunteering.
- (D) Ella's volunteer work did not make a big difference.

5. How does Ella make affect others through her volunteer work for polio patients?

____

____

____

____

6. How would you help your community during a time of crisis? How would this compare with what Ella Fitzgerald did?

____

____

____

____

____

____

____

____

____

____

Name: ______________________________ Date: ______________

Directions: Reread "A Heart Full of Happiness." Then, respond to the prompt.

Do you think Ella Fitzgerald was an important volunteer during World War II and the polio epidemic? Defend your claim with reasons and evidence from the text.

Name: ______________________________ Date: ________________

Volunteers Needed!

Join us and lend a helping hand to keep our beautiful beaches trash free!

Last year, our team helped remove over 8,000 pounds (3,629 kilograms) of garbage from our coastlines!

We are looking for enthusiastic people to help us pick up trash and sort the debris at French Beach this Sunday from 11 a.m. to 1 p.m.

Consider giving just an hour or two of your time, and it will make a huge difference for our ocean friends.

Our group likes to have a ton of fun, and you'll also get a chance to meet fellow volunteers.

Join us and help us take care of our planet.

Name: ______________________________ Date: ____________________

Directions: Read the "Volunteers Needed" poster. Then, answer the questions.

1. What is the purpose of the flyer?

- (A) to persuade
- (B) to entertain
- (C) to inform
- (D) to support

2. Who is the intended audience for the flyer?

- (A) People who like to go to the beach.
- (B) People who have extra time on their hands.
- (C) People who care about the environment.
- (D) all of the above

3. What does the word *debris* mean as used in the flyer?

- (A) marine life
- (B) garbage
- (C) shells
- (D) friends

4. How does the picture support the author's purpose?

- (A) It shows the effect trash has on the beach.
- (B) It supports the statistic.
- (C) It shows people working together to clean the beach.
- (D) It argues that the environment needs help.

5. What information would you add to the flyer to strengthen it and support its purpose?

____

____

____

____

6. What are some reasons people might want to respond to this flyer and join the effort?

____

____

____

____

Name: ______________________ Date: ______________

Directions: Closely reread the texts. Then, compare and contrast the actions of volunteers during COVID-19 to the actions of Ella Fitzgerald during World War II.

Close-Reading Texts

Who Are Volunteers?

Volunteers work at many different places. This can include animal shelters, schools, churches, and more! Some people volunteer at food banks or soup kitchens. These are places that provide food to people who struggle to get enough to eat. Volunteers can also work in parks or cities and clean up trash. Volunteers may help "beautify" spaces by painting or restoring areas. There are endless opportunities for volunteering in the world.

Emergency situations can also create a need for volunteers. During the COVID-19 pandemic, thousands of people signed up to volunteer. Volunteers provided care and support to vulnerable groups of people, such as the elderly. They sent them cards or delivered groceries to them. People who used to work as nurses came out of retirement and volunteered their time to help take care of people. In times of crisis like this, volunteers are a huge source of help. But volunteering is not only something people can do in an emergency. People can volunteer in their communities year-round, too!

A Heart Full of Happiness

At the end of our lives, do we look back and ask how we'd like to be remembered? Ella felt that question tug at her over the next decades as her singing career began to soar. She sang with Chick Webb's band until his death, and in time, the band became hers. With more time, she started to hear her voice on the radio, and her favorite tunes became her everyday companions.

When World War II struck, Ella knew she wanted to do her part, and the best way she knew how to help was to reach out with her voice. Ella decided to volunteer and sing for soldiers across the United States. When she put on her first performance for them, she looked out at a sea of young faces around her stage. Some of them would not return home, she knew, while others would return to their country with deep scars for memories. With her whole heart, Ella sang to the soldiers, reaching out with her melodies to boost their spirits and morale. She hoped she could bring even a small spoonful of comfort to them.

Volunteers during COVID-19	Similarities	Ella Fitzgerald during WWII

Name: ______________________________ Date: ______________

Directions: Closely reread the texts. Then, identify the transition words or prepositional phrases the authors use to organize the texts.

Close-Reading Texts

Who Are Volunteers?	A Heart Full of Happiness
Volunteers are people who help other people without being paid for it. Some volunteers give their time, while others share their abilities or resources. People can volunteer in many different ways. Volunteers work at many different places. This can include animal shelters, schools, churches, and more! Some people volunteer at food banks or soup kitchens. These are places that provide food to people who struggle to get enough to eat. Volunteers can also work in parks or cities and clean up trash. Volunteers may help "beautify" spaces by painting or restoring areas. There are endless opportunities for volunteering in the world. Emergency situations can also create a need for volunteers. During the COVID-19 pandemic, thousands of people signed up to volunteer. Volunteers provided care and support to vulnerable groups of people, such as the elderly. They sent them cards or delivered groceries to them. People who used to work as nurses came out of retirement and volunteered their time to help take care of people. In times of crisis like this, volunteers are a huge source of help. But volunteering is not only something people can do in an emergency. People can volunteer in their communities year-round, too!	*At the end of our lives, do we look back and ask how we'd like to be remembered?* Ella felt that question tug at her over the next decades as her singing career began to soar. She sang with Chick Webb's band until his death, and in time, the band became hers. With more time, she started to hear her voice on the radio, and her favorite tunes became her everyday companions. When World War II struck, Ella knew she wanted to do her part, and the best way she knew how to help was to reach out with her voice. Ella decided to volunteer and sing for soldiers across the United States. When she put on her first performance for them, she looked out at a sea of young faces around her stage. Some of them would not return home, she knew, while others would return to their country with deep scars for memories. With her whole heart, Ella sang to the soldiers, reaching out with her melodies to boost their spirits and morale. She hoped she could bring even a small spoonful of comfort to them.

Who Are Volunteers?	
A Heart Full of Happiness	

Name: ______________________________ Date: ________________

Directions: Reread "A Heart Full of Happiness." Then, respond to the prompt.

Imagine you are a newspaper reporter interviewing Ella Fitzgerald. Create a set of questions you would ask Ella Fitzgerald. Then, answer them as if you are Ella Fitzgerald. Use details from the text to support your ideas.

Name: ____________________ Date: ____________

Directions: Create a storyboard of Ella Fitzgerald's life with three or more sections. Be sure to include the effect music had on her and how her music affected others.

Name: ______________________ Date: ______________

Directions: Read the text, and answer the questions.

As You Read

Underline new or interesting information.

What Is Wearable Technology?

Technology continues to evolve at a rapid pace. In the past, a computer could take up 1,000 square feet (93 square meters) of space. That's roughly the size of a two-bedroom apartment! Nowadays, tiny computers and smart tech can fit into watches and phones. People are still learning how to design technology that fits into their lives. As people experiment, new inventions keep emerging.

One area that's seen a lot of recent growth is wearable technology. Wearable technology refers to electronic devices people can wear on their bodies. The most common example of wearable tech is a smartwatch. A smartwatch can conveniently display notifications right on your wrist. But wearable technology, or "wearables," are not limited to smartwatches. Other kinds include fitness trackers, smart jewelry, and smart clothing. Wearables are often fun to use and can make life a lot easier. But wearables may also change—and save—lives in the future. Many wearables are designed with a key goal in mind. They are supposed to help people manage and monitor their health.

1. What is the purpose of this text?

- (A) to entertain readers with a story about the topic
- (B) to describe and give background on the topic
- (C) to persuade the readers to purchase new technology
- (D) to compare and contrast types of smartwatches

2. What does the word *conveniently* mean in the text?

- (A) difficult
- (B) minute
- (C) superior
- (D) easily

3. According to the author, why was this kind of technology invented?

- (A) to fit into our lives
- (B) to be fashionable
- (C) to be an electronic device
- (D) to be cutting edge

4. What is the purpose of a smartwatch?

- (A) entertainment
- (C) convenience
- (B) design
- (D) business

5. How has technology evolved?

- (A) by expanding to the size of a two-bedroom apartment
- (B) by getting smaller and more powerful
- (C) by being more difficult to use
- (D) all of the above

Name: ______________________ Date: ______________

Directions: Read the text, and answer the questions.

As You Read

Put a star next to new or important vocabulary terms.
Use the clues in the text to help you define the new words.

Smartwatches, Smart Rings

Smartwatches are currently the best-known type of wearable technology, and they have become a powerful way for people to track and understand their health data. Smartwatches sit on your wrist and can track your heart rate, how many steps you take a day, and how many calories you burn. They can also track your blood oxygen levels and how long you sleep at night. For people who are struggling with their health, collecting this kind of data can be helpful and motivating. It creates a strong record, letting them know if they need to make a change to their daily routines. Smartwatches can do more than just track health data. They can also connect you to loved ones, let you listen to audiobooks, and much more.

If you're looking for smart jewelry that is more discrete than a smartwatch, a smart ring may be the way to go. These rings can collect data right from the pulse in your finger. Some smart rings can track your sleep, your heart rate at night, and your body temperature. Using this data, companies can give you insights on how to achieve deeper sleep. No matter if it is a watch or ring, these wearables are powerful tools to improve human health.

1. According to the text, why are wearables useful?
   - (A) They help people collect information in secret.
   - (B) They inspire people to exercise.
   - (C) They help people learn about their health.
   - (D) They are small enough to improve people's lives.

2. According to the text, why might someone choose a smart ring over a smartwatch?
   - (A) Smart rings are smaller.
   - (B) Smart rings are more fashionable.
   - (C) Smart rings are less expensive.
   - (D) Smart rings collect more data.

3. What does the word *data* mean as used in the text?
   - (A) improvement
   - (B) jewelry
   - (C) diet
   - (D) information

4. Which sentence best supports the reader's understanding of the word *data*?
   - (A) They can also connect you to loved ones, let you listen to audiobooks, and much more.
   - (B) Smartwatches are currently the best-known type of wearable technology.
   - (C) Some smart rings can track how deeply you sleep, your heart rate at night, and your body temperature.
   - (D) No matter if it is a watch or ring, these wearables are powerful tools to improve human health.

5. What is the author's tone in the paragraph?
   - (A) frustrated
   - (B) worried
   - (C) careful
   - (D) optimistic

135159—180 Days of Reading

Name: ______________________ Date: ______________

Directions: Read the text, and answer the questions.

As You Read

Circle interesting details about smart clothing.

Smart Clothing

Smartwatches and smart rings have the largest fanbase, but smart clothing is another kind of wearable on the rise. Many brands of smart clothing are looking for ways to improve the lives of their users. Brands often achieve this by tracking things that can improve health.

Smart clothing is usually made with unique textiles, or types of cloth. It is known as electronic textiles or e-textiles. Electronic textiles use sensors, circuits, and other hardware to track a person's activities. Smart clothing comes in various shapes with different purposes. These wearables range from yoga gear that can help you get into the right position to jean jackets that can play music. One brand of smart exercise gear can track your heart rate and assess your stress levels. Another brand offers baby clothes that track a little one's sleeping and breathing habits. One brand sells swimsuits that can alert someone to apply sunscreen or get out of the sun once they've had enough light exposure. Wearing smart clothing can be an innovative approach to taking care of your health.

1. What is the text structure of this passage?

- (A) description
- (B) cause and effect
- (C) problem and solution
- (D) compare and contrast

2. What makes smart clothing useful?

- (A) It can help protect users from sunburn.
- (B) It can be worn during any activity.
- (C) It can track users' movements.
- (D) all of the above

3. What is the meaning of the word *hardware* as used in the text?

- (A) equipment
- (B) thread
- (C) cloth
- (D) sparks

4. What is the main benefit of smart clothing?

- (A) It is fashionable.
- (B) It collects data that help people learn about their bodies.
- (C) It can protect people from getting hurt.
- (D) It is expensive and will increase in value over time.

5. Why might someone choose to wear smart clothing? Use the text to support your ideas.

____

____

6. What type of smart clothing sounds the most useful to you? Use details from the paragraph to support your ideas.

____

____

Name: ______________________________ Date: ____________________

As You Read

Underline details that inspire or interest you.

Medical Wearables

Wearable technology makes a big difference in people's lives. Wearables have even been created for medical technology. There are many examples of these wearables. Hearing aids are one common option. There are also devices that administer medication. Wearable medical tech often helps people live longer and healthier lives. When it comes to medical wearables, designers must consider their users. They must answer a couple of key questions. How will people use their products? How can they also make their products easy to use and more beautiful to look at?

Dr. Leah Heiss is a designer in Australia. She is focused on creating human-centered medical technology. Medical tech has helped improve the lives of many, but medical tech can also look awkward and bulky. For Heiss, her goal is to design with people in mind. One of her first products was a hearing aid called *Facett*. First, she surveyed users who had lost their hearing. She found they often did not want to be seen as having a disability. Also, they usually disliked the unattractive look of hearing aids. So, Heiss decided to design a hearing aid that is visually appealing. She designed her hearing aids in the shape of crystals. She also built the aids using rechargeable batteries. Each battery is magnetic, allowing users to simply click it into place. Many regular hearing aids use disposable batteries. These batteries are difficult to put in if someone has arthritis. Arthritis causes physical pain in the joints. By chatting with people who use hearing aids, Heiss discovered their problems with the technology. She used that information to design a product that sidestepped these issues and is also beautiful to look at.

Dr. Heiss and some of her jewelry designs

Next up on Heiss's list was to create diabetic jewelry. People who have diabetes must inject a medicine called *insulin* daily. Heiss had talked to teenagers who felt embarrassed by this daily process. They would slink away to the bathroom to administer their insulin so no one would see. Heiss began experimenting with creating diabetes jewelry. She wanted to make something that looked attractive. It also had to administer insulin discreetly. She ended up designing a shiny necklace that can do just that! It uses tiny needles, and the necklace looks like a regular piece of jewelry. However, users can wear it and feel more confident.

Designers like Dr. Leah Heiss are helping make medical tech useful and beautiful for people. Wearable technology is changing their lives. It is also making healthcare empowering and accessible.

Name: ______________________ Date: ______________

Directions: Read "Medical Wearables." Then, answer the questions.

1. Why does the author ask questions in paragraph 1?
   - (A) to model how to create smart clothing
   - (B) to highlight the importance of health
   - (C) to emphasize the goals of the designers
   - (D) to demonstrate how to use medial wearables

2. What motivated Dr. Heiss to create appealing hearing aids?
   - (A) She is a medical expert who was worried about her clients.
   - (B) She needs a medical device and wanted to make something better.
   - (C) She wanted to create devices that are focused on helping people.
   - (D) She wanted to help teens who need to inject insulin.

3. What is the most important step in Dr. Heiss's process of creating wearable medical technology?
   - (A) discovering a cure for illness
   - (B) learning about different medicines
   - (C) interviewing people who use it
   - (D) designing empowering jewelry

4. What is the author's opinion of Dr. Heiss?
   - (A) Dr. Heiss created beautiful medical devices.
   - (B) Dr. Heiss is a designer of medical jewelry.
   - (C) Dr. Heiss created a new type of hearing aids.
   - (D) Dr. Heiss created a type of insulin jewlery.

5. What did both groups that Dr. Heiss interviewed have in common?
   - (A) They were excited to be interviewed by a doctor.
   - (B) They were both looking for jewelry to help them administer their medication with pride.
   - (C) They were both seeking respect from the medical community.
   - (D) They both did not want to be seen as having a disability.

6. What does the word *discreetly* mean?
   - (A) loudly
   - (B) secretly
   - (C) beautifully
   - (D) creatively

7. Describe two causes and effects of Dr. Heiss inventing a stylish hearing aid.

Cause	**Effect**

Name: ______________________ Date: ____________

Directions: Reread "Smart Clothing." Then, respond to the prompt.

Imagine you are a designer who has been asked to create a brand-new piece of smart clothing. Write a pitch for your new item. Include the name of the item, its purpose, a description of it, and a drawing of what it would look like.

Name: ______________________ Date: ______________

Directions: Read the text, and answer the questions.

As You Read

Underline the details in the story that show the setting.

My Clothes Are Smart

It's 2060, and Jaden is just an ordinary teenager. He is a colossal fan of smart clothes, and he's always loved having a closet full of tech-savvy fabrics. All his friends agree that smart clothes are infinitely more fun to try on and try out. For this reason, Jaden knows he is beyond lucky to have a dad in the tech industry. His dad works for a company that loves sharing and testing out its latest smart products. Whenever there is a new smart sock, sneaker, or jacket in town, Jaden gets to try it on and tell all his friends about it. But, at dinner one night, after Jaden tells his dad about all the new smart clothes he wants to get, his dad gives him a gentle reminder.

"Remember," his dad says, "I want you to think about the *why* behind your smart clothes because function always comes first in design. Function is the ultimate purpose of a piece of clothing. What is the purpose of each piece of smart clothing in your life?"

1. How is the setting important to the story?

- (A) It shows the importance of technology.
- (B) It adds a futuristic feel to the story.
- (C) It gives details about Jaden's age.
- (D) It explains how smart clothes became popular.

2. What does *savvy* mean as used in the following sentence? *He's always loved having a closet full of tech-savvy fabrics.*

- (A) detailed
- (B) covered
- (C) interested
- (D) knowledgeable

3. Which word best describes Jaden's dad?

- (A) triumphant
- (B) intentional
- (C) intimidating
- (D) particular

4. Why does Jaden like smart clothes?

- (A) He wants to please his dad.
- (B) His dad buys them for him.
- (C) He thinks they are fun.
- (D) He likes to brag about the latest trends.

5. What does the word *colossal* mean in the text?

- (A) massive
- (B) popular
- (C) spoiled
- (D) grateful

6. How does Jaden's dad's job benefit Jaden?

- (A) Jaden's dad works at a tech company.
- (B) Jaden's dad loves all the smart clothes just like his son.
- (C) The company keeps the clothes secret.
- (D) Jaden gets to use the latest smart clothes.

Name: ______________________ Date: ______________

Directions: Read the text, and answer the questions.

As You Read

Circle words or phrases that show the main character's personality.

My Jacket Is Smart

Jaden's smart wardrobe is, without a doubt, the envy of many fellow classmates. But, ever since Jaden's conversation with his dad, he keeps hearing his dad's words echoing in his ears. Jaden wonders, *Do I like to wear smart clothes just to be on trend, or are they actually improving my life?*

Jaden's favorite piece of smart clothing has always been the five-pocket jacket his dad got him. The jacket employs conductive yarn to connect with the smartphone in his pocket. It allows Jaden to answer calls from his cousin and listen to music without ever pulling his smartphone out. His friends always gape and stare in awe at seeing the jacket in action, and no one else at school has a jacket even remotely similar. Jaden's dad told him the jacket was first made for cyclists so they could use their phones hands-free while cycling.

Jaden pulls on the jacket and looks inquisitively at himself in the mirror. He thinks back, remembering that the last time he went cycling was several years ago. Jaden furrows his brow. *Why do I need this jacket? If it weren't for my tech connection, would I really buy this with my own hard-earned money?*

1. How is Jaden's dad influencing Jaden?

- (A) He is helping Jaden become interested in cycling again.
- (B) He is teaching Jaden how to sell smart clothes.
- (C) He is challenging Jaden's ideas about smart clothes.
- (D) He is inspiring Jaden to show off his smart clothes.

2. What is Jaden's conflict?

- (A) He is angry at his dad for buying him smart clothes.
- (B) He is disappointed he has not been using his smart jacket for cycling.
- (C) His friends are jealous of his smart clothes.
- (D) He is questioning his interest in smart clothing.

3. Which line from the story best captures Jaden's conflict?

- (A) Jaden's smart wardrobe is, without a doubt, the envy of many fellow classmates.
- (B) Jaden's favorite piece of smart clothing has always been the 5-pocket jacket his dad got him.
- (C) His friends always gape and stare in awe at seeing the jacket in action, and no one else at school has a jacket even remotely similar.
- (D) *Why do I need this jacket?*

4. What does the jacket symbolize in the story?

- (A) status
- (B) friendship
- (C) carelessness
- (D) athleticism

Name: ______________________________ Date: ______________

Directions: Read the text, and answer the questions.

As You Read

Write a ∞ wherever you make connections. Summarize your connections in the margins.

My Socks Are Smart

Jaden is the third-fastest runner on his track team, and his fastest running time *just* lags behind Sasha's and Nathan's times. They are the school's top two runners. Jaden is planning to get faster though, and he's thinking he might get some help from his new smart socks.

All morning, Jaden's thoughts have bounced back and forth in his head as he considers how much smart gear he *actually* needs in his life. But he's excited to try out his new smart socks. His dad walked him through the ins and outs, pointing out each sock's pressure sensors, which will track the pressure Jaden puts on his feet when he runs. The socks collect data by monitoring his running pace and the distance he has traveled. An AI, or artificial intelligence, coach uses this data to give Jaden feedback via his smartphone. His dad thinks the socks will bolster Jaden's running speed and quicken his running pace.

At his afternoon track practice, Jaden gives the socks a try, and he checks the data on his phone afterward. The little AI coach gives him a virtual thumbs-up, along with some tips on how to improve his speed. Jaden's real-life coach gives him additional tips, too. Jaden pairs the feedback from both coaches together in his running plan.

1. Based on the text, what is artificial intelligence?

- (A) technology that is popular to use during sports
- (B) objects that are used to increase your running speed
- (C) objects that make running more comfortable
- (D) technology that collects data and provides answers

2. What does the idiom *ins and outs* mean in the second paragraph?

- (A) details
- (B) doors
- (C) data
- (D) focus

3. What does the word *bolster* mean in the text?

- (A) to provide traction
- (B) to quicken or strengthen
- (C) to reduce
- (D) to make consistent

4. How is Jaden responding to his conflict? Use details from the text to support your ideas.

____

____

____

5. How will Jaden improve his running speed? Use details from the text to support your ideas.

____

____

Name: ______________________________ Date: ______________

As You Read

Write a ∞ wherever you make connections. Summarize your connections in the margins.

Like Dad, Like Son

When Jaden returns home, his dad is waiting for him at the kitchen table with a big glass of iced tea. They talk about Jaden's running practice. His dad begins to gather the ingredients for a chili he's making for dinner that night.

"Dad," Jaden begins, "you told me last week to think about the *why* behind my smart clothes, and you told me to look out for the function of each piece. Did you say that because you think I should ditch some of my smart clothes?"

His dad looks thoughtful as he stirs red pepper flakes into their chili. "Jaden, I love sharing all this cutting-edge tech gear with you, especially because it's from an industry I'm passionate about. I do think that smart clothes are going to keep evolving and changing lives. But I think you and I might share this 'shiny-new-thing syndrome,' which means we often buy something without thinking about whether we need it. That's why I wanted to chat with you about the function of tech fashion. It was also to get us both reflecting on what technology will improve our lives and what tech we can probably leave behind."

Jaden replies, "I was looking at my jacket this morning—the one with that cool, conductive yarn—and I realized I don't really use it as a 'smart jacket,' you know? I mainly use it as a regular jacket that I sometimes use to play a couple songs, which I could easily do with my other devices."

Jaden's face brightens, though, when he thinks of his smart socks. "But I really like those smart socks you got me, the ones with the pressure sensors. Those socks are off the charts, and I already have so many ideas on how to outrun Sasha and Nathan after using them."

Jaden's dad laughs and says, "You see, that sounds like smart clothing with a clear function and purpose."

Jaden nods as his dad begins to stir more spices into the chili. "I think I might need to look again at what's in my closet and maybe donate a couple of things. Is that okay with you?"

"Absolutely, Jaden," his dad says. "And while you're at it, I might join you in decluttering my closet, too."

Name: ____________________ Date: ____________

Directions: Read "Like Dad, Like Son." Then, answer the questions.

1. What is the mood at the end of the story?

- (A) resigned
- (B) supportive
- (C) nonchalant
- (D) questionable

2. How has Jaden's dad challenged him?

- (A) by asking Jaden to reflect on his habits
- (B) by forcing Jaden to donate his smart clothes
- (C) by challenging Jaden to become a better runner
- (D) by giving Jaden smart socks

3. What does the following sentence show about Jaden? *Jaden's face brightens, though, when he thinks to his smart socks.*

- (A) Jaden is embarrassed.
- (B) Jaden is feeling happy.
- (C) Jaden is seeing his reflection.
- (D) Jaden is in the sunlight.

4. What does the prefix *de–* mean in the word *decluttering*?

- (A) over
- (B) apply
- (C) remove
- (D) before

5. What is the theme of the story?

- (A) Use smart clothes to help you be a better athlete.
- (B) Dad knows best.
- (C) Be mindful of your habits.
- (D) Donating is a great cause.

6. Which detail is most important to include in a summary of the story?

- (A) Jaden wants to be popular amongst his friends.
- (B) Jaden's dad asks him to think about the purpose of his smart clothes.
- (C) Jaden's dad makes chili for dinner while the two of them talk.
- (D) Sasha and Nathan are the two top runners at Jaden's school.

7. Summarize the story using the words in the graphic organizer as a guide for what to include in each section.

Somebody...	
Wanted...	
But...	
So...	
Then...	

Name: ______________________________ Date: ______________

Directions: Reread "Like Dad, Like Son." Then, respond to the prompt.

Imagine you are Jaden and you have been asked to write a persuasive speech about the importance of being mindful about the smart clothes that you purchase. Use details from the story to support your ideas.

Name: ______________________ Date: ______________

SMART EVOLUTION

1975 Pulsar Watch

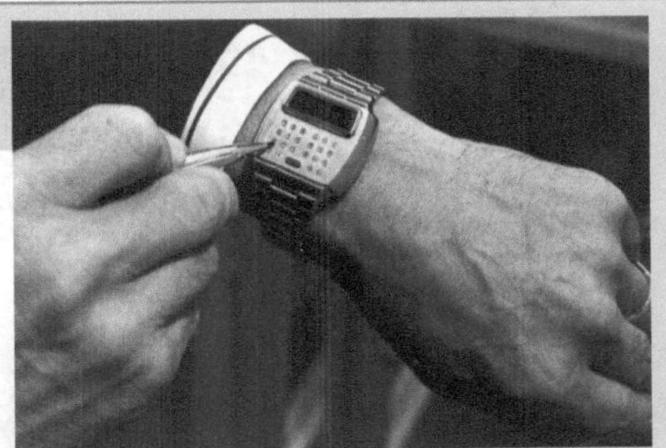

The first wristwatches to include electronic equipment were calculator watches. They were first released in 1975, and each one had a 9-digit display.

2004 SPOT Watch

Created in 2004, this was one of the first smartwatches. The watch notified you of weather and news updates using radio waves. You could also receive emails and messages, but there was no "reply" button.

2010-present Smartwatches

Smartwatches continued to evolve with releases in 2010 and 2015. These watches could connect to and receive data from a smartphone. Users could reply to many notifications received through the watch, such as text messages, emails, and phone calls.

Name: ______________________________ Date: ________________

Directions: Read "Smart Evolution." Then, answer the questions.

1. Based on the text, what is an "evolution"?

- (A) device
- (B) power
- (C) perfection
- (D) development

2. What is the author's purpose of this text?

- (A) to explain the first smartwatch and its display
- (B) to argue that the most recent watch is the best device
- (C) to show how smartwatches have developed over time
- (D) to challenge the idea that smartwatches are easy to design

3. How did the author structure the text?

- (A) by giving examples of smartwatches in chronological order
- (B) by showing the effects of smartwatches on their users
- (C) by explaining a problem with smartwatches and offering a solution
- (D) by comparing smartwatches

4. How are the most recent smartwatches different from previous watches?

- (A) The most recent smartwatches are worn around the wrist.
- (B) The most recent smartwatches display weather information.
- (C) The most recent smartwatches cannot reply to messages.
- (D) The most recent smartwatches connect to smartphones.

5. Complete the time line by adding three more pieces of smart, wearable technology that have come out after 2010. Do additional reserach to complete the graphic organizer.

Brand	Brand	Brand
Name	Name	Name
Purpose/Feature	Purpose/Feature	Purpose/Feature

Name: ______________________________ Date: ________________

Directions: Closely reread the texts. Then, record the adjectives and adverbs used in each, and answer the question.

Close-Reading Texts

Smartwatches, Smart Rings	Medical Wearables
Smartwatches can do more than just track health data. They can also connect you to loved ones, let you listen to audiobooks, and much more. If you're looking for smart jewelry that is more discrete than a smartwatch, a smart ring may be the way to go. These rings can collect data right from the pulse in your finger. Some smart rings can track your sleep, your heart rate at night, and your body temperature. Using this data, companies can give you insights on how to achieve deeper sleep. No matter if it is a watch or ring, these wearables are powerful tools to improve human health.	Next up on Heiss's list was to create diabetic jewelry. People who have diabetes must inject a medicine called *insulin* daily. Heiss had talked to teenagers who felt embarrassed by this daily process. They would slink away to the bathroom to administer their insulin so no one would see. Heiss began experimenting with creating diabetes jewelry. She wanted to make something that looked attractive. It also had to administer insulin discreetly. She ended up designing a shiny necklace that can do just that! It uses tiny needles, and the necklace looks like a regular piece of jewelry. However, users can wear it and feel more confident.

	Smartwatches, Smart Rings	Medical Wearables
Adjectives		
Adverbs		

What do you notice about the language used in these two texts?

____

____

____

____

Name: ______________________________ Date: ________________

Directions: Closely reread the texts. Then, list the type of data collected by each device.

Close-Reading Texts

My Socks Are Smart	Smartwatches, Smart Rings
All morning, Jaden's thoughts have bounced back and forth in his head as he considers how much smart gear he *actually* needs in his life. But he's excited to try out his new smart socks. His dad walked him through the ins and outs, pointing out each sock's pressure sensors, which will track the pressure Jaden puts on his feet when he runs. The socks collect data by monitoring his running pace and the distance he has traveled. An AI, or artificial intelligence, coach uses this data to give Jaden feedback via his smartphone. His dad thinks the socks will bolster Jaden's running speed and quicken his running pace. At his afternoon track practice, Jaden gives the socks a try, and he checks the data on his phone afterward. The little AI coach gives him a virtual thumbs-up, along with some tips on how to improve his speed. Jaden's real-life coach gives him additional tips, too. Jaden pairs the feedback from both coaches together in his running plan.	Smartwatches are currently the best-known type of wearable technology, and they have become a powerful way for people to track and understand their health data. Smartwatches sit on your wrist and can track your heart rate, how many steps you take a day, and how many calories you burn. They can also track your blood oxygen levels and how long you sleep at night. For people who are struggling with their health, collecting this kind of data can be helpful and motivating. It creates a strong record, letting them know if they need to make a change to their daily routines. Smartwatches can do more than just track health data. They can also connect you to loved ones, let you listen to audiobooks, and much more. If you're looking for smart jewelry that is more discrete than a smartwatch, a smart ring may be the way to go. These rings can collect data right from the pulse in your finger. Some smart rings can track your sleep, your heart rate at night, and your body temperature. Using this data, companies can give you insights on how to achieve deeper sleep. No matter if it is a watch or ring, these wearables are powerful tools to improve human health.

Device	Data Collected
Smart Socks	
Smartwatches	
Smart Rings	

Name: ______________________________ Date: ______________

Directions: Reread "My Clothes Are Smart." Then, respond to the prompt.

Write an argumentative essay in which you agree or disagree with Jaden's dad about smart clothes. Be sure to include your claim, reasons, and evidence to support your claim.

Name: ______________________________ Date: ______________

Directions: Reread "Medical Wearables." Then, respond to the prompt.

Create an award for Dr. Leah Heiss that recognizes and celebrates her accomplishments as a smart wearable designer. Write a short dedication that includes the title of the award, the purpose of the award, and why Dr. Heiss is receiving it. Then, sketch what the award would look like.

Name: ______________________ Date: ______________

Directions: Read the text, and answer the questions.

As You Read

Annotate the margins with your thoughts, questions, and connections.

The Soundtrack of Our Lives

People around the world listen to a diverse range of music. This includes rock, reggae, jazz, folk, classical, and many more genres! Across different decades and places, music provides the soundtrack to our lives. We listen to music that is upbeat to pump ourselves up before important events. Sad songs comfort us after deep and tender losses. Many road trips are accompanied by an endless playlist of sing-along songs. Partners on a dance floor might two-step to a country beat or sway to a classical waltz. Marching bands move to the beat and rhythm of their music. Many people like to whistle while they work. Some people test out the acoustics in their showers by singing their favorite songs.

Music is an integral part of our lives, and there are compelling reasons why people across the world love music. Researchers have found that music lights up different parts of the human brain, including parts of our brains that are connected to our emotions. Listening to music can shift how we feel, help us connect to long-lost memories, and make us feel more deeply connected to one another.

1. What does the word *diverse* mean?

- Ⓐ many
- Ⓑ different
- Ⓒ simple
- Ⓓ enjoyable

2. According to the text, why is there a diverse range of music in the world?

- Ⓐ Creative people make music.
- Ⓑ Music is for dancing.
- Ⓒ Music is listened to at different times.
- Ⓓ People sing different songs in the shower.

3. How can music affect our moods?

- Ⓐ It is different across the world.
- Ⓑ It connects to our emotions.
- Ⓒ People like music for different reasons.
- Ⓓ Some people listen to music when they work.

4. What is the author's tone?

- Ⓐ calm
- Ⓑ complicated
- Ⓒ melodic
- Ⓓ informational

5. What does the word *acoustics* mean?

- Ⓐ sounds
- Ⓑ water
- Ⓒ distances
- Ⓓ voice

6. What does the prefix *in*– mean as used in the word *integral*?

- Ⓐ not
- Ⓑ within
- Ⓒ above
- Ⓓ opposite of

Name: ______________________________ Date: ________________

Directions: Read the text, and answer the questions.

As You Read

Annotate the margins with your thoughts, questions, and connections.

Music and Mood

Music has the power to influence and shift our moods. Listening to music can help us feel more joy, comfort, or even a sense of relief. Different types of music can shape our moods in different ways.

In one study, researchers found that when people experience a loss, such as a break-up, they are more drawn to sad music. The researchers think sad music helps people feel less alone. Listening to sad music might make you feel like there's someone next to you who understands and empathizes with your loss. However, music is not only for times of sadness or despair.

Some studies have focused on how music can lift your mood. Have you ever noticed that you feel a bit more upbeat while listening to your favorite songs? When someone listens to their favorite songs, more dopamine, a neurotransmitter, is released in their brain. Some people call dopamine a "mood-enhancing" chemical. When dopamine is released, people tend to feel good or feel a sense of pleasure. The release of dopamine is only higher, though, when people are listening to music they personally love. If your mood needs a boost, make sure you turn to your playlist of favorites and not a friend's!

1. How does the author structure the text?

- (A) by listing the reasons why someone would listen to upbeat music
- (B) by offering a solution to being sad after a breakup
- (C) by describing different music types
- (D) by comparing music that is sad to music that is uplifting

2. What is the main idea of the text?

- (A) People listen to sad music after a breakup.
- (B) Listening to your music is better than listening to someone else's.
- (C) Different types of music support people in different ways.
- (D) Dopamine is a chemical in the brain.

3. Which line from the text best supports the main idea of the text?

- (A) Different types of music shape our moods in different ways.
- (B) However, music is not only for times of sadness or despair.
- (C) Some people call dopamine a "mood-enhancing" chemical.
- (D) If your mood needs a boost, make sure you turn to your playlist of favorites and not a friend's!

4. Which recommendation would be best to give to a friend who needs a pick-me-up?

- (A) Here! Listen to my favorite playlist.
- (B) Make a playlist of your favorite sad songs.
- (C) Listen to your favorite upbeat songs from your favorite artists.
- (D) Find a playlist that has happy songs on it.

Name: ______________________________ Date: ______________

Directions: Read the text, and answer the questions.

As You Read

Annotate the margins with your thoughts, questions, and connections.

Music and Memories

Music and nostalgia often go hand-in-hand. Holiday songs can conjure up memories of bonding with family or friends. Wedding songs can bring to mind fancy dresses and vows between two people in love. For most people, there is a playlist of songs that can transport them back in time. These special tunes are tied to emotional memories. Emotional memories have staying power in our brains. We are quicker to recall and reflect on memories that have layers of great feeling. This is because our brains are built to pair music with long-term memory. For instance, music is used to help improve the memory of people with Alzheimer's disease. People with Alzheimer's struggle with memory loss. Research suggests that hearing music tied to the past can help people with the disease connect with long-ago memories. In one study, people with Alzheimer's also scored higher on memory tests when they listened to classical music. Next time you feel nostalgic while listening to music, remember that music can be closely tied to our memories!

1. The author suggests music can ______.

- (A) affect memories
- (B) create stories
- (C) be played weddings
- (D) cause people to feel emotional

2. The author uses Alzheimer's disease as an example to emphasize ______.

- (A) how much people love music, regardless of age
- (B) music's ability to affect memories
- (C) the importance of music in the medical field
- (D) why doctors should use music as a research tool

3. What does the prefix *re–* mean as used in the words *recall* and *reflect*?

- (A) try
- (B) over
- (C) again
- (D) memory

4. According to the text, how can music be used as medicine?

- (A) It can be used to treat a cold.
- (B) It can make wounds heal faster.
- (C) It can help people with memory loss.
- (D) It can improve people's blood pressure.

5. Why is music considered a powerful force in our lives? Use details from the text to support your ideas.

____

____

____

____

____

Name: ________________________ Date: ____________

As You Read

Annotate the margins with your thoughts, questions, and connections.

Our Musical Bonds

Music has the ability to alter our moods. Certain melodies can reignite dormant memories. And music can help bring and bond people together. This can happen in different ways.

For our ancestors, music was not played through streaming services or smart devices. Instead, they listened to music live and in-person. They might have listened to tunes played on simple instruments with a group of people. Researchers think these group engagements helped create a sense of safety and connection for our ancestors. This camaraderie likely aided in their survival.

Music usually requires people to coordinate and function together as a unit. A band works best when the singer, drummer, and guitar player are in harmony. A song only comes together when all bandmates are on beat and harmonizing as a unit. Research shows that when we attempt to sync our sounds with others, we feel "positive social feelings" toward them. Playing music together helps us feel closer with our music mates. There is a sense of community when people match rhythms with each other.

Research has also shown that music can affect our oxytocin levels. Oxytocin is sometimes known as the "trust hormone." It encourages social bonds and trust between people. In this way, oxytocin can help build long-term relationships. Research has found that people who listen to music have higher levels of oxytocin. Another study found that when people sing, their oxytocin levels rise, too. Music appears to lift our levels of this hormone. This increase may help us trust and be more generous toward others. Both trust and generosity strengthen connections between people.

Music can also connect people from generation to generation. Every culture has songs or rhythms with great meaning. Passing along music through the years helps create a sense of belonging within a group or larger family.

Music may also help build empathy. Studies suggest that our brains do not simply hear sound when we listen to music. Our brains also try to guess what the musician is trying to "say" with their music. When we try to understand how others think and feel, this builds a social skill known as *theory of mind*, which is a skill connected to increased empathy.

Music is everywhere in our world. Melodies and lyrics bring us together, and music will continually connect us through heart and sound.

Name: ______________________________ Date: ______________

Directions: Read "Our Musical Bonds." Then, answer the questions.

1. Music can change our moods by ______.

- Ⓐ being played on radio
- Ⓑ releasing a chemical in our brains
- Ⓒ forcing us to trust people
- Ⓓ helping us understand musicians

2. Based on the information in the passage, it can be concluded that ______.

- Ⓐ music connects people
- Ⓑ music is different in every part of the world
- Ⓒ without music, people would never trust others
- Ⓓ everyone loves lyrics

3. Which word is a **synonym** for the word *camaraderie*?

- Ⓐ passion
- Ⓑ habit
- Ⓒ friendship
- Ⓓ entertainment

4. What is the central idea of the passage?

- Ⓐ People need music to socialize.
- Ⓑ Lyrics help people hear sounds when listening to music.
- Ⓒ Music is a tool that supports human relationships.
- Ⓓ Music is a welcome sound for people who feel lonely.

5. Summarize the details that support the main idea of the text.

____

____

____

____

____

6. Describe a time when music helped you connect with other people.

____

____

____

____

____

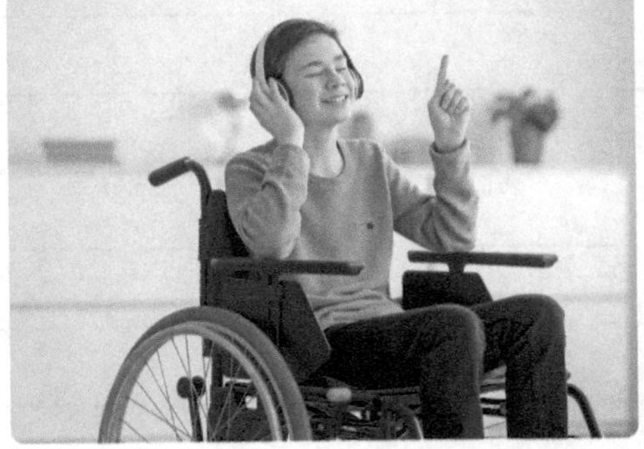

Name: ______________________________ Date: ______________

Directions: Reread "Music and Memories." Then, respond to the prompt.

Choose a song that makes you feel nostalgic and evokes a memory from your past. Then, write a paragraph about why this song is so powerful to you.

Name: ________________________________ Date: __________________

Directions: Read the text, and answer the questions.

As You Read

Put a star next to details in the story that surprise you.

A World without Music

It was just an ordinary Tuesday in October, or so I thought, when I woke up to find all the music in the world had *disappeared*. I came downstairs to eat breakfast—two eggs, scrambled, with a massive amount of spinach sliced in, as usual—and found my mom standing in the kitchen in complete and total silence. It was eerie, especially since my mom is the kind of melodic human who is always humming some country tune.

"Mom, where did you hide that old boombox?" I asked, peering around the dusty corners of our kitchen. "We should put some music on to get rid of this strange silence you have going on here."

My mom looked at me with wide, puzzled eyes, and she walked over to place her hand on my forehead.

"Oh dear, are you making up words because you're feverish, honey? You know there's no such thing as a 'boombox' or 'music.'"

And that was the moment, folks, that I, Melinda Williams, first suspected I was in a whole new world—one without music!

1. What does the word *eerie* mean?

- (A) bizarre
- (B) cheerful
- (C) outlandish
- (D) creepy

2. Which sentence punctuates the adjectives correctly, as modeled in the following sentence? *My mom looked at me with wide, puzzled eyes.*

- (A) It was a bright, warm morning.
- (B) It was a bright warm, morning.
- (C) It was a, bright warm morning.
- (D) It was a bright warm morning.

3. How has Melinda's setting changed?

- (A) She is bored by her mother's silence.
- (B) She is sick of eating spinach in her breakfast.
- (C) She is now in a world without music.
- (D) She wishes to hear her mother sing again.

4. Why does Melinda's mother think she is feverish?

- (A) Melinda is not eating enough of her breakfast.
- (B) Melinda is saying words she has never heard before.
- (C) Melinda's mother is feeling sick, too.
- (D) Melinda's mother is not used to Melinda making up words.

5. What is the mood of the story?

- (A) ordinary
- (B) unnerving
- (C) frustrated
- (D) silent

6. How does the characters' dialogue add to the mood?

- (A) It shows how the characters do not understand each other.
- (B) It explains why music doesn't exists.
- (C) It reveals that Melinda is feeling ill and her mother is worried.
- (D) It details Melinda's need for music.

Name: ______________________ Date: ______________

Directions: Read the text, and answer the questions.

As You Read

Circle details that add to or relate to the story's conflict.

Musical Karma?

I ought to explain why I was not surprised by this world without music development. Yesterday, I had one of those "I'm going to be grumpy with the whole wide world" days. I spent every hour chatting to my best friend, Eun-Ji, about every detail in our school that plagued me. And, yesterday, the biggest bee in my bonnet was the marching band music ringing through our school.

"Like, what is the point of us having a marching band if they're just going to ruin our eardrums?" I asked, pressing my hands to my ears as I tried to keep the band's mishmash of music out of my skull. "I'm just saying, this world would be endlessly better without this music, don't you think?"

Eun-Ji sometimes gets this strange look in her eyes, as if she's imagining and conjuring up another universe made of unusual rules. This was one of those times.

"Okay," she said, rubbing her hands together. "Let's make a world without music happen."

Upon hearing that, I just shook my head because Eun-Ji has been known to make these odd, magical-sounding statements.

But today, I was starting to doubt my sanity because here I was, post-chat with Eun-Ji, in that exact music-less world.

1. Which plot device does the author use?

- Ⓐ foreshadowing
- Ⓑ flash forward
- Ⓒ flashback
- Ⓓ recall

2. The line *I spent every hour chatting to my best friend, Eun-Ji, about every detail in our school that plagued me* reveals Melinda to be someone who _______.

- Ⓐ cherishes her friendships
- Ⓑ complains a lot
- Ⓒ is very outgoing
- Ⓓ likes her school

3. The description of the marching band suggests _______.

- Ⓐ they are a new club
- Ⓑ they are trying to annoy Melinda
- Ⓒ they need more practice
- Ⓓ they love a variety of music

4. What does the idiom *bee in my bonnet* mean in the text?

- Ⓐ loud music
- Ⓑ a new hat
- Ⓒ an annoyance
- Ⓓ a large bug

5. The term *post-chat* most likely refers to _______.

- Ⓐ Eun-Ji and Melinda leaving the lunchroom
- Ⓑ Eun-Ji making Melinda's wish come true
- Ⓒ Melinda leaving the conversation with Eun-Ji
- Ⓓ Melinda waking up the next morning without music

Name: ______________________________ Date: ______________

Directions: Read the text, and answer the questions.

As You Read

Underline the ways in which Melinda's school has changed.

This Is a Sad, Sad World

I've always found the beats and lyrics of most songs to sound like mosquitoes. I cannot stand marching bands, people who whistle, or any device that emits songs at loud volumes. But as I walked in this new world without music, I found myself second-guessing my stated hatred of most music.

No one whistled or hummed as they sauntered their way down the school halls. Timothy, who always bopped up and down the halls with a pair of earbuds in, instead shuffled by me with his gloomy head down. The sign for our school dance now read, "Come and Stand in Groups and Talk." Someone's phone went off, and instead of a random pop song playing, the phone rang with a blaring, *BEEEP-BEEEP-BEEEP.*

Feeling out of sorts, I ran to the school field, hoping to see a marching band player—or just anyone playing a tune—but there was no one. It felt like the whole world had fallen hopelessly out of rhythm, and with it, it had lost some of its soul, too.

1. The simile in the line *I've always found the beats and lyrics of most songs to sound like mosquitoes* suggests ________.
   - (A) Melinda lives in a tropical area
   - (B) music is annoying to Melinda
   - (C) Melinda hates mosquitos
   - (D) loud sounds hurt Melinda's ears

2. What is one conclusion that can be drawn about Melinda?
   - (A) She thinks people are sad.
   - (B) She is grateful for the silence.
   - (C) She likes a wide variety.
   - (D) She is regretting her wish.

3. What does the use of dashes suggest in the third paragraph?
   - (A) Melinda no longer wants to be alone.
   - (B) Melinda wishes to listen to good music again.
   - (C) Melinda is feeling desperate to hear music.
   - (D) The marching band is missing.

4. What does the word *sauntered* mean in the text?
   - (A) walk leisurely
   - (B) speed walk
   - (C) run quickly
   - (D) run at a steady pace

5. What does this text reveal about Melinda? Use details from the story to support your ideas.

____

____

____

6. What is the mood of this section? Use details from the story to support your ideas.

____

____

Name: ______________________________ Date: ________________

As You Read

Annotate the text with your questions, comments, or connections to the text.

A World of Music

After the school day finished up, I made my way home, and my music-less world got progressively worse. I turned on the radio and found every station only had anchors chatting about the latest local news, and even the way they spoke sounded more monotone. I went to the mall to buy an orange shirt for my school's pep rally, and the stores were silent except for the hush of a few voices and the occasional *bing* of a cash register. All elevator and escalator music had been banished from this new world. Terrible rock songs that used to follow me around the shopping center were eerily absent.

But what really seemed odd was how *apart* everything and everyone felt. It almost felt like, without music, we humans had this tendency to drift away from each other. I used to love bopping my head to a Whitney Houston tune in the food court and catching the eye of someone else enjoying the lyrics, too. But now, there was no music to share with anyone. As I got back in my car, I missed having songs on the radio that needed my sing-along voice. I felt oddly lonely in this world without music.

It was the birds that finally got to me. When I arrived home, I noticed my favorite blue jay was not humming or twittering a tune. I then realized none of the birds on my block were uttering a single sound. They all just pranced from branch to branch, completely silent, their voices seemingly gone with the wind. I'm brave enough to admit this was the point when I started crying big, fat tears.

"Are you ready to cry 'uncle' yet, my musically devoid friend?" a chipper voice asked behind me. I turned around to find Eun-Ji, who looked both mischievous and a tad bit worried about my overall well-being.

"Did you…how did you…Eun-Ji, putting me in a world without music is going *too* far!" I exclaimed shrilly.

My best friend (though I was rethinking this label) laughed a big belly laugh. She said, "I figure this experiment has probably gone on long enough, so there's no need to drag this out." She snapped her fingers, and my whole world went *poof* in a cloud of dark gray smoke.

I opened my eyes to find myself in my bed, waking up to a brand-new morning. My sleepy brain wondered, *Was it all a dream?* Then, outside my window, I heard the most beautiful sound in the world—the melodic *chirp-chirp-chirp* of my blue jay. It didn't matter whether it was real or not because the sound was music to my ears, and either way I would be more careful about telling my complaints to Eun-Ji!

Name: ______________________________ Date: ______________

Directions: Read "A World of Music." Then, answer the questions

1. What does music symbolize in the text?
   - (A) loving nature
   - (B) shopping
   - (C) human connection
   - (D) mistakes

2. What is the purpose of the description in paragraph 3?
   - (A) to emphasize the silence in the world
   - (B) to explain how Melinda sees the world
   - (C) to detail Melinda's frustration
   - (D) to encourage Melinda to change

3. What type of figurative language is used in the following sentence? *Terrible rock songs that used to follow me around the shopping center were eerily absent.*
   - (A) simile
   - (B) personification
   - (C) metaphor
   - (D) alliteration

4. Eun-Ji's dialogue reveals she ______.
   - (A) agrees with Melinda's opinion about music
   - (B) is tired of playing games with Melinda
   - (C) wanted to teach Melinda a lesson
   - (D) needed some silence in her life, too

5. What does the word *devoid* mean as used in the following sentence? *"Are you ready to cry 'uncle' yet, my musically devoid friend?" a chipper voice asked behind me.*
   - (A) determined
   - (B) without
   - (C) shared
   - (D) gloomy

6. Identify and record a major theme of the story, and cite details that support the theme.

Theme:
Detail 1:
Detail 2:
Detail 3:

Name: ______________________________ Date: ______________

Directions: Reread "A World of Music." Then, respond to the prompt.

Imagine you are Eun-Ji. Write a journal entry about your experiment with Melinda. Be sure to include details about the experiment, the purpose of the experiment, and the results.

Name: ______________________ Date: ______________

American Classics

Can you guess which songs Americans are most likely to recognize? Most people can quickly pick out the tune for "Happy Birthday" and "The Star-Spangled Banner." Did you know that "Take Me Out to the Ball Game" is yet another memorable melody? These three songs have stood the test of time—and are most likely to stick in your eardrums—because of their enduring melodies and simple, unforgettable lyrics.

Name: ______________________________ Date: ______________

Directions: Read "American Classics." Then, answer the questions.

1. The title "American Classics" suggests that _______.

Ⓐ the songs are loved by everyone
Ⓑ the songs have been around for a long time
Ⓒ the songs are set to classical music
Ⓓ the songs are catchy to Americans only

2. The phrase *stood the test of time* emphasizes _______.

Ⓐ the songs are longer than people expect them to be
Ⓑ the songs are still popular today
Ⓒ the songs are not important to the American people
Ⓓ the long memories of the songs' fans

3. What does the line *and are most likely to stick in your eardrums* reveal about the author's perspective of the songs?

Ⓐ These songs are going to be around for a long time.
Ⓑ The music is typically played too loudly.
Ⓒ The lyrics are too simple for the average listener.
Ⓓ The songs will play over and over in your head.

4. According to the writer, what makes a song memorable?

Ⓐ an event
Ⓑ sheet music
Ⓒ soft melody
Ⓓ simple lyrics

5. What does the word *enduring* mean?

Ⓐ adhesive
Ⓑ strong
Ⓒ lasting
Ⓓ boring

6. Describe the author's opinion of the three songs. Use details from the text or sheet music to support your ideas.

____

____

____

____

____

____

____

____

____

____

____

____

Name: ______________________________ Date: ________________

Directions: Closely reread the texts. Then, record the words and phrases the author choose to use to emphasize their view or opinion of music.

Close-Reading Texts

The Soundtrack of Our Lives	Our Musical Bonds
Many road trips are accompanied by an endless playlist of sing-along songs. Partners on a dance floor might two-step to a country beat or sway to a classical waltz. Marching bands move to the beat and rhythm of their music. Many people like to whistle while they work. Some people test out the acoustics in their showers by singing their favorite songs. Music is an integral part of our lives, and there are compelling reasons why people across the world love music. Researchers have found that music lights up different parts of the human brain, including parts of our brains that are connected to our emotions. Listening to music can shift how we feel, help us connect to long-lost memories, and make us feel more deeply connected to one another.	Research has also shown that music can affect our oxytocin levels. Oxytocin is sometimes known as the "trust hormone." It encourages social bonds and trust between people. In this way, oxytocin can help build long-term relationships. Research has found that people who listen to music have higher levels of oxytocin. Another study found that when people sing, their oxytocin levels rise, too. Music appears to lift our levels of this hormone. This increase may help us trust and be more generous toward others. Both trust and generosity strengthen connections between people. Music can also connect people from generation to generation. Every culture has songs or rhythms with great meaning. Passing along music through the years helps create a sense of belonging within a group or larger family. Music may also help build empathy. Studies suggest that our brains do not simply hear sound when we listen to music. Our brains also try to guess what the musician is trying to "say" with their music. When we try to understand how others think and feel, this builds a social skill known as *theory of mind*, which is a skill connected to increased empathy.

	The Soundtrack of Our Lives	Our Musical Bonds
Powerful Words and Phrases		

Name: ______________________________ Date: ________________

Directions: Closely reread the passages. Then, compare the moods of the two texts and the language used to create them.

Close-Reading Texts

This Is a Sad, Sad World	A World of Music
But as I walked in this new world without music, I found myself second-guessing my stated hatred of most music. No one whistled or hummed as they sauntered their way down the school halls. Timothy, who always bopped up and down the halls with a pair of earbuds in, instead shuffled by me with his gloomy head down. The sign for our school dance now read, "Come and Stand in Groups and Talk." Someone's phone went off, and instead of a random pop song playing, the phone rang with a blaring, *BEEEP-BEEEP-BEEEP.* Feeling out of sorts, I ran to the school field, hoping to see a marching band player—or just anyone playing a tune—but there was no one. It felt like the whole world had fallen hopelessly out of rhythm, and with it, it had lost some of its soul, too.	My best friend (though I was rethinking this label) laughed a big belly laugh. She said, "I figure this experiment has probably gone on long enough, so there's no need to drag this out." She snapped her fingers, and my whole world went *poof* in a cloud of dark gray smoke. I opened my eyes to find myself in my bed, waking up to a brand-new morning. My sleepy brain wondered, *Was it all a dream?* Then, outside my window, I heard the most beautiful sound in the world—the melodic *chirp-chirp-chirp* of my blue jay. It didn't matter whether it was real or not because the sound was music to my ears, and either way I would be more careful about telling my complaints to Eun-Ji!

	This Is a Sad, Sad World	A World of Music
Mood		
Words and Phrases that Reveal the Mood		
How do the moods compare?		

Name: ______________________ Date: ______________

Directions: Reread "American Classics." Then, respond to the prompt.

Think of a time you have heard one of these songs. If it has been awhile, have a listen now. Describe how it is a "classic" and what you think or feel when you hear the song.

Unit 6
WEEK 3
DAY
5

Name: ___________________________ Date: ______________

Directions: Reread "This Is a Sad, Sad World." Create a flyer for Melinda's school "dance." Be sure to capture the mood of the world she is living in through your use of images, colors, and words.

Name: ______________________________ Date: ________________

Directions: Read the text, and answer the questions.

As You Read

Underline information that is new to you. Put a star next to information you already knew.

Worldwide Sports

Across the world, people of all ages and abilities play sports. Sports give players a way to exercise and move their bodies. Sports also bring people—fans and players alike—together to work toward a common goal. This mutual purpose gives teammates a deep sense of connection with one another.

The most enduring and popular sport is fútbol, which translates in English to football. In the United States, this sport is called *soccer.* Around 3.5 billion fans across the world love to cheer on their favorite footballers.

Cricket, a team sport played with a bat and ball, has the second highest number of fans. At least 2.5 billion people watch and follow the sport worldwide.

Hockey, tennis, volleyball, baseball, and golf also have large, passionate fanbases. While these popular sports have the most fans, there are quite a few different sports played worldwide. Some people estimate there are more than 800 sports played across the globe! Are you ready to learn about some of the more unique sports played around the world?

1. Why is fútbol considered the most popular sport in the world?

- (A) There are many teams.
- (B) It has many names.
- (C) People love to watch their favorite footballers.
- (D) It has the most fans.

2. How is cricket played?

- (A) by kicking a ball
- (B) with a bat and ball
- (C) with fans
- (D) by exercising

3. According to the text, why are sports so popular?

- (A) They bring in a lot of money.
- (B) Many people worldwide watch sports.
- (C) They bring people together.
- (D) There are many types of sports

4. What does the word *unique* mean in the text?

- (A) popular
- (B) difficult
- (C) casual
- (D) different

5. What is the main idea of the passage?

- (A) Only popular sports are important.
- (B) Soccer is the most popular sport.
- (C) Cricket is the second most popular sport.
- (D) Many different sports have a following, big and small.

Name: ______________________ Date: ____________

Directions: Read the text, and answer the questions.

As You Read

Underline information that is new to you. Put a star next to information you already knew.

Sepak Takraw

Sepak takraw, a team sport that shares many common characteristics with volleyball, enjoys a huge popularity in Southeast Asia. However, there is one major difference between sepak takraw and volleyball. Sepak takraw players must hit the ball over a net with their feet (or other body parts) instead of their hands! This difference is why sepak takraw also goes by the name "kick volleyball."

To play sepak takraw, players must have a ball made of rubber or rattan, which are stems of a palm. They must also have a net that is five feet (1.52 meters) tall. Sepak takraw is played between two teams that can have up to three players. There is a server, a striker, and a bowler. Each player can touch or hit the ball with any part of their body, except their hands or arms. A team can touch the ball up to three times before they volley it over the net. Because players can hit the ball with different parts of their bodies, many players will stretch and flip to make contact with the ball. Sepak takraw is a sport that requires players to be agile and flexible!

1. How is sepak takraw different from volleyball?

- (A) Sepak takraw is played with the body, not the hands.
- (B) Sepak takraw is played with the hands, not the feet.
- (C) Sepak takraw is played with a net, not a fence.
- (D) Sepak takraw is played with more players than volleyball.

2. Where is sepak takraw popular?

- (A) North America
- (B) Southeast Asia
- (C) around the world
- (D) none of the above

3. Which skill would **not** help sepak takraw players?

- (A) a good throw
- (B) speed
- (C) flexibility
- (D) a strong kick

4. What part of speech is the word *volley* in the following sentence? *A team can touch the ball up to three times before they volley it over the net.*

- (A) noun
- (B) verb
- (C) adjective
- (D) adverb

5. What is the maximum number of total players that can play in a sepak takraw match?

- (A) 8
- (B) 4
- (C) 6
- (D) 3

6. How does the no-hands rule of sepak takraw affect how the players play?

- (A) They stretch and flip to make contact with the ball.
- (B) They only use their feet and legs to kick the ball.
- (C) They cannot hit the ball often.
- (D) They score fewer points.

Name: ______________________ Date: ______________

Directions: Read the text, and answer the questions.

As You Read

Underline information that is new to you. Put a star next to information you already knew.

Yukigassen

Yukigassen is a Japanese word that translates to "snow battle." While some people might picture a standoff between students in a schoolyard, yukigassen is an international sport played by professionals. The goal in yukigassen is to eliminate your opposing team's players by hitting them with snowballs. A game of yukigassen is played with two teams of seven players each. The game is played on a court with seven "bunkers," or obstructions, and each team has a flag at their court's end. Up to 90 snowballs are given to each team for use in the game. Each game features three rounds of three-minute sets.

There are three ways for a team to win a set in yukigassen. The first way is for a team to hit and eliminate every player on the opposing team with well-aimed snowballs. The second way is to have a greater number of players still on the court when the game's timer is up. The final way to win is for one team to capture the opposing team's flag.

1. What is the main idea of paragraph 2?

- Ⓐ *Yukigassen* is a real sport played by professionals.
- Ⓑ There are many rules in yukigassen.
- Ⓒ Teams can win yukigassen three different ways.
- Ⓓ Yukigassen is an international sport.

2. How does the author organize the text?

- Ⓐ by providing details about how yukigassen is played
- Ⓑ by showing the effects of yukigassen on Japan
- Ⓒ by comparing yukigassen to other sports
- Ⓓ by showing the problem with yukigassen and offering a solution

3. What is **most likely** the purpose of a bunker in yukigassen?

- Ⓐ to prevent players from hitting each other with snowballs
- Ⓑ to make it more challenging for teams to capture each other's flags
- Ⓒ to provide a hiding place as teams move across the court
- Ⓓ all of the above

4. How long is one game of yukigassen?

- Ⓐ 3 minutes
- Ⓑ 9 minutes
- Ⓒ 20 minutes
- Ⓓ 90 minutes

5. Which of the ways to win at yukigassen seems easiest to you? Why? Use details from the passage to support your ideas.

____

____

____

Name: ____________________ Date: ____________

As You Read

Underline information that is new to you. Put a star next to information you already knew.

More Unique Sports

Playing sports has a way of connecting players and fans to a team and a larger community. These unique and creative sports have become a means for people to move and compete with each other while having a ton of fun!

Kabaddi is a team sport played on a court or field divided into halves. The rules for the game were set and published in India in 1923. A single player from one team runs over to their rival's half of the court and repeatedly yells "kabaddi, kabaddi." The goal is for this player to tag out as many rival players as possible without getting captured or taking a breath. Yes, the player must keep repeating "kabaddi, kabaddi" or they're out! The single player must then race back to their team's half of the court within a 30-second time frame. Some people think the game of kabaddi began in prehistoric times. People may have played it to increase their reflexes so they could be better hunters. Kabaddi remains popular in India, and it is also the national game of Bangladesh.

People play kabaddi in Mumbai, India.

Chess boxing is a hybrid sport that pairs two (seemingly incongruous) activities together. The sport originally started as a performance art piece. A Dutch artist, Iepe Rubingh, envisioned a creative way to get people reflecting on a new sport. The result was chess boxing. Chess boxing started as a niche activity, but it has now grown in popularity. Two players face off in five rounds of boxing and six rounds of chess. Each chess or boxing round only clocks in at three minutes long. The winner of each round is crowned based on whoever reaches the first checkmate or lands the knockout punch. The biggest fanbases for this sport are found in Germany, the United Kingdom, India, and Russia.

Octopush, or underwater hockey, was first invented in Great Britain. Most people have seen ice or field hockey in action, but octopush takes the pucks down to the floor of a swimming pool. This team sport is usually played with six players on each side. Players put on fins, snorkel masks, and thick gloves to play against one another. Their objective is to move a weighted hockey puck into the opposing goal. A puck for octopush weighs around 3 pounds (1.4 kilograms)! Octopush started as a way for British divers to improve their skills maneuvering underwater, but it is now a well-loved sport.

These are just a few of the unique sports that are played around the world. Each game brings people together in fun and friendly competition. There are many more incredible sports to learn about—and you may have even played some of them!

Name: ______________________________ Date: ______________

Directions: Read "More Unique Sports." Then, answer the questions

1. What is the text structure of the passage?

- (A) cause and effect
- (B) problem and solution
- (C) description
- (D) compare and contrast

2. Why do people believe kabaddi may have been invented in prehistoric times?

- (A) It requires players to hold their breath.
- (B) The rules were published in 1923.
- (C) It is very popular and well known around the world.
- (D) It focuses on enhancing players' reflexes.

3. What does the word *incongruous* mean in the following sentence? *Chess boxing is a hybrid sport that pairs two (seemingly incongruous) activities together.*

- (A) congressional
- (B) popular
- (C) interesting
- (D) not alike

4. What does the word *niche* mean in the following sentence? *Chess boxing started as a niche activity, but it has now grown in popularity.*

- (A) small group
- (B) widely known
- (C) repetitive
- (D) vast

5. What do kabaddi, chess boxing, and octopush all have in common?

- (A) They all require referees.
- (B) They weren't originally created to be sports.
- (C) They are all played in water.
- (D) They are all popular in Germany.

6. What is the tone of the last sentence?

- (A) argumentative
- (B) excited
- (C) formal
- (D) worried

7. What is the author's perspective of the three sports? Support your claim by citing details from the text.

Author's Perspective:		
Detail 1	**Detail 2**	**Detail 3**

Name: ______________________________ Date: ______________

Directions: Reread "More Unique Sports." Then, respond to the prompt.

Imagine you have been asked to bring a new sport to your school. Choose a sport featured in the text. Then, create a flyer to advertise the sport. Be sure to include the name of the sport, the rules, why it would be fun to play at your school, and a picture of the sport in action.

Name: ______________________________ Date: ________________

Directions: Read the text, and answer the questions.

As You Read

Put a star next to details about Ravi, and put a check mark next to details about Eloise.

Ravi and Eloise Compete

Ravi and Eloise are the most competitive kids in their grade. Since they grew up as neighbors, the two of them have been each other's greatest friend—and enemy. Ravi is the fastest eater of ravioli, while Eloise can out-sprint her friend every day of the week. Eloise grows the best-tasting carrots in her family's vegetable garden, but Ravi makes the funniest papier-mâché masks. The two frenemies are fierce competitors, and they can pull a competition out of thin air. They love challenging each other to random matches, and they also love to ask innocent bystanders to crown a winner of said matches.

But, this school year, Ravi and Eloise are at a loss; they are unsure what they could hold a competition for. This past summer was their "sports summer." The two friends played 20 games of pick-up basketball (winner: Eloise) and 18 games of soccer (winner: Ravi). They even played two wobbly games of volleyball (winner: debatable). Ravi and Eloise have seemingly tried every sport their local gym has to offer.

They're both undecided until Eloise says, "Ravi, what if we make up our *own* sport?"

1. How do Eloise and Ravi interact with each other in the passage?

- Ⓐ They are jealous of each other's accomplishments.
- Ⓑ They are proud of each other's skills.
- Ⓒ They go to the gym together.
- Ⓓ They are always challenging each other.

2. What is the main conflict in the text?

- Ⓐ The two friends are envious of each other.
- Ⓑ The two friends have run out of ways to compete.
- Ⓒ Eloise and Ravi are no longer friends.
- Ⓓ The friends are bored with their gym.

3. What does the word *wobbly* suggest about the volleyball game?

- Ⓐ They do not like volleyball.
- Ⓑ Both are too competitive.
- Ⓒ Neither is very good at playing volleyball.
- Ⓓ They do not want to play volleyball anymore.

4. What is the mood of the story?

- Ⓐ dissatisfied
- Ⓑ thrilling
- Ⓒ confused
- Ⓓ peaceful

5. What does *they can pull a competition out of thin air* suggest about Ravi and Eloise?

- Ⓐ They have magical abilities.
- Ⓑ They are very fast athletes.
- Ⓒ They especially love to play dangerous sports.
- Ⓓ They can turn anything into a competition.

Name: ______________________ Date: ______________

Directions: Read the text, and answer the questions.

As You Read

Record any comments or questions you have in the margins.

Ravi and Eloise Have an Idea

Ravi and Eloise immediately jump to their feet. Creating their own sport—one where they can make up their own rules—might be the best idea they have ever had in their friendship. The two put their heads together and quickly start a brainstorm of approaches. Ravi and Eloise soon come to a couple of agreements. First, their new sport will need to involve some sort of skill or physical effort. There must be a set of rules that everyone follows (or else), and their new sport must involve a sense of healthy, hearty competition.

Ravi and Eloise then stare down a series of questions that need answering. Should their new sport be a two-player competition, or would a team sport encourage more community? Should their new sport have multiple rules, or should they keep it simple and stick to three rules at a maximum? Finally, what set of skills should their sport test the most? All the questions make their heads spin, but they keep working at them to determine the constraints of their new game.

1. What is the mood of the paragraph?

- (A) excited
- (B) nervous
- (C) nostalgic
- (D) competitive

2. How have Ravi and Eloise changed in this passage?

- (A) They are now working against each other.
- (B) They are now working together.
- (C) They have not changed.
- (D) They are now friends.

3. What do Ravi and Eloise need to do?

- (A) They need to determine the rules.
- (B) They need to decide how many players there will be.
- (C) They need to determine the number of rules.
- (D) all of the above

4. Why do Ravi and Eloise ask each other questions?

- (A) to learn to agree with each other
- (B) to test out hypotheses
- (C) to decide who has the best ideas for their sport
- (D) to help make decisions about their sport

5. What is the purpose of the dashes in the first paragraph?

- (A) to focus on the actions of the characters
- (B) to emphasize that Ravi and Eloise have control over the sport
- (C) to detail the specific rules of the sport
- (D) to show how the characters are different

Name: ______________________________ Date: ________________

Directions: Read the text, and answer the questions.

As You Read

Record any comments, questions, or connections you have in the margins.

Ravi and Eloise Do Some Research

Ravi and Eloise begin researching different sports around the world, trying to decipher which ones they could mix and match together. The two friends once watched a speech that reminded them that "everything is a remix." So, they figure their research is the most effective way to come up with a new sport. Ravi and Eloise learn about *kabaddi*, the team sport where people tag each other out while not taking a breath.

"I'd leave you in the dust, Ravi," chuckles Eloise.

Ravi and Eloise investigate chess boxing, the hybrid sport. But Ravi tells Eloise that they promised each other no violence. The two friends even briefly consider cheese-rolling, which is a sport in England involving people chasing rolls of cheese down a hill. But it's surprisingly rough. Some people actually break bones in the process.

"I like my knees too much, thanks," says Eloise.

However, the friends know they are on to something. They like the simplicity of *kabaddi*, the hybrid nature of chess boxing, and the goofiness of cheese-rolling.

"Surely," Eloise says to Ravi, "we can come up with a sport that combines all these elements together."

1. How does the dialogue affect the story?

- Ⓐ It reveals the intense conflict between Ravi and Eloise.
- Ⓑ It details the history of sports.
- Ⓒ It highlights Eloise's personality.
- Ⓓ It shows the characters' internal thoughts.

2. What does the word *decipher* mean?

- Ⓐ manipulate
- Ⓑ translate
- Ⓒ figure out
- Ⓓ sort through

3. What does the following line reveal about the friends' relationship? *"I'd leave you in the dust, Ravi," chuckles Eloise.*

- Ⓐ It reveals the competitive and fun nature of their friendship.
- Ⓑ It reveals they have not been friends for a long time.
- Ⓒ It reveals the serious and complicated nature of their friendship.
- Ⓓ It reveals the deep and trusting nature of their friendship.

4. According to the text, what is a *remix*?

____

____

5. How do Ravi and Eloise plan their sport? Use details from the story to support your ideas.

____

____

Name: ______________________________ Date: ______________

As You Read

Write a ∞ wherever you make connections.
Record details about the connections in the margins.

Ravi and Eloise Create a New Sport

The next day, Ravi and Eloise gather their friends and assign them to teams. There are two teams with two captains. Ravi is, of course, one of the team captains, and he is paired up with three of his friends. Eloise is, of course, the rival team captain, and she is also teamed up with three of her friends. Ravi and Eloise meet in the middle of the field near their neighborhood and shake hands firmly, a glint in their eyes.

"Let the games begin!" Ravi shouts, pumping his right fist, then his left, in the air.

"Umm, dude, we have no idea what we're playing," Virginia, one of Eloise's teammates, says.

Ravi grins, shrugging his shoulders, and says, "Yeah, I'm bit riled up and forgot the rules bit—but I'm excited, okay?"

Eloise shakes her head at Ravi and says, "Welcome, everyone, to our new sport, Tag with Pasta, or TWP for short. We wanted to keep the rules fairly simple, so Tag with Pasta is a game of tag combined with a pasta-eating competition. It must be completed while wearing papier-mâché masks."

"For three minutes, we play tag," Ravi continues, "in which one person from each team is the 'tagger' and tries to tag out everyone on the opposing team. The team with the most people left standing wins the round. Then, we move to the pasta-eating station, where you must first wear a papier-mâché mask and then try to eat as much pasta as you humanly can in three minutes. The team with the fewest noodles leftover wins the round."

"There will be four rounds of tag and three rounds of pasta-eating, all clocking in at three minutes each. The team who has won the most rounds will be our ultimate Tag with Pasta champion!" Eloise concludes, and she and Ravi give each other a high-five.

"This might be the most ridiculous game I've ever heard of," Virginia says. She then breaks into a massive grin and continues, "And, I love it!"

Ravi's and Eloise's teams face off, and, in time, the two teams lose track of the score as they play tag and eat a frankly enormous amount of pasta. Seven rounds turn into twenty, and finally, the teams disperse when they realize there is no more pasta left to eat.

Ravi and Eloise never play TWP again, but for years, they argue which of their teams actually won. They were so focused on winning that they forgot to pick someone to be an objective referee. But just between you and me: their teams won an equal number of rounds—so, yes, it was a draw!

Name: ______________________________ Date: ________________

Directions: Read "Ravi and Eloise Create a New Sport." Then, answer the questions.

1. Which detail would be **least** important to include in a summary of the text?
   - (A) Ravi is excited about Tag with Pasta and does not explain the directions well.
   - (B) Eloise and Ravi shake hands before playing Tag with Pasta.
   - (C) Tag with Pasta involves seven rounds of playing tag and eating pasta.
   - (D) No one wins the game, but everyone has a great time.

2. How does the mood shift from the beginning of the story to the end?
   - (A) from confused to competitive
   - (B) from exhausted to excited
   - (C) from nervous to frank
   - (D) from competitive to defeated

3. What is the theme of the passage?
   - (A) It can be difficult to convince people to follow your crazy ideas.
   - (B) You can accomplish anything if you persevere.
   - (C) Having fun with your friends is more important than winning.
   - (D) It's important to know who wins the game.

4. Which line from the text best captures the theme of the passage?
   - (A) "Umm, dude, we have no idea what we're playing," Virginia, one of Eloise's teammates, says.
   - (B) "We wanted to keep the rules fairly simple, so Tag with Pasta is a game of tag combined with a pasta-eating competition."
   - (C) Eloise concludes, and she and Ravi give each other a high-five.
   - (D) Ravi's and Eloise's teams face off, and, in time, the two teams lose track of the score as they play tag and eat a frankly enormous amount of pasta.

5. Compare and contrast Eloise and Ravi's personalities.

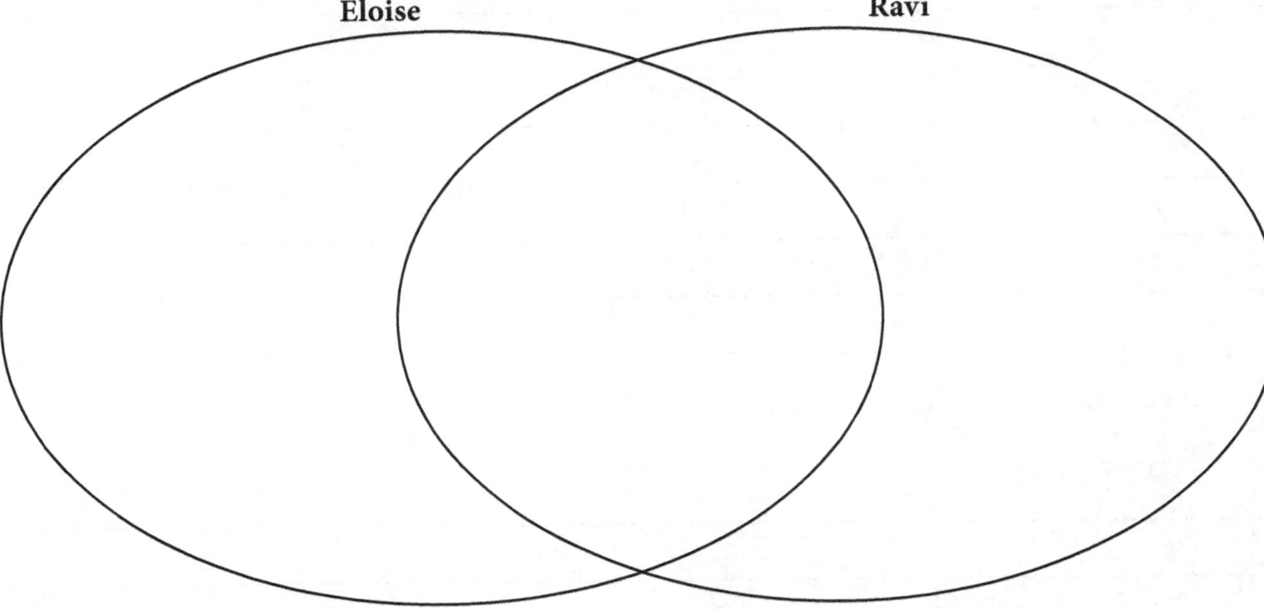

Name: ____________________ Date: ____________

Directions: Reread "Ravi and Eloise Create a New Sport." Then, respond to the prompt.

Imagine you are a teammate of Ravi or Eloise's during their game of Tag with Pasta. Write a diary entry detailing the events of the game.

A POSTCARD FROM ENGLAND

Gloucester, England

Greetings from Gloucester, England! I know, what a surprise it must be to hear from me, Mabel. But I just had to share with you that, for the first time in my life, I have witnessed grown humans chasing cheese down a hill. Since we're both from the "cheese capital of the world," Smithy told me I had to check out this cheese-rolling event when I visited England. So, I took the train from London (What a city! So big! So much tea!) and landed in Gloucester. Sandie, every year for this event, people chase a Double Gloucester cheese down this unbelievably steep hill. Someone told me the cheese can reach a speed of 70 miles (they tell me that is 113 kilometers) an hour, which seems completely absurd, don't you think? The players all sprinted down the hill, and my, so many took some serious tumbles in which they just kind of flew with their knees over their heads. It was quite a spectacle to see in person. Anyhow, I shall see you next Tuesday when I return—and I'll bring some tea!

Love always, Mabel

Sandie Sanders
123 Faux Street
Plymouth, Wisconsin
53073

Name: ______________________________ Date: ______________

Directions: Read "A Postcard from England." Then, answer the questions.

1. What is the tone of the text?
   - (A) disappointed
   - (B) nonchalant
   - (C) outraged
   - (D) amused

2. What is the purpose of the letter?
   - (A) to entertain
   - (B) to persuade
   - (C) to express oneself
   - (D) none of the above

3. What is Mabel's perspective of the cheese rolling event?
   - (A) It is an entertaining activity to see.
   - (B) It is a dangerous sport to play.
   - (C) It is far away in England.
   - (D) It takes a lot of skill to master the rules.

4. According to the text, where is the cheese capital of the world?
   - (A) England
   - (B) Wisconsin
   - (C) Gloucester
   - (D) London

5. What does the word *steep* mean in the text?
   - (A) short
   - (B) dirty
   - (C) sloped
   - (D) dangerous

6. Which word is an antonym for *absurd*?
   - (A) ridiculous
   - (B) scary
   - (C) unprepared
   - (D) practical

7. What part of cheese rolling do you find to be the most interesting? Use details from the text to support your thinking.

____

____

____

____

____

____

Name: ______________________________ Date: ________________

Directions: Closely reread the texts. Then, determine the common mood of the two texts, and record the author's word choice to express the mood.

Close-Reading Texts

A Postcard from England	Ravi and Eloise Create a New Sport
I know, what a surprise it must be to hear from me, Mabel. But I just had to share with you that, for the first time in my life, I have witnessed grown humans chasing cheese down a hill. Since we're both from the "cheese capital of the world," Smithy told me I had to check out this cheese-rolling event when I visited England. So, I took the train from London (What a city! So big! So much tea!) and landed in Gloucester. Sandie, every year for this event, people chase a Double Gloucester cheese down this unbelievably steep hill. Someone told me the cheese can reach a speed of 70 miles (they tell me that is 113 kilometers) an hour, which seems completely absurd, don't you think? The players all sprinted down the hill, and my, so many took some serious tumbles in which they just kind of flew with their knees over their heads. It was quite a spectacle to see in person.	"For three minutes, we play tag," Ravi continues, "in which one person from each team is the 'tagger' and tries to tag out everyone on the opposing team. The team with the most people left standing wins the round. Then, we move to the pasta-eating station, where you must first wear a papier-mâché mask and then try to eat as much pasta as you humanly can in three minutes. The team with the fewest noodles leftover wins the round." "There will be four rounds of tag and three rounds of pasta-eating, all clocking in at three minutes each. The team who has won the most rounds will be our ultimate Tag with Pasta champion!" Eloise concludes, and she and Ravi give each other a high-five. "This might be the most ridiculous game I've ever heard of," Virginia says. She then breaks into a massive grin and continues, "And, I love it!"

Mood:

A Postcard from England	Ravi and Eloise Create a New Sport

Name: ______________________ Date: ______________

Directions: Review "Ravi and Eloise Create a New Sport" on page 128. Closely reread the excerpts from "More Unique Sports." Then, complete the graphic organizer to show which ideas Ravi and Eloise used from kabaddi and chess boxing to create their new sport, Tag with Pasta.

Close-Reading Texts

More Unique Sports	More Unique Sports
Kabaddi is a team sport played on a court or field divided into halves. The rules for the game were set and published in India in 1923. A single player from one team runs over to their rival's half of the court and repeatedly yells "kabaddi, kabaddi." The goal is for this player to tag out as many rival players as possible without getting captured or taking a breath. Yes, the player must keep repeating "kabaddi, kabaddi" or they're out! The single player must then race back to their team's half of the court within a 30-second time frame. Some people think the game of Kabaddi began in prehistoric times. People may have played it to increase their reflexes so they could be better hunters. Kabaddi remains popular in India, and it is also the national game of Bangladesh.	Chess boxing is a hybrid sport that pairs two (seemingly incongruous) activities together. The sport originally started as a performance art piece. A Dutch artist, Iepe Rubingh, envisioned a creative way to get people reflecting on a new sport. The result was chess boxing. Chess boxing started as a niche activity but has now grown in popularity. Two players face off in five rounds of boxing and six rounds of chess. Each chess or boxing round only clocks in at three minutes long. The winner of each round is crowned based on whoever reaches the first checkmate or lands the knockout punch. The biggest fanbases for this sport are found in Germany, the United Kingdom, India, and Russia.

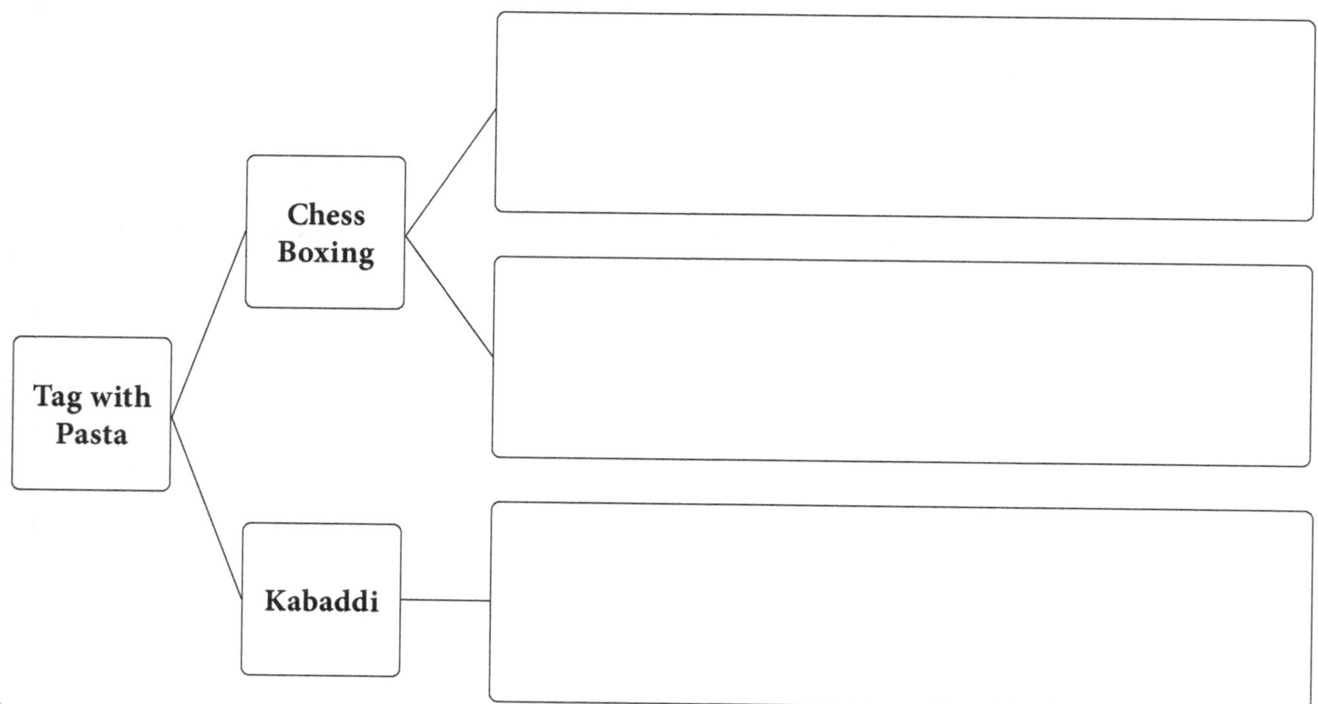

Name: ______________________________ Date: ______________

Directions: Reread "Ravi and Eloise Create a New Sport" and the postcard on page 131. Then, respond to the prompt.

Imagine you are a spectator at Ravi and Eloise's new sport, Tag with Pasta. Write a postcard back to Mabel describing the spectacle.

Name: ______________________ Date: ______________

Directions: Imagine you are attending a convention for unique sports around the world. Create a flyer that captures the topic, details, and purpose of the event. Do additional research on unique sports if you wish.

Name: ______________________ Date: ______________

Directions: Read the text, and answer the questions.

As You Read

Circle new information you learn about rainforests.

Rainforest Profile

Rainforests only grow on about six percent of our planet's surface, yet these forests are a source of wonder and awe for many. A rainforest is an area with many tall trees that receives a high annual rainfall. rainforests are home to a diverse range of organisms. Except for Antarctica, there are Rainforests on every continent. The largest is the Amazon Rainforest. This vast rainforest borders the Amazon River in South America. It covers an area larger than half of the United States! The Amazon stretches through nine countries in South America.

Every rainforest contains a rich biodiversity. This refers to the plants, animals, and other living things in a certain area. It's believed that the Amazon is home to a tenth of Earth's total biodiversity. Yes, 10 percent of all living things live in the Amazon!

There are several other large rainforests across the world, too. The second largest rainforest is near the Congo Basin in Central Africa. Thousands of species also live there. Rainforests worldwide are a welcoming home for many.

1. What does the root word *bio-* mean in the word *biodiversity*?

- (A) different
- (B) life
- (C) universe
- (D) trees

2. What does the word *vast* mean in the following sentence? *This vast rainforest borders the Amazon River in South America.*

- (A) large
- (B) wild
- (C) continent
- (D) life

3. What is the main idea of this text?

- (A) Rainforests are an important part of planet Earth.
- (B) Many animals live in the rainforest.
- (C) Rainforests are larger than people may think.
- (D) The Amazon is the largest rainforest in the world.

4. Why might there **not** be rainforests on Antarctica?

- (A) Antarctica is too large.
- (B) Too many animals already live in Antarctica.
- (C) Antarctic is too cold for many animals.
- (D) The Amazon is in Antarctica.

5. Based on the information in the passage, it can be concluded that _______.

- (A) rainforests take up a majority of Earth's surface
- (B) rainforests are important for Earth's species
- (C) no animals live in Antarctica
- (D) humans love to visit the rainforest

Name: ______________________________ Date: ______________

Directions: Read the text, and answer the questions.

As You Read

Circle the different types of rainforests. Then, underline what is different about them.

Types of Rainforests

Rainforests fall into two broad categories: tropical and temperate. Tropical rainforests occur in areas near the equator, and these areas have warm temperatures. Humidity remains high in these parts of the world. Tropical rainforests get at least 80 inches (203 centimeters) of rain per year! The Amazon is a well-known tropical rainforest. A few other tropical rainforests are found in Africa and Southeast Asia.

Temperate rainforests lie further from the equator. They are found in the "mid-latitudes." Temperatures in temperate rainforests are cooler compared to the tropics. These rainforests are often found near the coasts in mountainous areas. Rainfall is much lower there, and there is less sun. Temperate rainforests are home to fewer species than tropical ones. Regardless, they are still a key part of the world's ecosystem. Temperate rainforests are found in the Pacific Northwest of North America. They can also be found in Chile, the United Kingdom, Norway, Japan, New Zealand, and parts of Australia.

1. Why does the author use a colon in the first sentence?

- (A) to introduce evidence
- (B) to give examples
- (C) to list a definition
- (D) to separate ideas

2. What text structure does the author use to organize the paragraphs?

- (A) cause and effect
- (B) claim and evidence
- (C) problem and solution
- (D) compare and contrast

3. Which detail best supports the text structure of the paragraphs?

- (A) Tropics are areas near the equator.
- (B) The Amazon is a well-known tropical rainforest.
- (C) Temperate rainforests are home to fewer species than tropical ones.
- (D) Regardless, they are still a key part of the world's ecosystem.

4. What is the author's perspective on temperate rainforests?

- (A) Because temperate rainforests are so cold, many animals thrive there.
- (B) Because temperate rainforests are close to the equator, there is less rainfall.
- (C) Even though temperate rainforests don't have as many animals, they are still important to Earth.
- (D) Even though temperate rainforests aren't as close to the equator, they are still warm.

5. Which statement is true based on the text?

- (A) Tropical rainforests are warmer than temperate rainforests.
- (B) Temperate rainforests are warmer than tropical rainforests.
- (C) Temperate rainforests receive more rainfall than tropical rainforests.
- (D) Tropical rainforests receive less sunshine than temperate rainforests.

Name: ______________________________ Date: ______________

Directions: Read the text, and answer the questions.

As You Read

Circle the different parts of the rainforest. Then, underline the importance of each layer.

Rainforest Layers

A rainforest's structure is one of its defining characteristics. Every rainforest can roughly be divided into four layers. These layers are the emergent, canopy, understory, and forest floor. Each layer is home to different species and receives different levels of sunlight and rainfall. The tallest trees poke their heads up in the emergent layer, often towering at 200 feet (60 meters) tall. Branches here are thin, and they can only hold light animals that fly, such as bats or eagles. The canopy layer is often lush and dense, and sunlight can barely peek through this layer. Fruit grows here in abundance, and this source of food is why the canopy is home to most rainforest animals. The understory layer is much darker, and the plants that grow there have large, spacious leaves to catch the sun. Camouflaged animals, such as the python snake, can lurk and hunt in this layer. The forest floor is the darkest layer, and very few plants grow there due to the lack of sun. Leaves fall to the forest floor and decay quickly, much to the delight of the slugs and worms who live there.

1. What does the word *emergent* mean in the following sentence? *The tallest trees poke their heads up in the emergent layer, often towering at 200 feet (60 meters) tall.*

- (A) deep
- (B) under
- (C) natural
- (D) outer

2. What effect does the canopy layer have on the rainforest layers below it?

- (A) It surrounds the rainforest.
- (B) It provides food for the animals.
- (C) It supports plant growth.
- (D) It is thick and blocks the sunlight.

3. Why might different species live in the different layers of the rainforest? Cite the text to support your thinking.

____

____

4. What is the central idea of this paragraph? Use details from the passage to support your ideas.

____

____

____

5. Which layer of the rainforest would you like to explore? Use details from the passage to support your ideas.

____

____

____

Name: ______________________ Date: ______________

As You Read

Circle the reasons rainforests are important to Earth. Then, underline the evidence provided to support those reasons.

Why Rainforests Matter

Rainforests are diverse forests that conjure up awe for most visitors. While they are beautiful and inspiring, rainforests also serve a vital purpose in taking care of our well-being and our planet. Keeping rainforests whole and healthy is crucial.

Rainforests may only cover a small percent of Earth's surface, but they produce about 20 percent of our planet's oxygen. These forests can also take in and store large amounts of carbon dioxide due to the large number of green plants in rainforests. They absorb carbon dioxide and produce oxygen through photosynthesis. Some people have called rainforests Earth's "thermostat" or "lungs."

Earth's water cycle also relies on rainforests. Rainforests generate a huge amount of moisture. Much of this water is added back to the atmosphere. This rain then falls across the planet. Moisture that builds in the Amazon Rainforest might later turn into rainfall over Texas. In fact, more than half of the rain that falls on rainforests returns to the atmosphere. Rainforests have a far-ranging impact when it comes to our planet's water cycle.

Humans also depend on rainforests for many products. These products help us live healthier lives. Some rainforest plants produce medicines that treat diseases. Over 25 percent of our medicines come from tropical forest plants! For instance, more than half of the plants that treat cancer only grow in rainforests. From asthma to malaria, tropical plants treat many illnesses.

Rainforests also provide many people and animals with food needed for survival. Different fruits and nuts all come from rainforests. Some Indigenous communities have built their homes within rainforests, too. They rely on the forests for food, shelter, and medicine.

Rainforests around the world are being cut down so the land can be used for other purposes. Around 14 percent of Earth's surface was once covered in rainforests. That number has shrunk to just 6 percent. Humans cut down rainforests to make way for farms or for logging. This has led to the extinction of many rainforest species. The deforestation of rainforests is a pressing topic that was discussed at a climate change conference in 2021. Over 100 countries pledged to stop deforestation by 2030. Leaders from those countries recognized the value of keeping rainforests safe.

The ecosystem of a rainforest is diverse, but all living things there are interconnected. Many plants and animals rely on one another to survive. As we have seen, humans also depend on rainforests. Rainforests make a difference and help sustain our global community.

Name: ______________________________ Date: ________________

Directions: Read "Why Rainforests Matter." Then, answer the questions.

1. The main purpose of this passage is to _______.
   - (A) emphasize why humans have a negative effect on rainforests
   - (B) explain how important Earth's rainforests are to the planet
   - (C) entertain readers with a story about doctors discovering medicine in the rainforest
   - (D) inform readers that rainforests have medicinal plants

2. What does the metaphor in the following sentence show about rainforests? *Some people have called rainforests Earth's "thermostat" or "lungs."*
   - (A) Rainforests are the center of the Earth.
   - (B) Rainforests clean Earth's air.
   - (C) Rainforests help keep Earth moist.
   - (D) Without rainforests, the Earth would freeze.

3. What is the text structure of paragraph 6?
   - (A) description
   - (B) cause and effect
   - (C) narrative
   - (D) compare and contrast

4. Which statement about rainforests is true, according to the text?
   - (A) Rainforests produce much of Earth's carbon dioxide.
   - (B) Rainforests cover a large percent of Earth's surface.
   - (C) Rainforests are an important part of Earth's water cycle.
   - (D) Many countries pledged to increase deforestation.

5. Complete the chart to explain how rainforests support humanity.

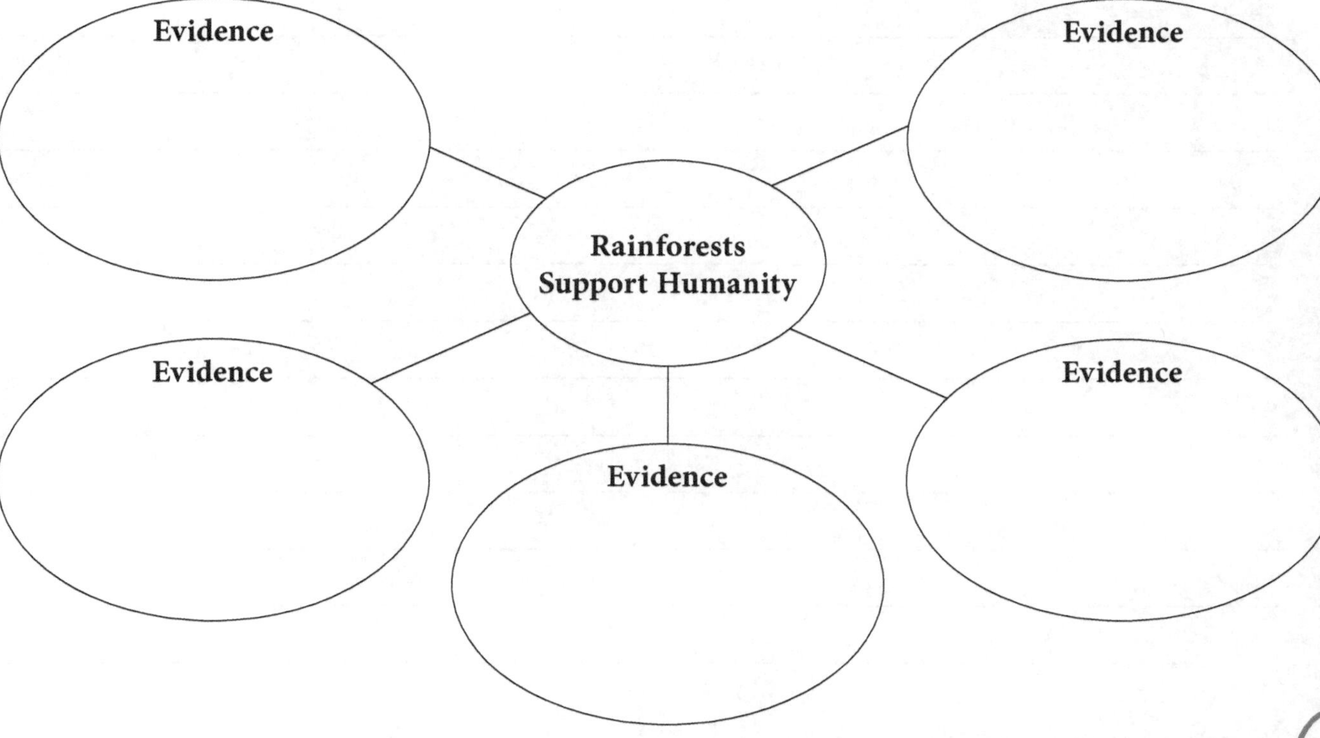

Name: ______________________________ Date: ________________

Directions: Reread "Why Rainforests Matter." Then, respond to the prompt.

Imagine you are a scientist sent to study the Amazon Rainforest. Write a report of what you have discovered there. Your report should include some of the wonderful things you would find and the problems you may find.

Name: ______________________________ Date: ______________

Directions: Read the text, and answer the questions.

As You Read

Underline details about the setting.

The Gift

The summer I turned 14, my grandma passed away, and we inherited a trip to the Amazon. I've never been particularly close to my grandma, especially since she lived in New York while we lived in Michigan. But when my dad was alive, he used to tell me stories of how my grandma traveled the world. She'd always send him trinkets from her global travels, usually bookmarks to encourage his reading. However, she and my mom were never close. I still remember the whispers of angry phone calls between them after my dad's funeral. My mom has spent the last seven years raising me, working as a teacher and a server to make ends meet. It seemed strange that my grandma paid for us to go on a trip to the Amazon when the money might have been better spent on a new washing machine. But when we received this "gift of a lifetime," my mom cried, and I had a feeling there was more to this gift than met the eye. And not even two weeks later, we were on a flight to Ecuador!

1. Why might the narrator's grandmother spend money on a trip to the Amazon instead of a new washing machine?

- (A) She missed her son too much.
- (B) She wished to teach her grandchildren about the value of money.
- (C) She did not want to share her money with her daughter-in-law.
- (D) She was passionate about traveling the world.

2. What does the word *trinkets* mean?

- (A) books
- (B) educational materials
- (C) small gifts
- (D) maps

3. What does the idiom *make ends meet* mean in the text?

- (A) earn just enough money
- (B) work many jobs
- (C) have many friends
- (D) earn an education

4. What point of view is this story told from?

- (A) first person
- (B) second person
- (C) third person limited
- (D) third person omniscient

5. Why is the narrator going to Ecuador?

- (A) Her father bought tickets before he passed away.
- (B) She won the trip in a contest.
- (C) Her mother saved up for years to afford it.
- (D) The family inherited the trip from her grandmother.

6. What did the grandmother usually send to the father from her travels?

- (A) spices
- (B) bookmarks
- (C) clothing
- (D) trips

Name: ______________________ Date: ______________

Directions: Read the text, and answer the questions.

As You Read

Put an exclamation point next to anything that you find surprising. Then, circle how the characters react.

A Talking Bird

"Seen any scrumptious crustaceans nearby, young one?" I looked around to see who was talking to me, and I saw a blue-green bird peering at me, a shield of fluffy orange fur covering its chest. I reared back; my eyes were wider than plates. I wondered if the bird was talking to me, and as if it had heard my thought, the bird chuckled in surprise and continued speaking.

"Ah yes, I could tell you were one of the few who could hear us. I figured it was an opportune time to welcome you to our rainforest."

Our tour guide turned to me and exclaimed, "That was the Amazon kingfisher, one of the millions of birds who live here in the rainforest. The green kingfisher likes to hunt by plunging headfirst into the water to nab fish and crustaceans."

I nodded my head at the explanation, still in slight disbelief at the fact that I'd heard an animal put a full sentence together. I looked over at my mom, who was smiling peacefully out at the water, and I thought maybe all the sun had gotten to my head.

1. Which detail would be most important to include in a summary of this passage?

- (A) The narrator hears a talking bird.
- (B) The bird eats fish and crustaceans.
- (C) The tour guide tells her the bird is an Amazon kingfisher.
- (D) The narrator's mother is at peace in the Amazon.

2. Which type of figurative language is the phrase *my eyes were wider than plates*?

- (A) hyperbole
- (B) personification
- (C) metaphor
- (D) alliteration

3. What do the author's actions in paragraph one reveal?

- (A) She thinks the bird is beautiful.
- (B) She hates boats and the Amazon.
- (C) She wants to get away from the bird.
- (D) She is shocked by the situation.

4. How has the narrator's mother begun to change in this section of the story?

- (A) She is crying now.
- (B) She is peaceful now.
- (C) She wants to experience more of life.
- (D) She is ready for adventure.

5. What do the narrator's thoughts in paragraph 4 reveal about her perspective of the situation?

- (A) She feels relieved for her mother when she sees her mother smile.
- (B) She thinks she may have imagined the conversation with the bird.
- (C) She wishes for the bird to come back and talk to her mother.
- (D) She knows she needs to get out of the sun because she is not used to it.

Name: ______________________________ Date: ________________

Directions: Read the text, and answer the questions.

As You Read

Circle words that describe how the characters feel.

Many Talking Birds

The next day, we climbed up a canopy tower located on the grounds of the lodge we were staying at. The idea was to get a glimpse of the complex rainforest ecosystem all around us. Our guide, Adan, kept redirecting our gaze to the colorful medley of birds that swooped in and out of the trees above our heads. Adan told us the birds loved the canopy layer for all the fruit that grew there. A black bird with a bright-yellow tail zipped past, which Adan quickly identified as an oropendola. A small, red bird pranced above my head, and Adan identified it as a tanager. It was only when Adan had moved to check in with the other guests that I began to hear the birds talk to me once again.

"Welcome, Francisca, young one," they hummed and sang. "Welcome to our rainforest home."

I prided myself on being an even-keel kind of human, but I felt a bit faint as I listened to the birds of the rainforest start to sing me a lullaby. It was a lullaby that had been sung to me before—by my dad.

1. How does the setting affect the story?

- (A) by allowing the narrator to be alone and communicate with the birds
- (B) by providing the narrator with a tour guide to explain the birds to her
- (C) by putting the narrator in a place where there are many birds
- (D) by putting the narrator far from the birds

2. What does the idiom *an even-keel kind of human* mean in the text?

- (A) someone who is wild
- (B) someone who is stable
- (C) someone who is confused
- (D) someone who is adventurous

3. How does the author build suspense in the story? Use details from the passage to support your answer.

____

____

____

4. Compare the narrator's perspective of the situation to the birds' perspectives. Use details from the passage to support your answer.

____

____

____

Name: ______________________________ Date: ________________

As You Read

Underline details that help reveal the theme of the story.

Connected

That evening, I looked up through the netting of our bungalow at the night sky, hearing the soft *whir* and *chirp* noises of thousands of birds. Our bungalow was built on stilts, and my mom and I were fully surrounded and secluded in this forest sanctuary.

I decided to launch right in and said, "Mom, the birds in this rainforest have been talking to me."

My mom turned over in her bed and looked at me with a calm seriousness.

"Yes, one of those toucans had a long chat with me this morning about your father."

"So…this feels normal to you, and you're not freaked out at all?"

My mom took her index finger and smoothed out her eyebrows, which is her habit when she's giving something great thought. "Your father came here, to this very lodge, with your grandma right before he died. They'd always wanted to travel together, and so, they finally came here when they knew he was likely to die in the next year or two from the cancer."

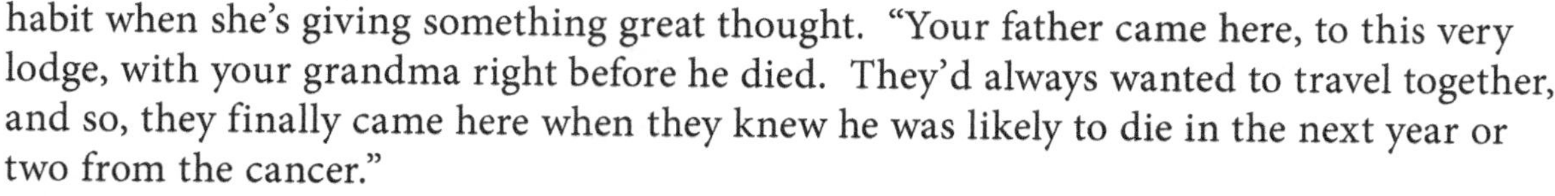

Her voice softened, and her smile turned nostalgic. "When he came back, he told me the birds had talked to him here. They had told him it would all be okay, that you and I would be okay, and that his mother would also be okay. At the time, I thought he was only talking nonsense, but maybe there is something a bit magical here in this rainforest."

"Is that why you think Grandma sent us here? To hear the talking birds?"

My mom laughed and gently said, "No, I think she just wanted us to experience a place that your father had, too. And, in a way, it might have been a slightly overdue apology for not bringing us along that last time." She paused and then continued, "I see and hear your father everywhere, and we will always be connected to him even if he's not with us anymore. Just like Adan said earlier, our lives are connected to this rainforest even if we're miles away. And maybe us hearing the birds speak is one way we stay connected to your father's memory."

I smiled and looked up again at the blanket of stars in the sky.

"Perhaps not everything needs an explanation, I guess."

My mom hummed in reply, and the two of us fell asleep under the night sky, connected with the rainforest around us—and my father's memory.

Name: ______________________________ Date: ______________

Directions: Read "Connected." Then, answer the questions.

1. What is the theme of the story?

- (A) It is important to be kind to others.
- (B) Make peace with yourself.
- (C) The Amazon is a magical place.
- (D) Shared experiences connect people.

2. Which line from the text best supports the theme of the story?

- (A) "So…this feels normal to you, and you're not freaked out at all?"
- (B) "Is that why you think Grandma sent us here? To hear the talking birds?"
- (C) My mom laughed and gently said, "No, I think she just wanted us to experience a place that your father had, too."
- (D) "Perhaps not everything needs an explanation, I guess."

3. Why might the mother and grandmother have fought after the narrator's father's death?

- (A) The mother did not get invited on the grandmother and father's last trip.
- (B) The mother was jealous she didn't talk to the birds.
- (C) The grandmother was insulted that the mother would not go to the Amazon.
- (D) They fought about money.

4. What is the mother's perspective on the grandmother now?

- (A) She is angry at the grandmother for apologizing after she passed away.
- (B) She is jealous of the grandmother because the birds do not speak to the mother.
- (C) She is grateful for the chance to connect with her husband in the rainforest.
- (D) She wishes the grandmother would have shared her money so she did not have to work so hard.

5. Why does the narrator's mother say, "And, in a way, it might have been a slightly overdue apology for not bringing us along that last time."

- (A) She wishes she could have apologized to the grandmother.
- (B) She is confused by the grandmother's actions.
- (C) She believes the grandmother wanted to make amends.
- (D) She misses her husband very much.

6. What are the words *whir* and *chirp* examples of?

- (A) hyperbole
- (B) alliteration
- (C) repetition
- (D) onomatopoeia

7. How does the backstory affect your understanding of the characters? Use details from the passage to support your answer.

____

____

____

____

____

Name: ______________________________ Date: ______________

Directions: Reread "Connected." Then, respond to the prompt.

Imagine you are the narrator's mother. Write a diary entry that expresses your feelings about the Amazon Rainforest trip. Reflect on past and present feelings of people, places, and events that are part of the narrative.

THE GLOBAL NEWS

World leaders pledge to end deforestation by 2030

Critics wonder if this promised target from COP26 is possible.

World leaders at the COP26 climate summit reached their first big deal this past week. More than 100 leaders from across the globe pledged to end deforestation by 2030. However, experts are uncertain if this target is possible. Many leaders have pointed to a similar climate deal in 2014 that failed to bring an end to deforestation.

People cut down trees for logging purposes and to make room for cows and other livestock to graze. Every tree cut down adds to the impact of climate change. Forests help take in a large amount of carbon dioxide. The loss of forests leads to a higher level of carbon dioxide in the air. This contributes to the planet's greenhouse effect.

Many people hope this pledge from COP26 will lead to sustained change. Only time will tell if our global community can reverse the effects of deforestation.

Name: ______________________________ Date: ______________

Directions: Read *The Global News* article. Then, answer the questions.

1. According to the article, what is deforestation?

- (A) carbon dioxide in the air
- (B) cutting down of trees for livestock
- (C) the 2014 climate deal that failed
- (D) climate change

2. What is a global community?

- (A) leaders from different nations
- (B) people making an effort to save forests
- (C) the people causing deforestation
- (D) countries across the world

3. How is this text structured?

- (A) problem and solution
- (B) cause and effect
- (C) chronological order
- (D) compare and contrast

4. Why might people think the new deal will not work?

- (A) The deal is not strong enough.
- (B) Deforestation is happening across the planet.
- (C) There was a failed attempt in the past.
- (D) The deal was not passed.

5. How does deforestation affect the climate?

- (A) It leads to higher levels of carbon dioxide.
- (B) It challenges world leaders to pledge to help the planet.
- (C) It causes plans to end climate change to fail.
- (D) It results in less carbon dioxide in the air.

6. Which word is a synonym for *pledged*?

- (A) refused
- (B) claimed
- (C) wrote
- (D) promised

7. Why is deforestation happening? Use details from the passage to support your answer.

____

____

____

Name: ______________________________ Date: ________________

Directions: Closely reread these paragraphs. Then, compare and contrast how the canopy is described in the texts.

Close-Reading Texts

Rainforest Layers	Many Talking Birds
Each layer is home to different species and receives different levels of sunlight and rainfall. The tallest trees poke their heads up in the emergent layer, often towering at 200 feet (60 meters) tall. Branches here are thin, and they can only hold light animals that fly, such as bats or eagles. The canopy layer is often lush and dense, and sunlight can barely peek through this layer. Fruit grows here in abundance, and this source of food is why the canopy is home to most rainforest animals. The understory layer is much darker, and the plants that grow there have large, spacious leaves to catch the sun. Camouflaged animals, such as the python snake, can lurk and hunt in this layer. The forest floor is the darkest layer, and very few plants grow there due to the lack of sun.	The next day, we climbed up a canopy tower located on the grounds of the lodge we were staying at. The idea was to get a glimpse of the complex rainforest ecosystem all around us. Our guide, Adan, kept redirecting our gaze to the colorful medley of birds that swooped in and out of the trees above our heads. Adan told us the birds loved the canopy layer for all the fruit that grew there. A black bird with a bright-yellow tail zipped past, which Adan quickly identified as an oropendola. A small, red bird pranced above my head, and Adan identified it as a tanager.

Canopy Descriptions	
Rainforest Layers	**Many Talking Birds**
Both	

Name: ______________________________ Date: ________________

Directions: Closely reread the paragraphs. Then, complete the cause-and-effects web with information from both texts.

Close-Reading Texts

Why Rainforests Matter	*The Global News* Article
Rainforests around the world are being cut down so the land can be used for other purposes. Around 14 percent of Earth's surface was once covered in rainforests. That number has shrunk to just 6 percent. Humans cut down rainforests to make way for farms or for logging. This has led to the extinction of many rainforest species. The deforestation of rainforests is a pressing topic that was discussed at a climate change conference in 2021. Over 100 countries pledged to stop deforestation by 2030. Leaders from those countries recognized the value of keeping rainforests safe.	People cut down trees for logging purposes and to make room for cows and other livestock to graze. Every tree cut down adds to the impact of climate change. Forests help take in a large amount of carbon dioxide. The loss of forests leads to a higher level of carbon dioxide in the air. This contributes to the planet's greenhouse effect.

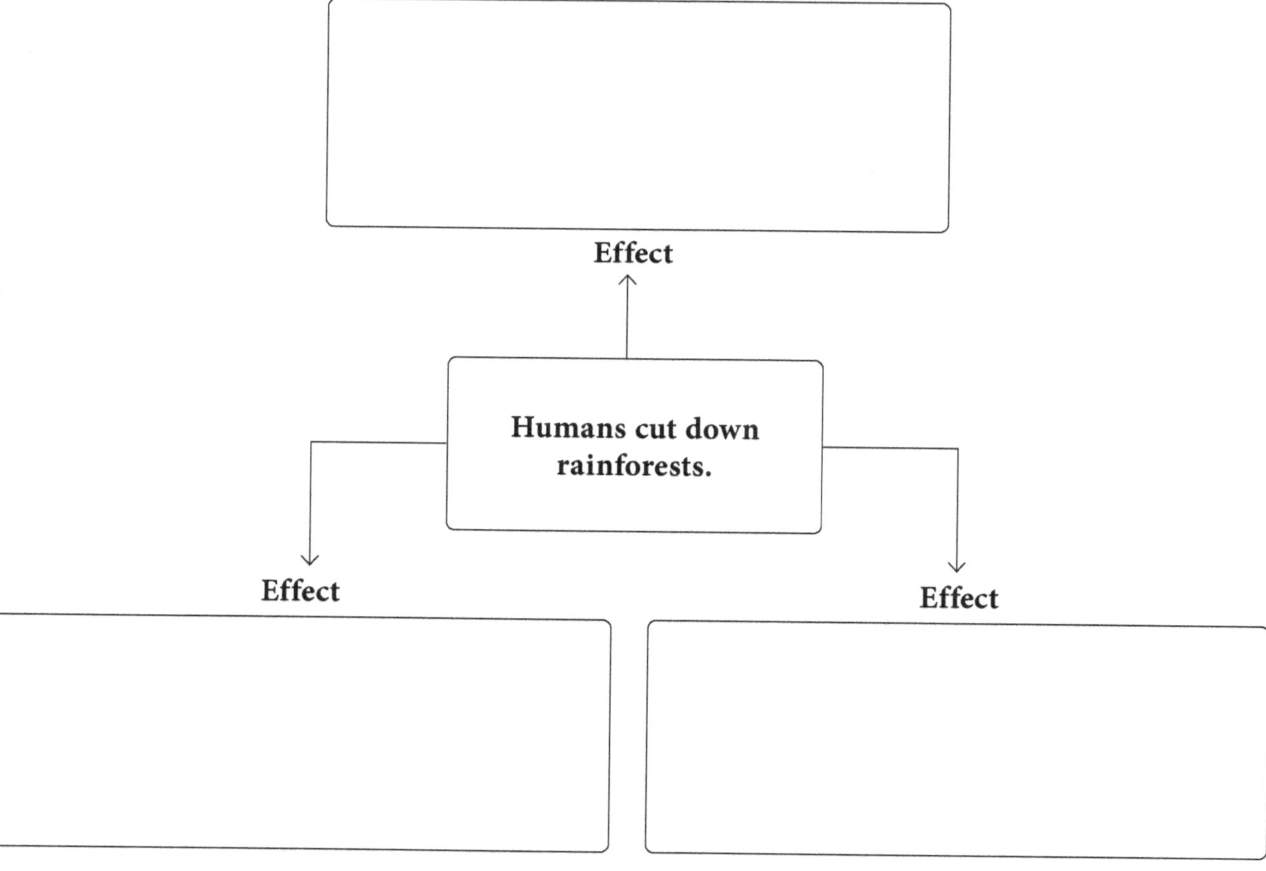

Name: ______________________________ Date: ________________

Directions: Think about the texts from this unit. Then, respond to the prompt.

Imagine you are travel agent. Create a travel itinerary for a visit to the Amazon Rainforest. Use the information from this unit and your imagination to recommended lodging, tours, and animal sightings. Include educational information about the ecosystem as well.

Name: ______________________________ Date: ____________________

Directions: Think about the texts from this unit. Then, respond to the prompt.

Imagine you live in a temperate rainforest. You have just become pen pals with an 8th grader who lives in a tropical rainforest. Write your new pen pal a letter in which you explain why your home is important and so is theirs. Be sure to use details from the texts to support your ideas.

Name: ____________________ Date: ____________

Directions: Read the text, and answer the questions.

As You Read

Underline important words and phrases. Record questions or comments you have in the margins.

Celebrations Around the World

Across the world, people love to gather with their communities to celebrate important holidays. Every culture hosts their own meaningful celebrations and festivals. These annual celebrations bring people together in joyous and connective ways. For instance, Saint Patrick's Day is celebrated in many countries on March 17. However, it wasn't always that way. The day was once a religious holiday for the people of Ireland. The day is meant to honor Saint Patrick, the patron saint of Ireland. He was born in the late fourth century. Now, Saint Patrick's Day is also about sharing Irish culture with people from many different cultures. To celebrate, people like to wear green, gather with others, and attend parades. Traditional Irish meals are also served. Common foods include soda bread, corned beef, and cabbage. Saint Patrick's Day is just one example of a holiday celebrated around the world. There are many more to learn about!

1. What is the main idea of the passage?

- (A) Saint Patrick's Day is an Irish holiday.
- (B) Holidays bring people together across the world.
- (C) Many holidays are religious celebrations.
- (D) Holidays are celebrated once a year.

2. Which detail is **most** important to include in a summary of the paragraph?

- (A) Holidays connect people and bring joy.
- (B) There are many more holidays to learn about.
- (C) Saint Patrick's Day was strictly a religious holiday.
- (D) People wear green when they celebrate Saint Patrick's Day.

3. How has Saint Patrick's Day changed over time?

- (A) It is now a religious holiday.
- (B) It now honors Saint Patrick, the patron saint of Ireland.
- (C) It is now only celebrated in Ireland.
- (D) It is now about sharing Irish culture around the world.

4. What does *traditional* mean in the text?

- (A) typical
- (B) delicious
- (C) different
- (D) religious

5. According to the author, why are holidays important?

- (A) The parties are exciting and fun.
- (B) They bring people together across cultures.
- (C) It is an important way to express your love of your culture.
- (D) People love to attend parades.

6. Why does the author discuss Saint Patrick's Day in the passage?

- (A) to argue that it is the best holiday
- (B) to describe many types of holidays
- (C) to give an example of a holiday that connects people
- (D) to demonstrate why Saint Patrick's Day is their favorite holiday

Name: ______________________ Date: ______________

Directions: Read the text, and answer the questions.

As You Read

Underline important words and phrases. Record questions or comments you have in the margins.

Loy Krathong Festival

The people of Thailand love to celebrate and often gather to share food and dance together. The country's *Loy Krathong* festival is one of their brightest and biggest celebrations. Also known as the "Festival of Lights," it is celebrated on the 12th full moon of the Thai lunar calendar. This is usually sometime in November. Loy Krathong is a day to give thanks to the goddess of water, Pra Mae Khongkha. On the day of the festival, Thai people join one another near bodies of water, such as lakes and rivers. They gently float *krathongs*, or tiny rafts shaped like lotus flowers, down the water. Krathongs are quite small. According to tradition, each one is usually made of banana leaves, flowers, and small candles. As they float on the water, the candle flames dance and reflect on the water with a warm glow. The release of krathongs is how the Thai people thank the goddess for providing. It is also a symbolic way to release negativity at the end of the year.

1. Why is Loy Krathong festival celebrated near water?

- (A) Rivers are convenient gathering places.
- (B) The festival honors the goddess of water, Pra Mae Khongkha.
- (C) The festival takes place in November.
- (D) The festival is on the 12th full moon of the year.

2. What does the word *symbolic* mean in the text?

- (A) releasing
- (B) praying
- (C) representative
- (D) positive

3. Which is the best alternative title for this text?

- (A) Thai Lunar Calendar
- (B) Celebrations in Thailand
- (C) The Full Moon
- (D) Celebrating the Goddess of Water

4. How is the Loy Krathong festival celebrated?

- (A) by meeting at a body of water
- (B) by releasing krathongs into the water
- (C) by creating krathongs out of traditional materials
- (D) all of the above

5. How did the author organize the passage?

- (A) cause and effect
- (B) problem and solution
- (C) description
- (D) chronological

Name: ______________________________ Date: ________________

Directions: Read the text, and answer the questions.

As You Read

Underline important words and phrases. Record questions or comments you have in the margins.

Día de los Muertos

Día de los Muertos translates to the Day of the Dead. Some people in Mexico celebrate this annual tradition over the span of two days. This is a meaningful holiday in which people remember and celebrate relatives who have died. It's believed Día de los Muertos marks the days when the spirits of deceased loved ones can briefly come back home. The first day of Día de los Muertos is when the spirits of children return. The second day is for the spirits of adults. While people honor the holiday in different ways across Mexico, many people set up altars in their homes to celebrate the people who've passed away. These altars are also known as *ofrendas*. They often hold marigold flowers, candles, and pictures of their loved ones. Traditional foods are also served, such as *pan de muerto* (bread of the dead) and *calaveras* (sugar skulls). Día de los Muertos is a joyful and lively celebration. It's a holiday where people can take the time to remember and honor loved ones who are no longer with them.

1. Why does the author use italics?

- Ⓐ to introduct Spanish terms
- Ⓑ to add additional information about the holiday
- Ⓒ to emphasize the author's opinion
- Ⓓ to highlight the food eaten during the holiday

2. Which two words form the contraction "who've"?

- Ⓐ who would
- Ⓒ who will
- Ⓑ who have
- Ⓓ none of the above

3. What does the word *span* mean in the text?

- Ⓐ celebration
- Ⓑ length
- Ⓒ prayer
- Ⓓ discussion

4. What is the mood this passage?

- Ⓐ regretful
- Ⓑ gloomy
- Ⓒ respectful
- Ⓓ informal

5. What is significant about the *ofrendas*, or altars, during Día de los Muertos? Use details from the text to support your ideas.

____

____

6. Why is Día de los Muertos an important holiday in Mexico? Use details from the text to support your ideas.

____

____

Name: ______________________________ Date: ______________

As You Read

Underline important words and phrases. Record questions or comments you have in the margins.

Diwali and Holi

India is home to more than 1.4 billion people. Faith is an important part of life for many Indians. The people of India practice a variety of religions and celebrate their faiths with a number of festivals. Let's learn about two of the largest festivals celebrated in the country.

Hindus, Jains, and Sikhs in India celebrate Diwali, or Divali. This five-day festival takes place in the fall, often in late October or November. The word *Diwali* comes from the word *dipavali* and translates to "row of lights." Diwali is nicknamed the "Festival of Lights" for its signature lamps that light up houses, temples, and rivers. Hindus light *diyas*, or lamps, which are usually made of clay and lit using oil. Diyas are hung in places where people live or practice their faith. The lanterns are also floated down rivers. For many, the festival marks the triumph of light over darkness, and it signifies the start of a new year in the Hindu calendar. People also come together during this holiday to eat large feasts, wear new clothes, and give gifts to one another.

Holi is a spring Hindu festival characterized by joyful, vibrant color. In fact, Holi is also known as the "Festival of Colors." This celebration usually ushers in the end of winter and takes place on the final full moon in the lunar month of *Phalguna*. This festival is usually celebrated in March. A large bonfire is often lit the day before Holi. It symbolizes the burning and letting go of negativity. People feed the flames with their own twigs and sticks. On Holi, people crowd the streets to throw colored powders at each other. These colored powders are called *gulal*. Many of these colored powders first came from different plants and spices. Roses gave pink powder its rosy hue, while turmeric gave yellow powder its sunny shade. All participants walk away from this festival coated in a medley of neon color. During this time, people also like to eat sweet treats and dance to folk music together. People embrace the delightful mess of Holi, and it is a celebration that welcomes all.

People celebrate Holi in India.

These festivals are just two of many others that are celebrated in India every year. Both Diwali and Holi serve to bring people together and celebrate life. Above all else, the festivals honor connection and a sense of celebration among people.

Name: ______________________________ Date: ____________________

Directions: Read "Diwali and Holi." Then, answer the questions.

1. What is the central idea of the text?

- (A) Diwali and Holi are important holidays in India.
- (B) India is home to people of many faiths.
- (C) Diwali is known as the "Festival of Lights."
- (D) Holi is known as the "Festival of Colors."

2. What is the text structure of the passage?

- (A) chronological
- (B) cause and effect
- (C) question and answer
- (D) description

3. What does the word *signifies* mean in the following sentence? *For many, the festival marks the triumph of light over darkness and signifies the start of a new year in the Hindu calendar.*

- (A) stops
- (B) provides
- (C) argues
- (D) represents

4. How are Diwali and Holi similar?

- (A) Both holidays honor the light overcoming the darkness.
- (B) Both holidays celebrate the beautiful colors of nature.
- (C) Both holidays bring people together.
- (D) Both holidays honor nature and all it has to offer.

5. What does the word *medley* mean in the following sentence? *All participants walk away from this festival coated in a medley of neon color.*

- (A) group
- (B) variety
- (C) celebration
- (D) sound

6. Compare and contrast Diwali and Holi.

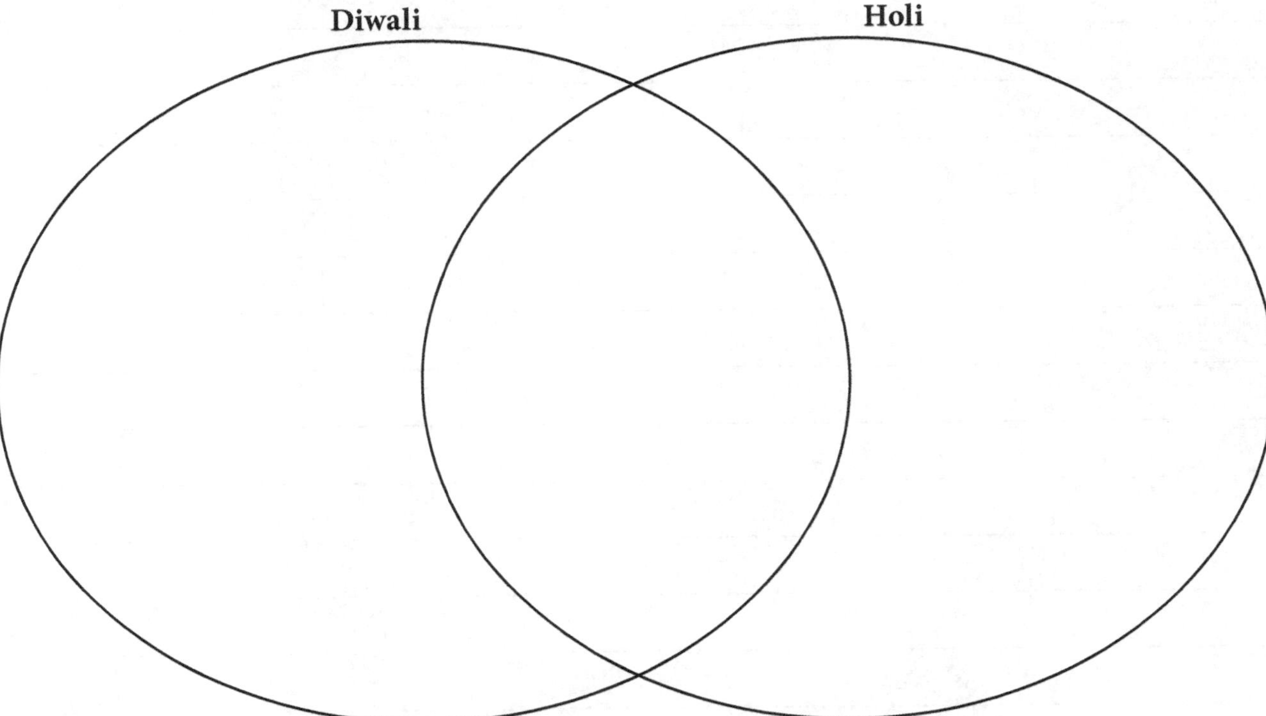

Name: ____________________ Date: ____________

Directions: Reread "Diwali and Holi." Then, respond to the prompt.

Imagine your teacher has assigned you a pen pal in India, and they have just told you all about Diwali and Holi. As you write back, explain a holiday that you celebrate. It can be a religious or national holiday. Then, explain how your holiday is both similar and different to Diwali or Holi.

Name: ______________________________ Date: ________________

Directions: Read the text, and answer the questions.

As You Read

Make predictions about what will happen in the story. Write your predictions in the margins, and underline the text that influenced the predictions.

Language Exchange

Benjamin was not the kind of guy to get nervous, but today, he felt all jittery and skittish. It was Benjamin's second year studying Mandarin in high school. His tongue still felt sluggish in his mouth when he tried to pronounce new Chinese characters. His teacher, Ms. Yeh, told him that learning a new language can take time. She reassured him that learning one so different from his first language could make everything more challenging.

So far, Benjamin had felt lucky that only his teacher and a few other classmates had seen him stumble through a sentence in Mandarin. But Ms. Yeh had decided that, starting on Fridays, he and the rest of his class were going to participate in a language exchange. Each student had been assigned to video chat with another student who had recently immigrated to their city from China.

Today marked the first day of their language exchange. Benjamin now needed to practice with someone his age who already spoke the language perfectly. In that moment, Benjamin looked and felt just like the queasy-faced emoji.

1. Why does Benjamin find Mandarin so difficult?

- (A) He is living in a new country.
- (B) It is very different from his first language.
- (C) Ms. Yeh is not a good teacher.
- (D) He is bad at the language exchange.

2. What is a language exchange?

- (A) Students studying each other's languages practicing together.
- (B) Students moving to a new country to learn a language.
- (C) Learning a new language in a classroom.
- (D) Studying a language very different from your own.

3. How does Benjamin feel about participating in the language exchange?

- (A) He is unbothered by the challenge.
- (B) He wishes Ms. Yeh was his Mandarin partner.
- (C) He is confident about speaking.
- (D) He does not think he is good enough at Mandarin.

4. How does Ms. Yeh interact with Benjamin?

- (A) She lets him skip the language exchange.
- (B) She offers him advice.
- (C) She provides him with learning opportunities.
- (D) She is critical of his progress.

5. What is the mood of the story?

- (A) depressing
- (B) stressful
- (C) joyful
- (D) optimistic

Name: ______________________ Date: ______________

Directions: Read the text, and answer the questions.

As You Read

Make predictions about what will happen in the story. Write your predictions in the margins, and underline the text that influenced the predictions.

Language Beginnings

Benjamin clicked the link in his email from Ms. Yeh so he could start the video chat. Benjamin was supposed to chat with Li Jie, another high school student who had just moved to New York City from Shanghai. Benjamin and Li Jie both had been given instructions from their teachers. For the first 20 minutes, Benjamin and Li Jie would ask and answer questions in Mandarin. For the last 20 minutes, they would ask and answer questions in English. If one person was struggling to pronounce a word, the other could gently prompt them with the correct pronunciation.

Benjamin wiped his sweaty palms on his lap as he waited for Li Jie to join the video conference. Then, with a *ding*, a face with a fringe of black hair popped up on the screen, a big grin on his face. Li Jie said "good morning" in Mandarin with perfect pronunciation.

"Good morning, Li Jie," Benjamin replied shakily in Mandarin, "I'm so excited to finally meet you."

To his surprise, as their conversation took off, Benjamin found he actually *was* excited to chat with his new language partner.

1. How does Benjamin change?

- (A) At first, he is uncomfortable, but then he loosens up.
- (B) At first, he is shy, but then he becomes disappointed.
- (C) At first, he is determined, but then he becomes disheartened.
- (D) At first, he is anxious, but then he feels challenged.

2. Why are Benjamin and Li Jie meeting?

- (A) to learn about New York City
- (B) to share information about Shanghai
- (C) to practice Mandarin and English
- (D) to show off their language skills

3. What does the word *pronounce* mean?

- (A) speed of talking
- (B) way of speaking
- (C) effort
- (D) sound

4. How does Li Jie affect Benjamin?

- (A) Li Jie embarrasses Benjamin.
- (B) Li Jie lifts Benjamin's mood.
- (C) Li Jie helps Benjamin sign on to the computer.
- (D) all of the above

5. How does Benjamin react when he must meet with Li Jie?

- (A) uneasy
- (B) argumentative
- (C) impatient
- (D) exhausted

6. Based on the text, what can you infer about Li Jie's feelings about the call?

- (A) He is feeling anxious about speaking English.
- (B) He is feeling frustrated about the assignment.
- (C) He is excited to talk to Benjamin.
- (D) He is too shy to talk to Benjamin.

Name: ______________________ Date: ______________

Directions: Read the text, and answer the questions.

As You Read

Make predictions about what will happen in the story. Write your predictions in the margins, and underline the text that influenced the predictions.

Language Partners

Benjamin had been positive that chatting with Li Jie would feel awkward and tense, but their conversations tended to flow. For the first half of the conversation, Benjamin had to think through his responses. It was a struggle to figure out the exact grammar and words to use. Sometimes, he stuttered and stopped as he talked his way through his answers.

Li Jie asked him about his dream job during their first chat, and Benjamin had to ask Ms. Yeh how to say the word *accountant* in Mandarin. Li Jie smiled at the reply and told Benjamin he was determined to become a firefighter, although his mom had high hopes he'd become a lawyer or dentist instead. Benjamin laughed in return. He told Li Jie his mom kept hinting she'd like him to follow in *her* footsteps and become a dentist, too.

In the second half of their conversations, Benjamin felt more at ease as he answered questions in English. He noticed it was more of a challenge for Li Jie to answer questions in his non-native language. But Benjamin and Li Jie both had an encouraging tone in their conversations. Benjamin could tell they both wanted to support each other in learning a new language.

1. How do Li Jie and Benjamin affect each other?

- (A) They disappoint each other when they cannot pronounce words.
- (B) They encourage each other to follow their dreams.
- (C) They meet each other's families.
- (D) They support each other as they learn new languages.

2. What is the message, or theme, of the passage?

- (A) It is important to consider the feelings of others.
- (B) Learning a new language can be difficult but rewarding.
- (C) Strong friendships are the key to success.
- (D) It is important to celebrate people's differences.

3. How are Li Jie and his mother different? Use details from the text to support your ideas.

____

____

4. What is similar about Li Jie and Benjamin during their language exchange practice? Use details from the text to support your ideas.

____

____

____

Name: ______________________________ Date: ______________

As You Read

Make predictions about what will happen in the story. Write your predictions in the margins, and underline the text that influenced the predictions.

Language Friends

It was the last language exchange of the school term, and Benjamin logged onto his computer feeling a bit morose that the end was near. He had gotten so used to seeing Li Jie that he felt like they were friends, and he knew he would miss seeing him.

Soon, Li Jie logged into their video call, and as they spoke, Benjamin could tell his Mandarin-speaking skills had improved. He spent less time second-guessing his sentences, and when it came time to discuss their favorite time of the year, it was easy for him to chat with his usual gusto.

"My favorite time of year is always, *always* Halloween," Benjamin said in Mandarin, "because I love to get creative and craft a costume no one's seen or done yet."

He pulled out his phone to show Li Jie the picture of him all costumed up from last year.

"I was a painter last year, a famous painter who used to have his own television show—"

"Bob Ross!" Li Jie replied excitedly, while Benjamin laughed and nodded his head.

"My favorite time of year is always Chinese New Year," Lie Jie began, speaking slowly as he switched to English. "When we lived in Shanghai, we would always leave the city and travel to my hometown. My *popo* made a big meal with all our favorite foods, and we would eat until our stomachs started to stretch. It is tradition to wear red, set off fireworks, and visit family during Chinese New Year. And since I'm young and not married, I get money in red envelopes from my family during the celebrations, too." Li Jie paused, his face growing somber. "But the best part was always eating with my whole family, and it is hard to think that next year we will not have that again."

"That is rough," Benjamin said, "I guess I kind of forgot that you'd be too far from home to celebrate with your extended family." Benjamin paused, wanting to ask Li Jie a question, but he was not sure what Li Jie's response would be. "Li Jie, I know we've only gotten to know each other through a screen, but I don't think we live that far away from each other. Maybe we can hang out over the holidays, and we could also do your New York version of Chinese New Year? I think it'd be cool to keep hanging out."

Li Jie looked back at him, smiled wide, and said, "Yes, let us do that—though I think we should keep speaking half Mandarin, half English."

Benjamin laughed and mimed putting his hand through the screen as he said, "You have yourself a deal, Li Jie."

Li Jie stretched his hand forward too, and they pretended to shake hands through the screen. "Deal," Li Jie said, trying out the word—and the two new friends smiled at each other.

Name: ______________________________ Date: ______________

Directions: Read "Language Friends." Then, answer the questions.

1. What does the word *morose* reveal about Benjamin in the following sentence?
It was the last language exchange of the school term, and Benjamin logged onto his computer feeling a bit morose that the end was near.

- Ⓐ Benjamin is saddened that he won't be speaking to Li Jie anymore.
- Ⓑ Benjamin is looking forward to the holidays.
- Ⓒ Benjamin is disappointed in the language exchange program.
- Ⓓ Benjamin is determined to keep speaking Mandarin because he feels more confident.

2. Which word best describes Benjamin toward the end of the passage?

- Ⓐ gloomy
- Ⓑ athletic
- Ⓒ uptight
- Ⓓ friendly

3. Which detail best supports the development of Benjamin's character?

- Ⓐ Benjamin's favorite holiday is Halloween.
- Ⓑ Benjamin likes to make his own costumes.
- Ⓒ Benjamin does not know how to say "Bob Ross" in Mandarin.
- Ⓓ Benjamin asks Li Jie if he wants to keep hanging out.

4. What is Li Jie's conflict?

- Ⓐ He does not like speaking English as much as Mandarin.
- Ⓑ He misses his extended family.
- Ⓒ His favorite holiday is the Chinese New Year.
- Ⓓ He does not know if Benjamin wants to be friends.

5. How does Benjamin respond to Li Jie's conflict?

- Ⓐ He does not understand it.
- Ⓑ He ignores it.
- Ⓒ He is empathetic about it.
- Ⓓ He talks about his own problems.

6. What is the theme of the story?

- Ⓐ Friendship can develop through a common goal.
- Ⓑ Learning a new language is important for building friendships.
- Ⓒ Halloween is a fun holiday in the United States.
- Ⓓ Chinese New Year is an important celebration.

7. How does the conclusion of the story help to develop the theme? Use details from the story to support your ideas.

____

____

____

____

____

Name: ______________________________ Date: ______________

Directions: Reread "Language Friends." Then, respond to the prompt.

Imagine you are either Benjamin or Li Jie. Write a narrative from one of their points of view about a day together in New York City celebrating the Chinese New Year. Research the holiday to include important details, if needed.

Name: ______________________ Date: ______________

Global FESTIVAL MAP

The Carnival of Venice is set in Italy. Parades of people, dressed in elegant finery, glide through the canals of the city by gondola.

Chinese New Year marks the start of a new year on the lunar calendar, and it is the most important festival in China.

Mardi Gras is a two-week celebration in New Orleans that is packed with parades, live music, and big parties.

Carnival is held in Brazil, and this massive festival is nicknamed the "Greatest Show on Earth." It is an annual and colorful celebration with costumes, dancing, and lots of food.

The Abu Simbel Sun Festival is a bi-annual festival that is celebrated in February and October. For two days every year, people come together to watch the sun light up the central part of the Ramses II temple in Egypt.

Name: ______________________ Date: ______________

Directions: Read "Global Festival Map." Then, answer the questions.

1. How do the images of the holidays relate to each other?

Ⓐ They give a description of each holiday's purpose.
Ⓑ They capture the history of each holiday.
Ⓒ They are all photographs of the festivals or where they take place.
Ⓓ They explain the meanings of the festivals.

2. Which holidays are the most similar?

Ⓐ Carnival and Mardi Gras
Ⓑ Carnival and the Abu Simbel Sun Festival
Ⓒ the Carnival of Venice and the Abu Simbel Sun Festival
Ⓓ Chinese New Year and the Carnival of Venice

3. What is the central idea of the text?

Ⓐ With large events, everyone across the country celebrates together.
Ⓑ Different cultures of the world celebrate holidays with large, extended events.
Ⓒ Once a year, countries around the world celebrate holidays at the same time.
Ⓓ Celebrations are the same in different countries.

4. Which word best supports the central idea of the text?

Ⓐ festivals
Ⓑ parades
Ⓒ parties
Ⓓ all of the above

5. What do the holidays on the map have in common?

____

____

____

6. Which holiday celebration would you like to attend and why? Use details from the text to support your ideas.

____

____

____

____

____

Name: ______________________________ Date: ____________________

Directions: Closely reread the texts. Then, compare and contrast the two holidays.

Close-Reading Texts

The Loy Krathong Festival	Diwali and Holi
The people of Thailand love to celebrate and often gather to share food and dance together. The country's *Loy Krathong* festival is one of their brightest and biggest celebrations. Also known as the "Festival of Lights," it is celebrated on the 12th full moon of the Thai lunar calendar. This is usually sometime in November. Loy Krathong is a day to give thanks to the goddess of water, Pra Mae Khongkha. On the day of the festival, Thai people join one another near bodies of water, such as lakes and rivers. They gently float *krathongs*, or tiny rafts shaped like lotus flowers, down the water. Krathongs are quite small. According to tradition, each one is usually made of banana leaves, flowers, and small candles. As they float on the water, the candle flames dance and reflect on the water with a warm glow. The release of krathongs is how the Thai people thank the goddess for providing. It is also a symbolic way to release negativity at the end of the year.	Hindus, Jains, and Sikhs in India celebrate Diwali, or Divali. This five-day festival takes place in the fall, often in late October or November. The word *Diwali* comes from the word *dipavali* and translates to "row of lights." Diwali is nicknamed the "Festival of Lights" for its signature lamps that light up houses, temples, and rivers. Hindus light *diyas*, or lamps, which are usually made of clay and lit using oil. Diyas are hung in places where people live or practice their faith. The lanterns are also floated down rivers. For many, the festival marks the triumph of light over darkness, and it signifies the start of a new year in the Hindu calendar. People also come together during this holiday to eat large feasts, wear new clothes, and give gifts to one another.

Loy Krathong Festival	Similarities	Diwali

Name: ______________________________ Date: ______________

Directions: Closely reread the texts. Then, record the common central idea or theme of the texts. Write details to support your conclusion.

Close-Reading Texts

Language Friends	Global Festival Map
"My favorite time of year is always, *always* Halloween," Benjamin said in Mandarin, "because I love to get creative and craft a costume no one's seen or done yet." He pulled out his phone to show Li Jie the picture of him all costumed up from last year. "I was a painter last year, a famous painter who used to have his own television show—" "Bob Ross!" Li Jie replied excitedly, while Benjamin laughed and nodded his head.	Carnival is held in Brazil, and this massive festival is nicknamed the "Greatest Show on Earth." It is an annual and colorful celebration with costumes, dancing, and lots of food. Mardi Gras is a two-week celebration in New Orleans that is packed with parades, live music, and big parties. The Carnival of Venice is set in Italy. Parades of people, dressed in elegant finery, glide through the canals of the city by gondola.

Common Central Idea	
Detail	
Detail	
Detail	

Name: ______________________________ Date: ________________

Directions: Reread "Global Festival Map" on page 167. Then, respond to the prompt.

Choose one of the images and summaries on the map. Conduct additional research on this celebration. Then, summarize your findings. Include details about how the holiday is celebrated and why.

Name: ______________________ Date: ______________

Directions: Create an invitation for your favorite holiday that you celebrate. Include name of the holiday, the purpose of the holiday, and activities you do during the holiday.

Name: ______________________________ Date: ________________

Directions: Read the text, and answer the questions.

As You Read

Circle important details about the topic.

Tiny Towns

Most people can pinpoint the most bustling and populous U.S. cities on a map. New York City in New York has a worldwide reputation. "The Big Apple" is home to more than 8 million people. Los Angeles in California has many famous places, including Hollywood. "The City of Angels" is home to more than 3.8 million people. But while America's biggest cities are easy to spot on a map, the country has plenty of small towns, too.

Every state has some towns that have small populations. Thousands of these small towns in the United States have fewer than 1,000 residents. And there are some tiny towns across the country that have even smaller populations than that! These towns are home to just a short list of locals and usually have fewer than 50 residents in total. Although they're small in size, each of these towns are incorporated places. This means they have a local government and are recognized in the U.S. census, or population count. From the town of Stockholm in Wisconsin to Monowi in Nebraska, there are many tiny towns in the United States to discover!

1. Why are "The Big Apple" and "The City of Angels" capitalized?

Ⓐ They are in quotation marks.
Ⓑ They are adjectives.
Ⓒ They are common nouns.
Ⓓ They are proper nouns.

2. Why does the author use quotation marks around "The Big Apple" and "The City of Angels?"

Ⓐ to show they are unofficial names
Ⓑ to show that someone else called them those names
Ⓒ to emphasize their preference for the names
Ⓓ to inspire humor

3. What are residents?

Ⓐ people who live in a small town
Ⓑ people who travel to an area
Ⓒ people who live in an area
Ⓓ groups of 50 or fewer people

4. What does the author mean by *From the town of Stockholm in Wisconsin to Monowi in Nebraska*?

Ⓐ Small towns are only in a specific part of the country.
Ⓑ There are small towns across the U.S.
Ⓒ Small towns are hard to travel to.
Ⓓ These two states have large cities.

5. How are small towns similar to larger cities?

Ⓐ They both have a large population.
Ⓑ They both have a local government.
Ⓒ They both require people to vote.
Ⓓ all of the above

6. What is the author's perspective of small towns?

Ⓐ They have large populations.
Ⓑ They are easy to find on a map.
Ⓒ Most people live in small towns.
Ⓓ They are important parts of the U.S.

Name: ________________________ Date: ______________

Directions: Read the text, and answer the questions.

As You Read

Star new, interesting facts about the topic.

The Town of Stockholm

The town of Stockholm, Wisconsin, lays claim to fame as being one of the state's oldest towns. According to 2021 census estimates, it is also the state's least populated place with only 76 people calling the small village home. The town has just two streets of shops and restaurants, but it's a well-known day trip destination. The town is close to the Maiden Rock Bluff, which is a limestone cliff that hovers over Lake Pepin. This natural area is a bird migration corridor, and a variety of birds swoop past the town during the year. Visitors to the area can hike to the top of the bluff and may glimpse Peregrine falcons nesting nearby.

Maiden Rock Bluff also features in the town's origin story. In 1851, a Swedish adventurer named Erik Petterson climbed the bluff. He felt that the land that lay before him was the perfect place to live, so he purchased some of the land. A couple of years later, he and a group of immigrants from Sweden built a community there. They named the town Stockholm after the capital of their home country.

1. What makes Stockholm famous?

- (A) It is Wisconsin's oldest town.
- (B) It is close to Maiden Rock Bluff.
- (C) It borders on Lake Pepin.
- (D) all of the above

2. Why might people visit Stockholm?

- (A) to hike and see the falcons
- (B) to see the oldest town in the United States
- (C) to have a Swedish adventure
- (D) to volunteer on the farms

3. Which is the best alternative title for this text?

- (A) Small Town Draws Bird Watchers
- (B) The History of a Swedish Adventurer
- (C) The Cliffs
- (D) The Smallest Town in America

4. What is the significance behind the city's name?

- (A) It is named after the birds that call it home.
- (B) It honors the town the original settlers were from.
- (C) It is named after a limestone cliff.
- (D) all of the above

5. What does the word *origin* mean in the text?

- (A) adventure
- (B) traveling
- (C) beginning
- (D) dedication

6. How does the author organize the first paragraph of the passage?

- (A) cause and effect
- (B) chronological
- (C) problem and solution
- (D) description

Name: ________________________ Date: ______________

Directions: Read the text, and answer the questions.

As You Read

Star new, interesting facts about the topic.

Rendville, Ohio

The tiny town of Rendville, Ohio, has only 33 residents. While the town's population is small, Rendville has a long history of housing important leaders. Rendville was once a coal mining town, and it was first established in 1879. William P. Rend helped establish the town's mine. As the owner, he welcomed people from all backgrounds to work in his mine. This led to a diverse community in Rendville.

Isaiah Tuppins was Rendville's first mayor. He was the first Black mayor of an Ohio town, and he was the first Black man to earn a medical degree in Ohio. He was elected to lead the town in 1888. Roberta Preston also lived in Rendville. She became the first Black female postmaster in Ohio when she took on the position in 1953. Later, Sofia Mitchell would become Rendville's mayor and the first Black female mayor in Ohio.

There is an important legacy of Black leadership in this small town. While the town's population has dwindled since the days of coal mining, it remains a place of important history.

1. What does the word *diverse* mean as used in the following sentence? *This led to a diverse community in Rendville.*

- (A) with similar backgrounds
- (B) with different backgrounds
- (C) cooperative
- (D) hardworking

2. What do Sofia Mitchell and Isaiah Tuppins have in common?

- (A) The town was named after them.
- (B) They both loved coal.
- (C) They were both postmasters.
- (D) They were both mayors in Rendville.

3. In the second paragraph, how does the author structure the text?

- (A) chronological
- (B) cause and effect
- (C) problem and solution
- (D) description

4. What does the word *legacy* mean in the text?

- (A) a lasting impact or memory
- (B) money left to someone
- (C) someone's children
- (D) an official document

5. Why is Rendville, Ohio, an important small town in the United States? Use details from the text support your idea.

____

____

6. What is the central idea of the text? Use details from the text support your ideas.

____

____

Name: ______________________ Date: ______________

As You Read

Underline information that is new to you. Put a star next to information you find most interesting.

Gilbert and Monowi

Tiny towns can be found across the United States. While these towns may have small populations, they often have a sense of pride and connection that keeps the communities alive. Let's look in-depth at two tiny towns.

First, the town of Gilbert is known as the "coolest town of Arkansas." This is meant literally because the town's weather is regularly the coolest in the state! With only 25 residents as of 2021, this town is home to a tiny population. The town lies along the Buffalo National River, and it has a long history. Founded in 1902, the town started off as a railroad construction camp. The town was once a bustling stop for cotton, logs, and grain that arrived by train. While the railroad no longer runs to the town, Gilbert now has a new claim to fame. Buffalo National River was recently named an International Dark Sky Park. Since the area is found far from city lights, the skies at night are often clear and lit with thousands of stars. The residents of Gilbert hope more stargazers will come by their town with this Dark Sky Park designation.

Another town in Nebraska has an even smaller population than Gilbert. Monowi, Nebraska is America's only incorporated town with a single resident. Yes, that's right—there is a tiny town with a population of one! As of 2023, Monowi's sole resident is Elsie Eiler, who is in her late 80s. Her husband, Rudy, died in 2004, leaving Eiler as the town's solitary occupant. Eiler is the town's mayor and treasurer. Her résumé also lists her as the town's clerk, secretary, librarian, and tavern owner!

Elsie Eiler in Monowi

Like other tiny towns, Monowi was once a more crowded community. In the 1930s, it was a railroad town filled with businesses and people. But over time, people moved away until Eiler was the town's only remaining resident. She has run the town's tavern since she and her husband bought it in 1971. Even now, Eiler opens the tavern six days a week, only taking Mondays off. The tavern has become what she calls a "community watering hole," and Eiler says she's hardly ever alone. Eiler once said, "The bar is the town, and I'm the town. We're all so intermeshed, you can't quite imagine one without the other." Eiler is committed to her community, and she files the paperwork every year to keep her town incorporated. She's the town's only taxpayer, and she pays taxes to herself to keep the town's water and electricity running.

Across the United States, there are residents who are deeply connected to their tiny towns—and one another. The people living in Gilbert and Monowi are just two examples; there are many more tiny towns you can learn about!

Name: ______________________ Date: ______________

Directions: Read "Gilbert and Monowi." Then, answer the questions.

1. What is the author's perspective of small towns?

- (A) Every small town should have a tavern for locals to meet at.
- (B) Small towns are not interesting.
- (C) Small communities have big impacts on their residents.
- (D) There should be more small towns in the United States.

2. What does the phrase *claim to fame* mean in the following sentence? *While the railroad no longer runs to the town, Gilbert now has a new claim to fame.*

- (A) the way a town changes through progress
- (B) the beginning of their small town
- (C) the reason people leave the town
- (D) the reason the town is well-known

3. How did Buffalo National River earn its International Dark Sky Park title?

- (A) Stargazers love to visit the park.
- (B) It is the darkest park in the United States.
- (C) All the lights from the city help the stars shine.
- (D) It is far from city lights, making the skies clear at night.

4. Why is Eiler the only resident of Monowi?

- (A) She prefers to live alone.
- (B) Many people moved away.
- (C) She is the mayor and treasurer of the city.
- (D) She owns the town's tavern.

5. How does the Monowi tavern affect Eiler's life?

____

____

6. Write proper nouns from the passage in the chart. Write a related word or phrase from the text next to each proper noun.

Proper Nouns	Related Words or Phrases

Name: ______________________ Date: ____________

Directions: Reread "Gilbert and Monowi." Then, respond to the prompt.

Imagine you are interviewing Elsie Eiler from Monowi. Create questions that you would ask Eiler about her experience living in her small town. Then, imagine what Eiler would say, and answer the questions from her point of view.

Name: ______________________ Date: ______________

Directions: Read the text, and answer the questions.

As You Read

Put an exclamation point near information that surprises you.

Welcome to Wellspring

July 22

So, it's official: my parents and I have moved to an extremely small town south of Minneapolis. Nancy, my therapist back home in Boston, told me a journal might be a nice way to process my feelings about the move. I'm not really sure what to write here, but let's just say it already feels weird to live in a place with fewer than 2,000 people. I'm so used to going to the grocery store and not knowing our cashier's name. But now, we live in Wellspring, a town with exactly one grocery store, one post office, and one school. There's nowhere to hide, and it feels like everyone knows my name and what I like to order for lunch at Sammie's Diner.

Last year, my parents started to feel trapped and caged in the concrete maze of Boston. My mom told us she wanted to live somewhere with more space and tranquility. Both of my parents have remote jobs, so they can work anywhere with internet service. They were excited to move, but now that we're here and faced with the reality of Wellspring, I feel like they *must* be regretting the move…right?

1. Which line from the text best supports the narrator's point of view of their family's move?

- Ⓐ I'm not really sure what to write here, but let's just say it already feels weird to live in a place with fewer than 2,000 people.
- Ⓑ It feels like everyone knows my name and what I like to order for lunch at Sammie's Diner.
- Ⓒ My mom told us she wanted to live somewhere with more space and tranquility.
- Ⓓ They were excited to move, but now that we're here and faced with the reality of Wellspring, I feel like they *must* be regretting the move…right?

2. How is the narrator's new home different from their previous home?

- Ⓐ Everyone seems to know each other.
- Ⓑ It is a confusing place to live.
- Ⓒ The town has a diner.
- Ⓓ It is an exciting place to live.

3. What is the narrator writing?

- Ⓐ a letter to his grandparent back home
- Ⓑ a letter to his friends back home
- Ⓒ a creative story
- Ⓓ a journal entry

4. How has the setting affected the narrator?

- Ⓐ He's uncomfortable being recognized.
- Ⓑ He wishes he could make more friends his age.
- Ⓒ He wants to order different food at Sammie's Diner.
- Ⓓ He thinks his parents should work at an office instead of at home.

Name: ______________________ Date: ____________

Directions: Read the text, and answer the questions.

As You Read

Underline information in the story that you make connections to. Describe the connections in the margins.

Small Steps

August 1

Bad news: my parents love life here in this tiny, little, itty-bitty town, and all my plots to get them to hate Wellspring are failing. I tried pointing out to them that we were hours and hours *and hours* away from the nearest ice cream shop, but my dad just laughed. Then, he pulled me into his pickup truck and took us on a road trip for gelato. (I refuse to admit to him that this road trip was actually pretty fun.)

To be fair, there are a few small parts of Wellspring that I don't mind at all, such as the great basketball court a block from us. And, last weekend, my mom and I spent hours browsing the shelves at the local library. I discovered they have an incredible mystery collection. What I really appreciate, though, is how quiet this town is compared to Boston. I'm so used to hearing cars honking and getting jostled by people on the sidewalks that the silence and space is kind of amazing.

It's now August, and if I'm being honest with myself, I'm feeling terrified about starting at a new school. It's probably going to be way harder to make friends in a small town, right?

1. What is the narrator's external conflict?

- (A) He likes the library.
- (B) The gelato is delicious.
- (C) His parents like the small town.
- (D) He is nervous about a new school.

2. What does *jostled* mean in the text?

- (A) left alone
- (B) annoyed by
- (C) bumped around
- (D) talked to

3. How is the setting affecting the narrator?

- (A) He is annoyed by everyone knowing him.
- (B) He wishes the town were smaller.
- (C) He is reluctant to like anything.
- (D) He wishes his parents didn't want to move.

4. What makes the narrator a complicated character?

- (A) He wants to be angry but is happy about his new school.
- (B) He is upset about moving but is starting to like the town.
- (C) He hates ice cream but loves gelato.
- (D) He wishes to move to a small town, but his parents won't let him.

5. What does the information in the parentheses reveal about the narrator's internal conflict?

- (A) He is relieved.
- (B) He is shy.
- (C) He is grateful.
- (D) He is stubborn.

Name: ______________________ Date: ______________

Directions: Read the text, and answer the questions.

As You Read

Put an exclamation point near information that surprises you.

Me and Shira

August 15

I biked over to the basketball court to meet up with my cousin, Shira, today. I told my mom right before I left, and she had that secretive "I'm-so-proud-of-my-son" look on her face. She's been bugging me to get together with Shira for a while, especially because she figures we're going to immediately become best friends.

We partly moved to Wellspring because my mom's sister, Aunt Mags, lives here, too. Shira is a year older than me, but we have never lived close enough to actually hang out. As Shira and I shot some hoops together, she told me what school is like here. I have to admit, I'm feeling a little less worried! It turns out my new school isn't huge, unlike my old one back in Boston, and I get the vibe that other kids are usually very friendly.

Shira told me if I wanted to connect with people that I should work on being "interested, instead of interesting." She thinks most people try to be interesting by talking about all the cool things they've done in their lives. But she believes it is more important to be genuinely interested in other people and what makes them tick. I've been thinking about that a lot today.

1. Why is the narrator's mother proud of him?

- Ⓐ She is grateful he likes his family members.
- Ⓑ She is happy he is trying to be social.
- Ⓒ She is excited that he is playing basketball.
- Ⓓ She is proud of him for learning about his new school.

2. What does the word *genuinely* mean in the third paragraph?

- Ⓐ popularly
- Ⓑ inclusively
- Ⓒ purposely
- Ⓓ honestly

3. Why is Shira's advice important to the narrator? Use details from the text to support your ideas.

____

____

4. What advice would you give the narrator and why? Use details from the text to support your ideas.

____

____

____

Name: ______________________ Date: ______________

As You Read

Underline information in the story that you make connections to. Describe the connections in the margins.

A New Home

August 22

I've been thinking a lot about what Shira said last week. I also have a funny feeling she was maybe trying to say that I sometimes talk a lot about myself and don't ask enough questions about the people I'm talking to. I've hung out with Shira a lot this last week, and she's introduced me to a few of her friends, including Cyrus and Sebastian. People have been friendly, and I've reminded myself to try to ask more questions when I meet new people. In this small town, it feels like everyone knows everyone, and that's been helpful for me to remember. Here, you're definitely not anonymous, and how you treat other people gets around.

I find I really get along with Cyrus because we both desperately want to beat Shira on the basketball court. But that's probably not going to happen though since she's miles ahead of us skills-wise. But I find that I'm pretty curious about Shira, Cyrus, and Sebastian, especially since their lives have been so different from mine. It's nice because they're curious about my life back in Boston, too. And I must admit, I've been thinking of Wellspring as home.

August 30

I had my official first day of school today, and what do you know, it wasn't half bad! It turns out I'd already met my math teacher a few times at the grocery store, and I've always liked settling into the rhythms of a new school year. I'm still talking to Nancy, my therapist back in Boston, but getting these words down on paper has been kind of helpful, too. I'm starting to think that learning how to ask questions about others is maybe the key to making new friends. I mean, there are plenty of other ways to make friends, but I think being genuinely curious about someone else makes a big difference. Since I'm the new kid in my grade, I've been introducing myself to everyone, but I do seem to already know most people around here—and that feels nice.

I do miss Boston sometimes, especially when I think of missing a hockey game or the next big blockbuster movie. Nancy told me a while back that everything comes with pros and cons. She says it comes down to accepting that there are upsides and downsides to every decision. I do feel pretty happy my family moved here, but there will always be things I miss from my old city life. But for the most part, I think this new chapter in Wellspring is going to be a lot of fun for me!

Name: ______________________________ Date: ____________________

Directions: Read "A New Home." Then, answer the questions.

1. What does the word *anonymous* means in the following sentence? *Here, you're definitely not anonymous, and how you treat other people gets around.*

- Ⓐ popular
- Ⓑ unknown
- Ⓒ different
- Ⓓ rude

2. Which line from the text provides a context clue to help the reader determine the meaning of *anonymous*?

- Ⓐ She's introduced me to a few of her friends.
- Ⓑ People have been friendly.
- Ⓒ How you treat other people gets around.
- Ⓓ I find I really get along with Cyrus.

3. What role does journaling play in the narrator's life?

- Ⓐ Writing his thoughts helps him figure out his emotions.
- Ⓑ It gives him a list of things to discuss with Nancy, his therapist.
- Ⓒ It helps him stay in contact with his friends in Boston.
- Ⓓ It makes him hate small town life.

4. What benefit does the narrator see about his new town?

- Ⓐ He does not know many people.
- Ⓑ He knows many people in town.
- Ⓒ School feels bigger than he thought.
- Ⓓ He wants to see a blockbuster movie.

5. How is the narrator adjusting to his new town?

- Ⓐ He is keeping to himself.
- Ⓑ He is asking questions and making new friends.
- Ⓒ He is pretending to like the town for his parents.
- Ⓓ He is attending hockey games.

6. What is the significance of the title "A New Home"?

- Ⓐ The narrator is making new friends.
- Ⓑ The narrator is beginning to accept Wellspring as his home.
- Ⓒ The narrator is curious about life outside his new town.
- Ⓓ The narrator's family does not like Wellspring.

7. List events that inspired the narrator to change and the changes he made because of those events.

Event	Change

Name: ______________________ Date: ______________

Directions: Reread "Me and Shira" on page 181. Then, respond to the prompt.

Write a dialogue between Shira and the narrator at the basketball court. Include Shira's advice and the narrator's reactions, both internal and external.

Name: ______________________ Date: ______________

VOCABULARY

community / **kə-ˈmyü-nə-tē** / ***noun***
1: a group of people who reside in one particular area (such as a city or town)
2: a group of people who share interests, engage in the same activity, practice the same faith, etc.

village / **ˈvil-lij** / ***noun***
1: a place where people live and work that is often smaller than a town and found in the countryside

town / **ˈtau̇n** / ***noun***
1: a place where people live and work that is often larger than a village but smaller than a city

city / **ˈsi-tē** / ***noun***
1: a place where many people live and work that is larger than a town

neighborhood / **ˈnā-bər-ˌhu̇d** / ***noun***
1: (count): an area that is part of a city or town
2: (noncount): a group of people who live near each other

suburb / **ˈsə-ˌbərb** / ***noun***
1: a town or other small area where people live in houses, outside but near a big city

borough / **ˈbər-(ˌ)ō** / ***noun***
1: a town, village, neighborhood, or part of a large city that has its own government
*Boroughs can be found in many English-speaking countries. They are more common in Great Britain than in the United States.

Name: ______________________________ Date: ____________

Directions: Read "Vocabulary." Then, answer the questions.

1. What is the purpose of the colon (:) in each dictionary entry?

- Ⓐ to highlight the purpose of a dictionary
- Ⓑ to separate the word from the pronunciation
- Ⓒ to separate the word from the pronunciation
- Ⓓ to introduce a definition

2. Why does *neighborhood* have more than one definition?

- Ⓐ The word is complicated and needs more explanation.
- Ⓑ The word has more than one meaning.
- Ⓒ The word is not always a noun.
- Ⓓ The word has changed over time.

3. What is the purpose of this text?

- Ⓐ to teach
- Ⓑ to persuade
- Ⓒ to entertain
- Ⓓ to challenge

4. What is the central idea of this text?

- Ⓐ There are many different places to live and call home.
- Ⓑ Community is important no matter where you live.
- Ⓒ Everyone lives in the same place no matter what it is called.
- Ⓓ A borough is a section of a city.

5. Why does the last entry have an asterisk (*)?

- Ⓐ to highlight the pronunciation
- Ⓑ to compare the United States to Great Britain
- Ⓒ to show the importance of boroughs
- Ⓓ to add extra, important information

6. How could this text be a useful resource? Use details from the text to support your ideas.

____

____

____

____

____

____

Name: ______________________________ Date: ________________

Directions: Closely reread the texts. Then, answer the questions.

Close-Reading Texts

Tiny Towns	Gilbert and Monowi
Every state has some towns that have small populations. Thousands of these small towns in the United States have fewer than 1,000 residents. And there are some tiny towns across the country that have even smaller populations than that! These towns are home to just a short list of locals and usually have fewer than 50 residents in total. Although they're small in size, each of these towns are incorporated places. This means they have a local government and are recognized in the U.S. census, or population count. From the town of Stockholm in Wisconsin to Monowi in Nebraska, there are many tiny towns in the United States to discover!	Another town in Nebraska has an even smaller population than Gilbert. Monowi, Nebraska is America's only incorporated town with a single resident. Yes, that's right—there is a tiny town with a population of one! As of 2023, Monowi's sole resident is Elsie Eiler, who is in her late 80s. Her husband, Rudy, died in 2004, leaving Eiler as the town's solitary occupant. Eiler is the town's mayor and treasurer. Her résumé also lists her as the town's clerk, secretary, librarian, and tavern owner! Eiler is committed to her community, and she files the paperwork every year to keep her town incorporated. She's the town's only taxpayer, and she pays taxes to herself to keep the town's water and electricity running.

1. How is Monowi an incorporated town even though there is only one resident?

____

____

____

2. How are these two texts similar? How are they different?

____

____

____

____

____

____

____

Name: ____________________ Date: ____________

Directions: Closely reread the texts. Then, complete the graphic organizer by explaining how the narrator in "A New Home" is experiencing community.

Close-Reading Texts

Vocabulary	A New Home
community / kə-'myü-nə-tē / *noun* **1:** a group of people who reside in one particular area (such as a city or town) **2:** a group of people who share interests, engage in the same activity, practice the same faith, etc.	I find I really get along with Cyrus because we both desperately want to beat Shira on the basketball court. But that's probably not going to happen though since she's miles ahead of us skills-wise. But I find that I'm pretty curious about Shira, Cyrus, and Sebastian, especially since their lives have been so different from mine. It's nice because they're curious about my life back in Boston, too. And I must admit, I've been thinking of Wellspring as home.

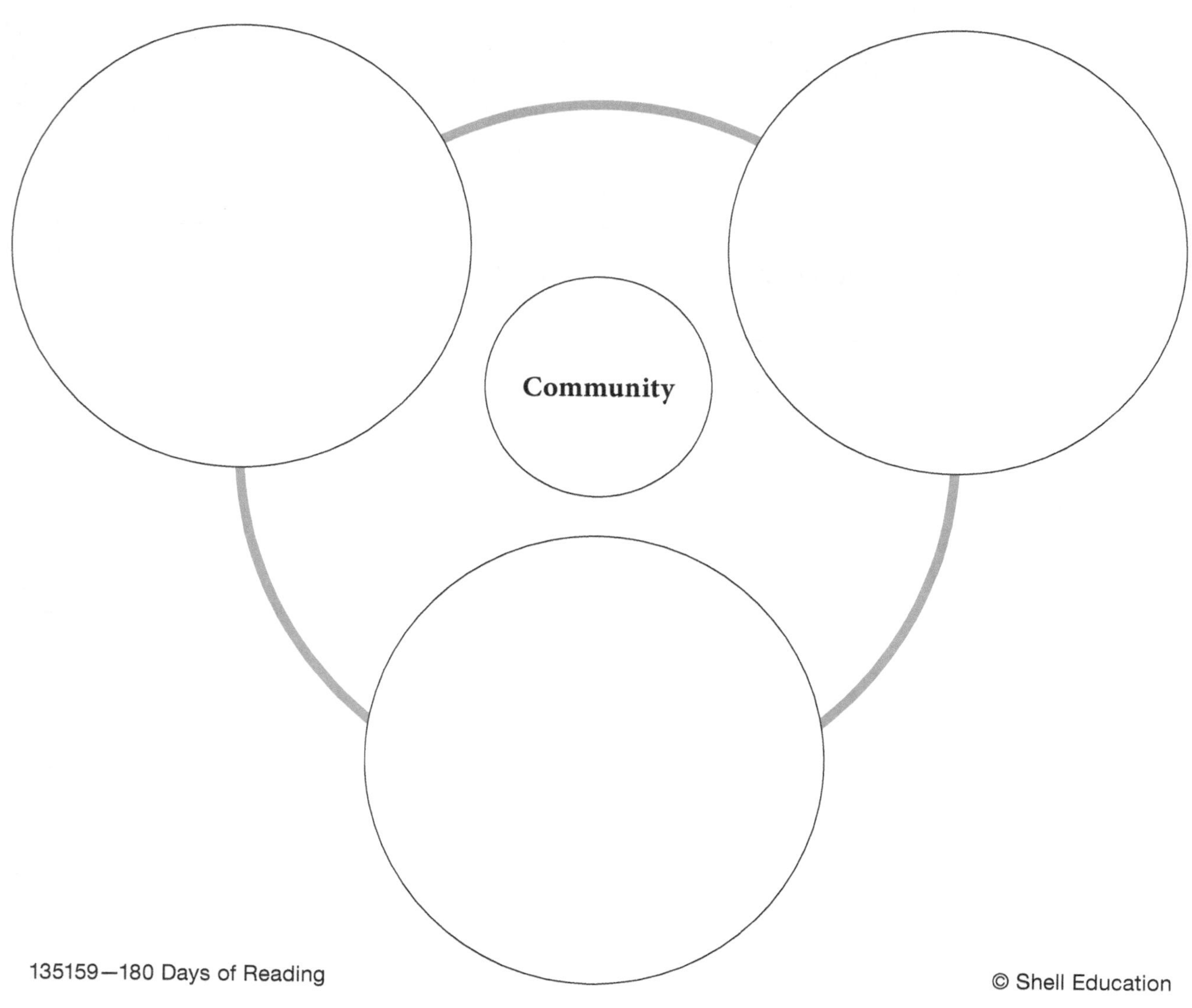

Name: ____________________________ Date: ______________

Directions: Reread "Small Steps" on page 180. Then, respond to the prompt.

The narrator of "Small Steps" is a complicated character. He is grappling with his new home while simultaneously liking it. Write a short essay that explains his internal conflict. Be sure to include your claim about how or why he is a complicated character, reasons to support your claim, and evidence from the text.

Name: ______________________________ **Date:** ________________

Directions: Review the texts from this unit. Then, respond to the prompt.

Create a social media advertisement for a small town. It can be one you learned about in this unit, one you look up, one you already know, or one you make up! Be sure to include the name of the town, its population, interesting facts about the town, and persuasive devices that encourage tourists to visit.

Name: ______________________________ Date: ________________

Directions: Read the text, and answer the questions.

As You Read

Underline important vocabulary that is related to money management.

What Is Money Management?

No matter a person's age, most people know that money plays a big role in their lives. Most people in the United States use money to pay for items and services they use every day. Money is how people pay for their homes and the food they put on their tables. People also use money to pay for services. These may include oil changes for cars and trips to the dentist. A large part of people's lives is usually spent earning money through work. But while most people focus on the earning of money, there is sometimes less emphasis placed on how they manage their money.

While most young students likely do not have jobs yet, many of them often receive allowances or small financial gifts from others. In that way, most young people are already earning or receiving money. Money management is about making an intentional plan for your money that reflects your values and priorities. Money management usually involves budgeting for the present and saving for the future.

1. According to the text, why is money important?
   - (A) We need it to buy items for everyday use.
   - (B) We enjoy buying luxury items.
   - (C) We inherit money.
   - (D) People do not manage their money well.

2. Which statements best captures the author's opinion of money?
   - (A) We should think more about how we spend our money.
   - (B) It is important to have a job so you understand the value of money.
   - (C) Young people do not have money because they aren't working yet.
   - (D) Earning money is more important than money management.

3. What is the meaning of the word *budgeting* in the text?
   - (A) buying things you like
   - (B) saving money for a long-term goal
   - (C) planning how money is used
   - (D) deciding where to work

4. Who is **most** likely the author's intended audience?
   - (A) adults
   - (B) people who are employed
   - (C) very wealthy people
   - (D) young people

5. Where does the author think people should place more focus?
   - (A) why they want to have money
   - (B) who they give their money to
   - (C) how they earn their money
   - (D) how they manage their money

Name: ______________________ Date: ____________

Directions: Read the text, and answer the questions.

As You Read

Circle new ideas about the topic.

Creating a Budget: Part 1

Money management often begins with creating a budget. A budget is a plan for how someone will use their money in a set period of time. Some people create monthly budgets for themselves. Other people create yearly budgets for their finances. Within a budget, a person or family allocates money to different categories. For many people, there are two main ways to use money: spending or saving.

People spend their money for many reasons. They might spend money on a take-out meal, the latest video game, or movie tickets on a Friday night. Part of creating a budget involves deciding what you want to spend your money on and how much money you want to spend on that particular item or activity. However, people can also choose to save their money. Many people have their eyes on big purchases they cannot pay for with the money they currently have. Instead, they must save their money on a month-to-month basis. People might save up for big trips, new cars, or the latest computer. Many people also see saving money as a way to take care of their future selves. They may save up money for retirement or potential emergencies.

1. What are finances?

- (A) time
- (B) plans
- (C) money
- (D) goals

2. What does the word *allocates* mean as used in the text?

- (A) portions out
- (B) changes
- (C) spends
- (D) earns

3. How is a budget helpful?

- (A) It lets you buy everything you want at the store.
- (B) It prevents you from buying everything you want at the store.
- (C) It provides insight into the latest trends.
- (D) It helps you decide how much money you want to spend.

4. Why do people save money?

- (A) to be prepared for an emergency in the future
- (B) to purchase something expensive
- (C) both A and B
- (D) none of the above

5. According to the text, how often should people save money?

- (A) daily
- (B) monthly
- (C) when they aren't interested in buying anything
- (D) when they have a big trip planned

6. What is the text structure of paragraph 2?

- (A) problem and solution
- (B) cause and effect
- (C) compare and contrast
- (D) chronological order

Name: ____________________ Date: ____________

Directions: Read the text, and answer the questions.

As You Read

Put stars next to claims the author makes. Underline the author's evidence that supports their claims.

Creating a Budget: Part 2

A budget can help a person decide how much money they want to spend and save. But there is one final category they can allocate money to: sharing. People can choose to share their money with people in need. One common way is to donate money to non-profit organizations. People can support causes that are close to their hearts. Or, they might also choose to share their money with someone who is going through a tough time and needs financial support.

Budgets are flexible plans for how a person can use money. If someone is creating a monthly budget, they might decide that 45 percent of their money will go to spending, while another 45 percent will go toward saving. The remaining 10 percent could then go to sharing their money. Budgeting is often a helpful way to become more intentional with spending money. A budget lines up with a person's values and priorities, and it can be referred back to when it comes time to spend money.

1. How are budgets flexible?

- Ⓐ They restrict you into spending and saving a certain amount each month.
- Ⓑ They make you share your money with people in need.
- Ⓒ They give you choice in how to portion out your money.
- Ⓓ all of the above

2. What does the idiom *close to their hearts* mean in the following sentence? *People can support causes that are close to their hearts.*

- Ⓐ common
- Ⓑ vital to life
- Ⓒ romantic
- Ⓓ important to them

3. What is the author's perspective on sharing money? Support your ideas with details from the text.

____

____

4. How are the three categories for budgeting connected? Support your ideas with details from the text.

____

____

____

Name: ______________________________ Date: ____________________

As You Read

Underline information that is new to you. Put a star next to information you already knew.

What Are Your Priorities?

When you're making a plan for how you will spend, save, and share your money, it helps to first figure out your priorities. Your list of priorities often starts with identifying your needs versus your wants. A need is something that is necessary for someone to live, including safe places to sleep or meals to eat. Everyone shares certain basic needs, including food, water, shelter, and clothing. Medical needs can vary from person to person, and they can potentially have a huge impact on one's finances and budget. A want, on the other hand, is something that can improve your quality of life, but it is not needed for survival. Wants can include smartphones or rollerblades. While these items are not needed to live, they can help you stay connected or get to new places.

Your needs are a top priority when it comes to budgeting. When you're deciding how to use your money, it's helpful to first put the money toward your needs. You can then decide how you will use the rest of your money based on your list of wants. Everyone has their own set of priorities. For example, one person might love eating out, but they are less excited about owning the latest tech gear. Spending money at a new restaurant is therefore a higher priority to them rather than buying the latest smartwatch. Before you use your money, it's helpful to decide what your priorities are. These priorities can help you plan your overall budget.

If you have decided to use 40 percent of your money for spending, calculate the total amount of money you have to spend every month. Once you have that number, you can then make a plan for how you will spend that money. Try writing a list of all the things you want to spend your money on in a month. Do you like buying take-out meals from a local shop, or do you like thrifting clothes? Once you have your list of wants, you can then begin to plan how much money you want to spend on each want every month.

Creating a budget is a helpful way to avoid impulse purchases, too. When we are out running errands or walking through a mall, we can make quick decisions about what to buy. You might decide to buy something because it's on sale, or you feel as though you have to buy the latest gadget. Having a budget that focuses on your priorities gives you a way to step back from that. It can help you stop making purchases you might later regret.

A budget is your personal, intentional plan that guides how you will spend, save, and share your money. It's an empowering tool to help you put your money toward what matters most to you!

Name: ______________________ Date: ______________

Directions: Read "What Are Your Priorities?" Then, answer the questions.

1. What is a priority?

Ⓐ something a person needs, not wants
Ⓑ something important to a person
Ⓒ a way to budget money
Ⓓ something a person wants, not needs

2. Which statement would the author **most strongly** agree with?

Ⓐ It is just as important to spend money on wants as well as needs.
Ⓑ Spend money on what you need first.
Ⓒ Budgets are not efficient tools to plan your spending habits.
Ⓓ Without a budget, it is safe to spend money in the moment.

3. Why does the author use different examples of ways to spend money?

Ⓐ to list ways for readers to spend money
Ⓑ to convince readers to budget
Ⓒ to judge readers' spending habits
Ⓓ to connect to their audience's different interests

4. What is one of the author's claim?

Ⓐ Budgeting your money is an empowering tool.
Ⓑ Spending is the most important part of a budget.
Ⓒ Buy what you want on a budget.
Ⓓ List what you want to spend money on each month.

5. Why are a person's needs the first thing they should consider when managing their money?

Ⓐ It is useful to think about which wants are most important to you.
Ⓑ People need to be safe and healthy first.
Ⓒ Managing money helps people know how much to spend on food.
Ⓓ People want to budget for many different reasons.

6. Budget how you would spend, save, and share $100 in a month. Include the name and price of each item.

Spend		Save	Share
Needs	**Wants**	**Future Investment**	**Person/Group Close to Your Heart**

Name: ______________________________ Date: ______________

Directions: Reread "What Are Your Priorities?" Then, respond to the prompt.

Imagine you have a friend who just started getting an allowance. You notice that they spend all their money quickly each month. Use ideas from the text to write a dialogue between you and your friend in which you explain how to budget their money.

Name: ______________________________ Date: ____________________

Directions: Read the text, and answer the questions.

As You Read

Put stars next to words that show the mood of the text.

Budgeting Setbacks

From: deja2002@fauxmail.com

To: merritt_barlowe@fauxmail.com

Subject: Colorado May Be Canceled?!

Aunt Merritt,

I come to you full of bad news: I'm already behind on our financial challenge. Frankly, I barely feel brave enough to send you this email. I'm so embarassed!

I was so excited when we made our plan to go camping in Colorado this summer, and I know I need to save at least $500 to make it happen. It meant so much to me that you helped me make a budget (or a plan for my money, as you say) so we could make this magical aunt and niece trip happen. But *ugh*, I am struggling to stick to my budget, and I honestly don't know how you do it! I'm not used to watching what I spend my money on, and I have a habit of dropping by the local shop and just throwing money at them for a chai latte. I added up my income and expenses for this month, just like you showed me, and I'm $50 behind on my savings target for our trip. Are we going to have to cancel our Colorado plans? Or do you have some wise wisdom to dispense, my dear aunt and budget master?

Love,
Deja

1. What role does Deja's aunt play in Deja's life?

- (A) Her aunt is someone Deja looks to for guidance.
- (B) Her is aunt is fun-loving and free-spirited.
- (C) Deja wishes she could live closer to her aunt.
- (D) Deja does not have much contact with her aunt.

2. How does Deja contribute to the conflict?

- (A) She spends money on things she does not need.
- (B) She donates money to her local coffee shop.
- (C) She throws her money in the trash.
- (D) She does not like being on a budget.

3. Why does the author use parentheses in the second paragraph?

- (A) to add inner thinking
- (B) to define a term
- (C) to create dialogue
- (D) to show the conflict

4. Which word best describes Deja's personality?

- (A) reflective
- (B) selfish
- (C) kind
- (D) lazy

5. Why does Deja write to her aunt?

- (A) to prove she cannot save money
- (B) to clear her guilt
- (C) to ask for money
- (D) to ask for support

Name: ______________________ Date: ______________

Directions: Read the text, and answer the questions.

As You Read

Put stars next to words that show Aunt Merritt's personality.

Getting Flexible

From: merritt_barlowe@fauxmail.com

To: deja2002@fauxmail.com

Subject: Colorado Is Not Canceled

Hi Deja,

You are hilarious and wonderful, even if I do not quite understand your love for chai lattes. Thank you for letting me know your concerns about Colorado, but there really is no need for you to worry because your budget is all about being flexible. The plan we made for how you were going to spend, save, and share your money is not set in stone. If you veer off track, there is no need to get too worried. It might just involve some creativity on your part to meet your financial goals.

Now, missing $50 to meet your goal is not insurmountable. I'd suggest that you look at how you spent your money this month and see if there are any expenses you could let go for next month. For me, if I have a big target goal, that usually means I let go of getting take-out tacos for the month.

Also, is there a way to remind yourself every day of your goal of getting to Colorado with me? I sometimes keep a little sticky note in my wallet that lists my big budgeting goals. I find this helps me remember my budgeting plan—and stick with it!

Much love,
Aunt Merritt

1. What does the word *veer* mean in the text?
   - (A) follow
   - (B) return
   - (C) remain
   - (D) deviate

2. What advice does Aunt Merritt give Deja?
   - (A) Stick to the same budget.
   - (B) Stop spending money all together.
   - (C) Stop ordering take out.
   - (D) Reevaluate your budget.

3. How does Aunt Merritt help Deja?
   - (A) by providing examples of how she rebudgets
   - (B) by scolding her
   - (C) by laughing at her
   - (D) by asking Deja questions to better understand the situation

4. What is Aunt Merritt's perspective of Deja?
   - (A) Deja is just like her.
   - (B) Deja can fix the problem if she tries.
   - (C) Deja is disappointing her by spending too much money.
   - (D) Deja is doing well in school.

5. What is the mood of Aunt Merritt's email?
   - (A) disappointed
   - (B) awkward
   - (C) reassuring
   - (D) glad

6. What does the word *insurmountable* mean?
   - (A) unwilling to
   - (B) unchanging
   - (C) not challenging
   - (D) not able to overcome

Name: ______________________________ Date: ________________

Directions: Read the text, and answer the questions.

As You Read
Circle anything that surprises you.

Changing Behavior

From: deja2002@fauxmail.com
To: merritt_barlowe@fauxmail.com
Subject: Thanks for the Pep Talk!

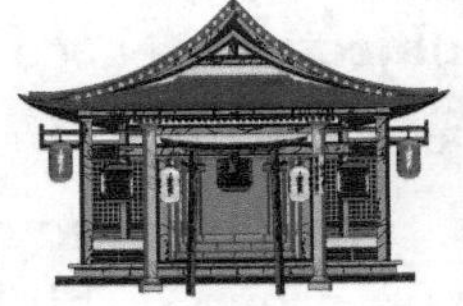

Aunt Merritt,

Do people compliment you on your wisdom every day? That last email of yours really got me thinking, and I realized that to hit this savings target, I'm going to have to change how I usually spend my money. I'm going to have to make some habit changes, aren't I? Like you once told me, saving is not rocket science, it just involves putting some of my money aside for a future goal. I know you have so many cool savings goals—such as your retirement and that trip to Japan—and I can tell these are top priorities for you. It's important for you to save enough to see a real-life temple in Kyoto, so you make sure you always put money aside for that trip.

I think I've been prioritizing my chai latte habit over our trip to Colorado, if I'm being honest with myself. I'm going to change things up this month though, I promise.

Your favorite niece,
Deja

1. How has Deja's tone shifted?

- (A) Deja is now determined.
- (B) Deja is now remorseful.
- (C) Deja is now reserved.
- (D) Deja is now excited.

2. How does Aunt Merritt's letter affect Deja?

- (A) It inspires Deja to meet her goals.
- (B) It reminds Deja that chai lattes are expensive.
- (C) It helps Deja save for Japan.
- (D) It shows Deja how to spend more money.

3. What does the chai latte symbolize in the story?

- (A) the connection between age and money habits
- (B) the reasons spending is more important than saving
- (C) the difficulty of changing spending habits
- (D) the encouragement of a relative

4. What is Deja's perspective of her aunt? Use details from the text to support your ideas.

____

____

____

Name: ______________________ Date: ______________

As You Read

Write a ∞ wherever you make connections. Briefly describe the connections in the margins.

Long-Term Thinking

From: merritt_barlowe@fauxmail.com
To: deja2002@fauxmail.com
Subject: My Niece Is the Wise One

Dearest Deja,

I am so proud of you. I'm always proud of you, of course, but today I will say that I am extra proud. I think you have touched on one of the most difficult parts of saving money because, yes, it does involve changing some of our habits. If we are used to spending money on anything that catches our eye, it is difficult to begin changing that habit. But having an awareness of how we spend our money is such a helpful place to start.

I was not always someone who made a budget, you know. But after your uncle and I went our separate ways, I discovered I needed to take care of myself. In many ways, it was empowering for me to choose new financial goals. I spent a lot of time learning how to set new priorities and stick to them, and it was hard at the beginning! I liked to have fun with my friends, and it was sometimes tough for me to tell them I could not afford to do all the activities they wanted to do. But I knew I wanted to get out of debt, and I also wanted to save my money for the future and for my retirement. I also wanted to save for my big solo adventures because travel is my favorite activity in the world, and it is my top priority.

I know you, Deja, and I know our adventure in Colorado will happen. We are going to have a blast together! Keep me posted on how everything goes with your budget, and always know I am only a quick call or email away.

Love,
Aunt Merritt

From: deja2002@fauxmail.com
To: merritt_barlowe@fauxmail.com
Subject: Photos from Our Colorado Adventure!

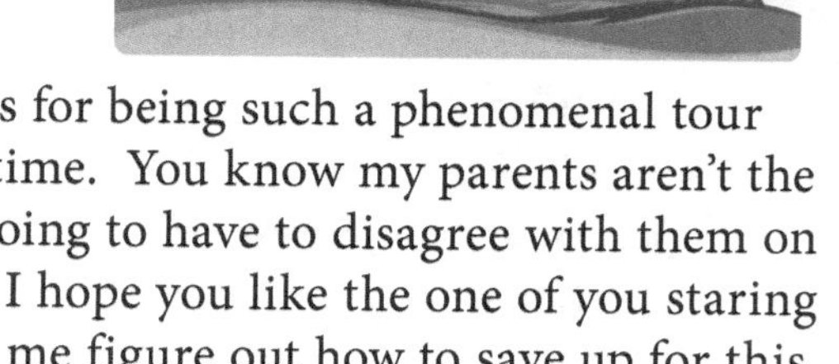

Aunt Merritt,

That was the best trip I have EVER been on! Thanks for being such a phenomenal tour guide and showing me how to set up a tent for the first time. You know my parents aren't the biggest fans of camping, but after this trip, I think I'm going to have to disagree with them on that one. I've attached all the photos from our trip, and I hope you like the one of you staring down that black-billed magpie. Thanks also for helping me figure out how to save up for this big trip. Learning how to budget has been so empowering, like you said, and I can't wait to set my next financial target: our trip to Yosemite!

Talk to you soon,
Deja

Name: ______________________________ Date: ________________

Directions: Read "Long-Term Thinking." Then, answer the questions.

1. When did Aunt Merritt learn to budget?

(A) after she became single
(B) before she wanted to travel to Japan
(C) when Deja asked to go to Colorado
(D) after she was in debt

2. Why does Aunt Merritt budget?

(A) to be independent
(B) to teach people how to be like her
(C) to party with her friends
(D) to spend as much as she earns

3. What obstacle did Aunt Merritt need to overcome?

(A) going through a breakup
(B) telling her friends she could not afford activities
(C) paying off her debt
(D) all of the above

4. What effect does budgeting have on Aunt Merritt and Deja?

(A) They can buy whatever they want.
(B) The share their money.
(C) They feel empowered.
(D) They feel restricted.

5. What does the line *I know you, Deja* suggest about Aunt Merritt?

____

____

____

6. Write a theme of the story, and support your answer with details from the text.

Theme
Detail 1
Detail 2
Detail 3

Name: ______________________ Date: ____________

Directions: Reread "Long-Term Thinking." Then, respond to the prompt.

Create a time line that sequences the events in the email for both Deja's and Aunt Merritt's stories. Your time line should include the past and present storylines for both characters.

Name: ______________________ Date: ______________

SAMIR'S MONTHLY BUDGET

Different computer programs offer a variety of templates for managing your finances. Most templates offer a good starting place and can be altered to meet your needs. They have built-in formulas to help you calculate everything and avoid mistakes. There are also a wide range of financial management apps for phones and other devices. Many of them can track your spending to give ideas of where you could possibly save. It is important to find a template or app that works for you. Luckily, there are a lot of options to choose from! Below is a simple template used to plan and track Samir's finances.

Samir's Income	$100

Expenses	Budget	Actual	Notes
coffee (*spending*)	$20	$28	Oops. I spent a little extra money on coffee this month. Luckily, I spent less on paint supplies this month.
paint supplies (*spending*)	$25	$12	
new bike (*saving*)	$45	$45	Woot! I now have $200 saved up for my new bike. I'm on track to buy my new wheels in March.
donation to World Wildlife Fund (*sharing*)	$10	$10	I love animals!

	Budget	Actual
Total Income	$100	$100
Expenses	– $100	– $95
Leftover	$0	$5

Name: ______________________ Date: ____________

Directions: Read "Samir's Monthly Budget." Then, answer the questions.

1. According to the text, why is it easy to budget your money?

- (A) There are many complicated tools to use.
- (B) The apps are free to use.
- (C) Budgeting is smart.
- (D) There are many templates and apps.

2. How did Samir save money this month?

- (A) He stuck to his budget.
- (B) He spent less money on paint supplies.
- (C) He donated his extra money.
- (D) He did not save any money this month.

3. What is the author's opinion about budgeting?

- (A) Use an app to help you.
- (B) Always donate your extra money.
- (C) Be flexible with your spending.
- (D) Find a format that works for you.

4. Why does Samir donate to World Wildlife Fund?

- (A) He likes to share money.
- (B) He gets extra credit at school.
- (C) He cares about animals.
- (D) His parents ask him to.

5. The line *Most templates offer a good starting place and can be altered to meet your needs* suggests ______.

- (A) users need a template to show them what to do
- (B) users should change templates to work for them
- (C) a template is not helpful
- (D) users should create their own budget format

6. How are Samir's paint supply expenses different from his new bike expenses?

- (A) He spent his money on paint supplies, but he is saving up money for a new bike.
- (B) He spent his money on a new bike, but is saving up money for paint supplies.
- (C) He needed twice as much money for his paint supply expenses as his new bike expenses.
- (D) He saved less money for his new bike than he budgeted, and he spent more money on paint supplies than he budgeted.

7. What lesson could be learned from Samir's budget? Use details from the passage to support your ideas.

____

____

____

____

____

____

Name: ______________________________ Date: ________________

Directions: Closely reread the texts. Then, reread "Samir's Monthly Budget" on page 203. Identify the examples of flexibility in each text, and record them in the chart.

Close-Reading Texts

Creating a Budget: Part 2	Getting Flexible
People can support causes that are close to their hearts. Or, they might also choose to share their money with someone who is going through a tough time and needs financial support. Budgets are flexible plans for how a person can use money. If someone is creating a monthly budget, they might decide that 45 percent of their money will go to spending, while another 45 percent will go toward saving. The remaining 10 percent could then go to sharing their money. Budgeting is often a helpful way to become more intentional with spending money. A budget lines up with a person's values and priorities, and it can be referred back to when it comes time to spend money.	If you veer off track, there is no need to get too worried. It might just involve some creativity on your part to meet your financial goals. Now, missing $50 to meet your goal is not insurmountable. I'd suggest that you look at how you spent your money this month and see if there are any expenses you could let go for next month. For me, if I have a big target goal, that usually means I let go of getting take-out tacos for the month.

Flexibilities of a Budget	
Creating a Budget: Part 2	
Getting Flexible	
Samir's Monthly Budget	

Name: ______________________________ Date: ______________

Directions: Closely reread the texts. Write three pieces of advice from the texts in order of how important they are to you. Explain your reasoning.

Close-Reading Texts

What Are Your Priorities?	Samir's Monthly Budget
Creating a budget is a helpful way to avoid impulse purchases, too. When we are out running errands or walking through a mall, we can make quick decisions about what to buy. You might decide to buy something because it's on sale, or you feel as though you have to buy the latest gadget. Having a budget that focuses on your priorities gives you a way to step back from that. It can help you stop making purchases you might later regret. A budget is your personal, intentional plan that guides how you will spend, save, and share your money. It's an empowering tool to help you put your money toward what matters most to you!	Different computer programs offer a variety of templates for managing your finances. Most templates offer a good starting place and can be altered to meet your needs. They have built-in formulas to help you calculate everything and avoid mistakes. There are also a wide range of financial management apps for phones and other devices. Many of them can track your spending to give ideas of where you could possibly save. It is important to find a template or app that works for you. Luckily, there are a lot of options to choose from!

Budgeting Advice		
Ranking	**Advice from Texts**	**Your Reasoning**
1		
2		
3		

Name: ____________________________ Date: ________________

Directions: Think about the texts from this unit. Then, respond to the prompt.

What do you believe about money management based on what you read? Write a short essay about money management. Include a claim about money management and evidence to support your claim.

Name: ______________________________ Date: ________________

Directions: Create a template for a budget that works for you. Include categories for spending, saving, and sharing.

Name: ______________________ Date: ______________

Directions: Read the text, and answer the questions.

As You Read

Circle the topic. Underline the words that show the author's perspective, or opinion, of the topic.

What Is Self-Compassion?

Compassion is an expression of caring toward someone who is going through a challenging time. When people feel compassion toward others, they feel compelled to empathize with their struggles. Some people may want to help them in some way. Most people work to practice compassion with others. However, people are often less likely to practice compassion with themselves.

Dr. Kristin Neff is a professor and author who led some of the first studies in self-compassion. According to her, self-compassion "involves treating oneself with warmth and understanding in difficult times." She says it also means recognizing that "making mistakes is part of being human." Self-compassion is defined as a self-attitude. At the heart of self-compassion is treating ourselves like we would a good friend or loved one. When a friend is struggling, we speak to them with an encouraging tone. We approach them with kindness and understanding. Self-compassion is about speaking to ourselves with the same gentle care and attention.

1. Which line from the text best supports the central idea of the passage?

- (A) Compassion is an expression of caring toward someone who is going through a challenging time.
- (B) Most people work to practice compassion with others.
- (C) However, people are often less likely to practice compassion with themselves.
- (D) We approach them with kindness and understanding.

2. Which act would the author agree is an example of self-compassion?

- (A) criticizing yourself after a hard day
- (B) speaking gently to yourself after a test
- (C) arguing internally during an easy task
- (D) helping a friend in need by giving them advice

3. What is the author's perspective of the topic?

- (A) People should be more caring.
- (B) Compassion is new and exciting, and we should all learn about it.
- (C) Doctors have been studying compassion for a long time.
- (D) It is important to be understanding with yourself.

4. Which is a synonym for *compassion*?

- (A) criticism
- (B) sympathy
- (C) indifference
- (D) utility

5. Why does the author include quotes from Dr. Kristin Neff?

- (A) to explain the topic
- (B) to include an example
- (C) to illustrate an experience with an anecdote
- (D) to provide an expert opinion

Name: ______________________ Date: ______________

Directions: Read the text, and answer the questions.

As You Read

Draw a heart next to details that you strongly agree with. Write additional thoughts in the margins.

Why Practice Self-Compassion?

Every person goes through hard and challenging times. It is often in the tough chapters of our lives that we are most critical of ourselves. When we are feeling low after a failure, we might judge ourselves for messing up. Or if we have trouble standing up to someone who is disrespectful, we might later criticize ourselves for not being braver. Our instinct is usually to inwardly beat ourselves up for our mistakes and failures. But self-compassion offers an alternate strategy.

Research shows that being kind to oneself helps in a myriad of ways. People who practice self-compassion are able to see their mistakes with calmness and clarity. They are more likely to correct their mistakes and believe they can improve. Research shows that when we are critical of ourselves, our stress hormones increase. Using a critical voice to talk to ourselves can prevent us from learning from our failures. On the other hand, when we use a kind voice to encourage ourselves, we are more able to soothe ourselves and decrease our stress levels. Self-compassion also leads to greater emotional resilience. It appears to be correlated with increased optimism and curiosity, too.

1. Which is **not** something the text says about people who practice self-compassion?

- (A) They are able to see their mistakes with calmness and clarity.
- (B) They have higher levels of stress hormones.
- (C) They are more likely to correct their mistakes.
- (D) They have greater levels of emotional resilience, optimism, and curiosity.

2. Which text structure is used in this text?

- (A) problem and solution
- (B) cause and effect
- (C) compare and contrast
- (D) chronological order

3. What does the author mean by a *critical voice* in the second paragraph?

- (A) arguing
- (B) being kind
- (C) judging
- (D) silencing

4. What does the word *soothe* mean in the text?

- (A) argue
- (B) challenge
- (C) calm
- (D) joyful

5. What effect could positive self-talk have on people?

- (A) People will learn from their mistakes and be more confident.
- (B) People will not trust themselves.
- (C) People will have a hard time making lasting friendships.
- (D) People will have elevated stress hormones.

6. What is the author's point of view?

- (A) We should speak kindly to others.
- (B) Without compassion, friends would feel lonely.
- (C) People should forgive others.
- (D) People are often too hard on themselves.

Name: ______________________ Date: ______________

Directions: Read the text, and answer the questions.

As You Read

Circle ideas that you think are important to try. Write additional thoughts in the margins.

Misgivings about Self-Compassion

Some people are reluctant to practice self-compassion. They may think self-compassion is the same as self-pity. But self-pity and self-compassion are different practices. When we feel self-pity, our focus remains *only* on our challenges. We forget that everyone experiences struggles. Instead, we might believe we are the only person going through something hard. Self-pity focuses on the separation between oneself and others. Self-compassion emphasizes our connection to ourselves and others. When we practice self-compassion, we look at our situations with a kind and balanced outlook. Self-compassion involves reminding ourselves that we are not alone in our struggles.

Another misgiving about self-compassion is that it involves self-indulgence. Some people think that if they are kind to themselves, they'll become selfish. When they want to make a change in their lives, they might think that they can criticize themselves into action. But this usually does not translate to an effective or long-term practice.

When we treat ourselves with compassion, we can see our weak points with kindness and clarity. This allows us to get back on track if we experience setbacks—which we often do in pursuit of a goal.

1. What does the word *reluctant* mean?

- (A) hesitant
- (B) stressed
- (C) frightened
- (D) forgetful

2. Why does the author use italics in the first paragraph?

- (A) to show dialogue
- (B) for emphasis
- (C) to give a definition
- (D) to challenge the reader

3. What is the central idea of the passage?

- (A) Self-compassion is about supporting yourself during challenging times.
- (B) Self-compassion is being easy on yourself.
- (C) Self-compassion and self-pity are essentially the same thing.
- (D) When you are kind to yourself, it can be seen as selfish.

4. Why might it be beneficial to reflect on our own weak points with compassion? Use details from the text to support you answer.

____

____

5. How are self-pity and self-compassion different? Use details from the text to support your answer.

____

____

Name: ______________________ Date: ______________

As You Read

Underline information that is new to you. Put a star next to information you already knew.

How to Practice Self-Compassion

Dr. Kristin Neff led some of the first studies on the subject of self-compassion. She says there are three key elements of self-compassion: self-kindness, common humanity, and mindfulness.

To practice self-compassion, it's key to treat oneself with kindness. This can sit in contrast with self-judgment. When people make mistakes, they may come to a crossroads in their minds. They have to choose between speaking gently or harshly to themselves. Talking to yourself with kindness, instead of judgment, means using warm and understanding language. Everyone makes mistakes, and it's helpful to not judge yourself too harshly when life goes awry. If you are going through a tough time, a simple phrase you can say to yourself is, "May I be kind to myself." You can also try placing your hand on your heart as a comforting gesture. Above all else, keep in mind that self-kindness is not about ignoring our struggles. Rather, it involves acknowledging our pain without criticism.

The second element of self-compassion is common humanity. Common humanity is opposite to isolation. When we are going through challenging times, our perspectives can shrink. We can only see our problems and challenges and forget that everyone else struggles, too. Part of self-compassion is recognizing there is a shared human experience. Every person experiences suffering, difficulties, and failure. Every person has shortcomings and feels pain. So, next time you are going through a tough time, try to remember this shared human experience. Common humanity can help us feel connected to others instead of isolated. Two simple phrases you can use are, "Other people have experienced this, too," or "I am not alone."

The final element of self-compassion is mindfulness. Mindfulness is about observing our thoughts and feelings without judgment. It's a practice in which a person does not deny their feelings, but they also do not hold onto them too tightly. As Dr. Neff says, "We cannot ignore our pain and feel compassion for it at the same time." Therefore, mindfulness can help us see our feelings and thoughts with perspective. Part of self-compassion is not over-identifying with our thoughts and feelings. Sometimes, we can get caught in a spiral of rumination. We might go over a thought repeatedly in our heads. Mindfulness is about observing our thoughts and feelings—and then letting them go. Mindful statements you could say to acknowledge what you are experiencing are, "This hurts," or "This is a moment of suffering."

The next time you go through a hard time, check with yourself to see whether you are practicing self-compassion. Ask yourself, "Am I treating myself with kindness and understanding? Do I remember everyone makes mistakes and feels pain? Am I observing my thoughts and feelings with perspective?" You might find that answering these questions can help you move through a tough time with more compassion for yourself.

Name: ______________________________ Date: ________________

Directions: Read "How to Practice Self-Compassion." Then, answer the questions.

1. What is the author's purpose in this text?

- (A) entertainment
- (C) informative
- (B) persuasive
- (D) both B and C

2. Which line from the text contains a metaphor?

- (A) When people make mistakes, they may come to a crossroads in their minds.
- (B) Everyone makes mistakes, and it's helpful to not judge yourself too harshly when life goes awry.
- (C) If you are going through a tough time, a simple phrase you can say to yourself is, "May I be kind to myself."
- (D) Rather, it involves acknowledging our pain without criticism.

3. Why does the author use quotation marks in the follow sentence? *Mindful statements you could say to acknowledge what you are experiencing are, "This hurts," or "This is a moment of suffering."*

- (A) to quote an expert opinion on self-compassion
- (B) to model positive self-talk as inner dialogue
- (C) to emphasize a how easy positive self-talk is
- (D) to set off a list of ideas for mindfulness

4. How might remembering that you are not alone in your struggles help you practice self-compassion?

____

____

____

5. Give examples of situations when you could apply the three key elements of self-compassion.

Key Element	Situation	What You Might Say

Unit 12
WEEK 1
DAY
5

Name: ______________________ Date: ____________

Directions: Reread "How to Practice Self-Compassion." Then, respond to the prompt.

Write a letter to a friend explaining a time that you used one, two, or all the key elements of self-compassion. If you have never used them, explain how you hope to incorporate them into your internal thoughts.

Name: ______________________________ Date: ________________

Directions: Read the text, and answer the questions.

As You Read

Mark the cause-and-effect relationships in Chantelle's life.

Keeping a Stiff Upper Lip

Chantelle had a long list of slogans that buoyed her through life's turbulence. "Keep a stiff upper lip," her grandfather always told her. "Failure is never an option," she once overheard her father tell her mother. While Chantelle was not the sort of person to list out these life slogans, she kept them close to her heart. She always referred to them when life started to hand out lemons.

In junior year of high school, when Chantelle's dad lost his job and her mom started cleaning houses to keep the family afloat, Chantelle kept a "stiff upper lip." She persisted by adding more classes to her schedule and updating her to-do list app. Chantelle had a list of 27 projects on the go at any given time, and she adhered to a rigid study schedule. Failure was not an option, and Chantelle knew there was no space for her to feel upset or fall behind in school. Her father and mother were already dealing with too much, and her little sister looked up her as a role model. Everyone was counting on Chantelle, so Chantelle pushed herself harder and harder. But in December, everything began falling apart.

1. What does the idiom *keep a stiff upper lip* mean in the text?

- (A) to not show that you are upset or bothered
- (B) to keep a steady expression on your face
- (C) to never give into the drama
- (D) to stay busy

2. What is Chantelle's perspective on her family's situation?

- (A) Her sister is too busy to give her advice.
- (B) Her parents are thrilled by the progress she is making at school.
- (C) She needs to stay focused and not get upset.
- (D) A schedule can solve any problem.

3. How is Chantelle affected or influenced by her family?

- (A) She works hard because they work hard.
- (B) She wants to get good grades like her parents did.
- (C) They push her to do her best always.
- (D) She knows she'll be in trouble if she doesn't succeed.

4. Which word best describes Chantelle's personality?

- (A) determined
- (B) unmotivated
- (C) resentful
- (D) gloomy

5. Which is an example of the "lemons" in Chantelle's life?

- (A) Chantelle's busy schedule
- (B) taking many classes
- (C) Chantelle having to clean houses
- (D) Chantelle's father losing his job

Name: ______________________________ Date: ______________

Directions: Read the text, and answer the questions.

As You Read

Write a ∞ wherever you make connections. Briefly describe your connections in the margins.

When Everything Falls Apart

On December 6th, Chantelle accidentally dropped her phone in a puddle of water. *No, no, no,* she silently screamed in her head as she tried to revive her phone. But it was literally dead in the water. With this tech demise, Chantelle lost her carefully structured project list and detailed calendar.

So, on December 8th, Chantelle missed an essay deadline for history class. She also forgot to pick up her little sister from school. Her parents scolded her behavior. Chantelle's stomach dropped when she thought of telling her parents about the zero she got on the history assignment. Ultimately, she decided not to tell them. *Best to ignore the zero completely,* she figured. *You have been totally useless lately, so get yourself together!*

Then, on December 10th, Chantelle was feeling under the weather and forgot about her calculus assignment. Her teacher offered her another chance to finish up the assignment, but Chantelle could already feel everything in her life falling apart.

1. What does the word *demise* mean as used in the text?

- (A) end
- (B) death
- (C) problem
- (D) puddle

2. What caused Chantelle to start missing her deadlines?

- (A) not using her calendar
- (B) not sticking to her detailed project list
- (C) breaking her phone by dropping it in a puddle
- (D) ignoring her responsibilities

3. Why do Chantelle's parents scold her?

- (A) They want Chantelle to work harder.
- (B) They are angry they are working so much.
- (C) They think Chantelle is being irresponsible.
- (D) Chantelle is getting bad grades.

4. What does this sentence reveal about Chantelle? *Chantelle's stomach dropped when she thought of telling her parents about the zero she got on the history assignment.*

- (A) She wishes to be a better student.
- (B) Her stomach is upset.
- (C) She is sick with the flu and needs to lie down.
- (D) She is afraid of disappointing her parents.

5. Why does the author include dates in this part of the story?

- (A) to sequence the building of negative events in Chantelle's week
- (B) to emphasize the effects of time passing on Chantelle's feelings
- (C) to highlight Chantelle's problem with negativity
- (D) to compare Chantelle's mistakes each day

Name: ______________________________ Date: ________________

Directions: Read the text, and answer the questions.

As You Read

Underline the places you connect, or emphathize, with what Chantelle is experiencing.

Asking for Help

During lunch, Chantelle paced up and down the hallways, trying to collect her thoughts. She kept beating herself up, thinking of every mistake she'd made and what a terrible daughter and sister she was turning out to be. Chantelle wandered, not watching her steps, when she collided into someone. It was Ms. Iona, the school's counselor and head of the debate squad. She took one look at Chantelle's face and, with a gentle smile, invited Chantelle to sit in her office.

Chantelle sat down in the office's red leather chair and felt mortified as tears began to stream down her face. It was like she couldn't stop them from happening, and Ms. Iona handed her a box of tissues.

"Chantelle, I've heard you've been going through a tough couple of weeks," Ms. Iona said. "Would you like to tell me about what's going on?"

Chantelle looked into Ms. Iona's kind eyes and found herself disclosing everything: her dad's unemployment, her fears around meeting deadlines, and the critical voice in her head that would not leave her alone. Ms. Iona simply listened and nodded her head, and as Chantelle talked, she felt a small weight leave her chest.

1. How does Ms. Iona affect Chantelle?

- (A) Chantelle likes Ms. Iona's office enough to spend time there.
- (B) Chantelle is embarrassed about her problems.
- (C) Chantelle feels comfortable talking about what is bothering her.
- (D) Ms. Iona offers good advice.

2. What does the word *disclosing* mean in the text?

- (A) helping
- (B) revealing
- (C) changing
- (D) observing

3. Which word does **not** use the prefix *dis–* correctly?

- (A) disband
- (B) discourage
- (C) disconnect
- (D) disread

4. What is one possible theme or message of the story?

- (A) Sharing personal things with other can be dangerous.
- (B) It is important to celebrate our differences.
- (C) We don't have to try and do everything on our own.
- (D) We should not forget the past but learn from it.

5. How does Ms. Iona help Chantelle? Use details from the story to support your answer.

____

____

____

Name: ______________________________ Date: ________________

As You Read

Place a star next to the most helpful information Ms. Iona gives Chantelle.

Being Kind to Herself

When Chantelle finished talking, Ms. Iona took a deep breath and said, "Thank you so much for sharing all that, Chantelle. It sounds like you're going through a difficult time right now, and maybe we can figure out a schedule for you that's less taxing. But I also want to suggest a way for you to deal with that voice in your head that's intent on criticizing and judging everything you do."

"But doesn't that voice keep me from failing?" Chantelle asked.

Ms. Iona shook her head, her black hair swinging from side to side. "You know, I had a voice very similar to yours in my head, too. The voice judged everything I did and was relentlessly critical of my actions. But then I had a mentor ask me if I'd ever talk to my son or my friends the way I do to myself. Instantly, I realized I'd never use the same language."

Chantelle thought of her little sister, Liza, and she could never picture herself talking to Liza the way she did to herself.

Ms. Iona continued, "My mentor suggested I work on being compassionate toward myself and treat myself with the same kindness I showed others. He taught me to mindfully notice when I was struggling and to remind myself that other people were struggling, too."

Ms. Iona's voice softened as she smiled gently at Chantelle. "We all make mistakes, and there are always other people who are going through similar challenges. It's helpful to remember this because we often feel alone when we're going through a tough time. But you're not alone, Chantelle, not even a little bit."

Chantelle felt tears welling up again in her eyes and fought to keep them back. She whispered, "I don't really know how to talk kindly to myself, Ms. Iona."

"Ah, I would gently disagree with you there. I've seen you with your younger sister, and I know you speak to her with kindness, warmth, and encouragement. Your tone and your words toward her are always kind. Being self-compassionate is about extending that same kindness and warmth to ourselves."

Ms. Iona reached into her desk and pulled out a sheet of paper, which she slid across the table to Chantelle. "This evening, try writing yourself a letter and using the same language you'd use if you were writing a letter to your sister. Remind yourself that you can make it through this tough time and that others share your pain."

Chantelle smiled at Ms. Iona and put the paper in her backpack. She thanked her counselor and left the office. In some ways, nothing had changed about her circumstances, but already Chantelle felt lighter and more optimistic.

Name: ______________________ Date: ______________

Directions: Read "Being Kind to Herself." Then, answer the questions.

1. What does the word *taxing* mean in the following sentence? *It sounds like you're going through a difficult time right now, and maybe we can figure out a schedule for you that's less taxing.*

(A) engaging
(B) appetizing
(C) emotional
(D) stressful

2. Why does Ms. Iona feel compassion for Chantelle?

(A) She had a similar experience when she was younger.
(B) She is a counselor and is supposed to care about students.
(C) She is an expert on self-compassion.
(D) She is uncomfortable with Chantelle crying in her office.

3. Which is the best example of a mentor?

(A) a friend
(B) a teacher
(C) a doctor
(D) a peer

4. Which line from the text best captures Chantelle's growth?

(A) "But doesn't that voice keep me from failing?"
(B) Chantelle felt tears welling up again in her eyes and fought to keep them back.
(C) Ms. Iona reached into her desk and pulled out a sheet of paper, which she slid across the table to Chantelle.
(D) In some ways, nothing had changed about her circumstances, but already, Chantelle felt lighter and more optimistic.

5. What does the line "But doesn't that voice keep me from failing?" reveal about Chantelle's thinking? Do you agree with her thinking?

____

____

____

6. Summarize Chantelle's visit to Ms. Iona's office by completing the chart. Use the words in the first column as guides for what information to include.

Somebody...	
Wanted...	
But...	
So...	
Then...	

Name: ____________________ Date: ____________

Directions: Reread "Being Kind to Herself." Then, respond to the prompt.

Imagine you are Chantelle. Write a letter to yourself, incorporating the advice from the school counselor, Ms. Iona.

Name: ______________________________ Date: ________________

A Letter to Myself

Dear Aubrey,

Yeah, it's kind of weird to start writing a letter to yourself, but I know you're going through a tough time. So, I wanted to write and chat with you like I would with Skylar or Julie.

You have a lot on your plate right now, and dude, the plate is practically flooding! I know you're doing your best to be a solid friend and not fall behind on your epic amount of work, but it's not really working out, is it? You missed that deadline last week, and then you completely forgot Julie's birthday, which was pretty upsetting. Right now, it feels like you just keep falling behind and letting people down.

All these things hurt right now, and this is a difficult chapter of your life, so I don't want to sugarcoat any of this stuff. But I also want to remind you there are definitely other students who are struggling to keep up, too. There are other people who also forgot birthdays this week. You are not alone. You are 100 percent not alone.

I also want you to know you can be kind to yourself. You are a kind friend to Julie; remember that time you took her out for pancakes after Alex broke her heart? You've learned from your mistake this time because you took the time to add Julie's birthday to your calendar, and you'll never forget again. Plus, this is the first time you have missed a deadline, and I have faith you will hit the rest of your deadlines.

It's okay to make mistakes—everyone does. I'm going to tell you to put your hand over your heart (yes, literally), which I know you think is kind of cheesy. But hey, give it a go—it feels comforting, admit it! ☺

You've got a good heart, Aubrey, and you will make it through this tough chapter. I know you will. I've got your back.

Love,
Aubrey

Name: ______________________________ Date: ____________________

Directions: Read "A Letter to Myself." Then, answer the questions.

1. What does the idiom *a lot on your plate* mean in the following sentence? *You have a lot on your plate right now.*

- (A) to have many obligations
- (B) to have a lot of food
- (C) to care about others
- (D) to be unorganized

2. What point of view is this letter written in?

- (A) first person
- (B) second person
- (C) third-person limited
- (D) third-person omniscient

3. What does the term *sugarcoat* mean in the following sentence? *So I don't want to sugarcoat any of this stuff.*

- (A) make it sound interesting
- (B) put a layer of sugar on it
- (C) make it seem worse than it really is
- (D) make it seem better than it really is

4. The line *I've got your back* suggests ______.

- (A) Aubrey is not a kind person
- (B) Aubrey is determined to be a better person
- (C) Aubrey will help her friends out from now on
- (D) Aubrey will be compassionate toward herself in the future

5. What is the tone of the letter? What words or phrases make you think this?

____

____

____

____

____

____

6. How did the writer show self-compassion in this letter? Support your ideas with details from the passage.

____

____

____

____

____

____

Name: ________________________________ Date: ________________

Directions: Closely reread the texts. Then, list the tips for self-compassion, and write how Aubrey applies these tips in her letter.

Close-Reading Texts

How to Practice Self-Compassion	A Letter to Myself
To practice self-compassion, it's key to treat oneself with kindness. This can sit in contrast with self-judgment. When people make mistakes, they may come to a crossroads in their minds. They have to choose between speaking gently or harshly to themselves. Talking to yourself with kindness, instead of judgment, means using warm and understanding language. Everyone makes mistakes, and it's helpful to not judge yourself too harshly when life goes awry. If you are going through a tough time, a simple phrase you can say to yourself is, "May I be kind to myself." You can also try placing your hand on your heart as a comforting gesture. Above all else, keep in mind that self-kindness is not about ignoring our struggles. Rather, it involves acknowledging our pain without criticism.	I also want you to know you can be kind to yourself. You are a kind friend to Julie; remember that time you took her out for pancakes after Alex broke her heart? You've learned from your mistake this time because you took the time to add Julie's birthday to your calendar, and you'll never forget again. Plus, this is the first time you have missed a deadline, and I have faith you will hit the rest of your deadlines. It's okay to make mistakes—everyone does. I'm going to tell you to put your hand over your heart (yes, literally), which I know you think is kind of cheesy. But hey, give it a go—it feels comforting, admit it!

Tips for Self-Compassion	Aubrey's Application

Name: ______________________________ Date: ______________

Directions: Closely reread the texts. Then, identify and record powerful adverbs and verbs that help you understand the mood of the texts.

Close-Reading Texts

When Everything Falls Apart	Asking for Help
On December 6th, Chantelle accidentally dropped her phone in a puddle of water. *No, no, no,* she silently screamed in her head as she tried to revive her phone. But it was literally dead in the water. With this tech demise, Chantelle lost her carefully structured project list and detailed calendar. So, on December 8th, Chantelle missed an essay deadline for history class. She also forgot to pick up her little sister from school. Her parents scolded her behavior. Chantelle's stomach dropped when she thought of telling her parents about the zero she got on the history assignment. Ultimately, she decided not to tell them. *Best to ignore the zero completely,* she figured. *You have been totally useless lately, so get yourself together!* Then, on December 10th, Chantelle was feeling under the weather and forgot about her calculus assignment. Her teacher offered her another chance to finish up the assignment, but Chantelle could already feel everything in her life falling apart.	During lunch, Chantelle paced up and down the hallways, trying to collect her thoughts. She kept beating herself up, thinking of every mistake she'd made and what a terrible daughter and sister she was turning out to be. Chantelle wandered, not watching her steps, when she collided into someone. It was Ms. Iona, the school's counselor and head of the debate squad. She took one look at Chantelle's face and, with a gentle smile, invited Chantelle to sit in her office. Chantelle sat down in the office's red leather chair and felt mortified as tears began to stream down her face. It was like she couldn't stop them from happening, and Ms. Iona handed her a box of tissues. "Chantelle, I've heard you've been going through a tough couple of weeks," Ms. Iona said. "Would you like to tell me about what's going on?" Chantelle looked into Ms. Iona's kind eyes and found herself disclosing everything: her dad's unemployment, her fears around meeting deadlines, and the critical voice in her head that would not leave her alone. Ms. Iona simply listened and nodded her head, and as Chantelle talked, she felt a small weight leave her chest.

	When Everything Falls Apart	Asking for Help
Powerful Adverbs		
Powerful Verbs		

Name: ______________________________ Date: ______________

Directions: Reread "How to Practice Self-Compassion" on page 212. Then, respond to the prompt.

Write yourself a letter in which you show yourself self-compassion. Follow the three key elements in the passage.

Name: ________________________________ Date: ________________

Directions: Review the texts from this unit. Then, follow the prompt.

Imagine your school counselor has asked you to create an informational flyer to help students practice about self-compassion. Include helpful tips, suggestions, and images to support your ideas.

Standards Correlations

Shell Education is committed to producing educational materials that are research and standards based. To support this effort, this resource is correlated to the academic standards of all 50 states, the District of Columbia, the Department of Defense Dependent Schools, and the Canadian provinces. A correlation is also provided for key professional educational organizations.

To print a customized correlation report for your state, visit our website at **www.tcmpub.com/administrators/correlations** and follow the online directions. If you require assistance in printing correlation reports, please contact the Customer Service Department at 1-800-858-7339.

Standards Overview

The Every Student Succeeds Act (ESSA) mandates that all states adopt challenging academic standards that help students meet the goal of college and career readiness. While many states already adopted academic standards prior to ESSA, the act continues to hold states accountable for detailed and comprehensive standards. Standardware is also used to develop standardized tests to evaluate students' academic progress. State standards are used in the development of our resources, so educators can be assured they meet state academic requirements.

College and Career Readiness

Today's college and career readiness (CCR) standards offer guidelines for preparing K–12 students with the knowledge and skills that are necessary to succeed in postsecondary job training and education. CCR standards include the Common Core State Standards as well as other state-adopted standards such as the Texas Essential Knowledge and Skills. The standards found on page 228 describe the content presented throughout the lessons.

TESOL and WIDA Standards

English language development standards are integrated within each lesson to enable English learners to work toward proficiency in English while learning content—developing the skills and confidence in listening, speaking, reading, and writing. The standards found in the digital resources describe the language objectives presented throughout the lessons.

Standards Correlations *(cont.)*

180 Days of Reading for Eighth Grade offers a full page of daily reading comprehension and word analysis practice activities for each day of the school year.

Every eighth grade unit provides questions and activities tied to a wide variety of language arts standards, providing students the opportunity for regular practice in reading comprehension, word recognition, and writing. The focus of the first two weeks in each unit alternates between nonfiction and fiction standards, with the third week focusing on both, as students read nontraditional texts and complete paired text activities.

Reading Comprehension
Read and comprehend complex literary and informational texts independently and proficiently.
Read closely to determine what the text says explicitly. Ask and answer questions about the text and make logical inferences; cite specific textual evidence when writing or speaking to support conclusions drawn from the text.
Determine central ideas or themes of a text and analyze their development; summarize the key supporting details and ideas.
Analyze how and why individuals, events, or ideas develop and interact over the course of a text.
Recognize and analyze genre-specific characteristics, structures, and purposes within and across diverse texts.
Use metacognitive skills to both develop and deepen comprehension of texts.
Analyze how two or more texts address similar themes or topics to build knowledge or to compare the approaches the authors take.
Analyze how two or more texts address similar themes or topics to build knowledge or to compare the approaches the authors take.
Assess how point of view or purpose shapes the content, style, and tone of texts.
Language and Vocabulary Acquisition
Determine or clarify the meaning of unknown and multiple-meaning words and phrases by using context clues, analyzing meaningful word parts, and consulting general and specialized reference materials, as appropriate.
Demonstrate understanding of figurative language, word relationships, and nuances in word meanings.
Demonstrate command of the conventions of standard English grammar, capitalization, punctuation, and spelling.
Writing
Produce clear and coherent writing in which the development, organization, and style are appropriate to task, purpose, genre, and audience.
Respond to and draw evidence from literary or informational texts to show analysis, reflection, and research.

Writing Rubric

Score students' written response using the rubric below. Display the rubric for students to reference as they write. A student version of this rubric is provided in the digital resources.

Points	Criteria
4	• Uses an appropriate organizational sequence to produce very clear and coherent writing. • Uses descriptive language that develops or clarifies ideas. • Engages the reader. • Uses a style very appropriate to task, purpose, and audience.
3	• Uses an organizational sequence to produce clear and coherent writing. • Uses descriptive language that develops or clarifies ideas. • Engages the reader. • Uses a style appropriate to task, purpose, and audience.
2	• Uses an organizational sequence to produce somewhat clear and coherent writing. • Uses some descriptive language that develops or clarifies ideas. • Engages the reader in some way. • Uses a style somewhat appropriate to task, purpose, and audience.
1	• Does not use an organized sequence; the writing is not clear or coherent. • Uses little descriptive language to develop or clarify ideas. • Does not engage the reader. • Does not use a style appropriate to task, purpose, or audience.
0	• Offers no writing or does not respond to the assignment presented.

References Cited

Gough, Philip B., and William E. Tunmer. 1986. "Decoding, Reading, and Reading Disability." *Remedial and Special Education* 7 (1): 6–10.

Marzano, Robert. 2010. "When Practice Makes Perfect...Sense." *Educational Leadership* 68 (3): 81–83.

National Reading Panel. 2000. *Report of the National Reading Panel: Teaching Children to Read. Report of the Subgroups*. Washington, D.C.: U.S. Department of Health and Human Services, National Institutes of Health.

Scarborough, Hollis S. 2001. "Connecting Early Language and Literacy to Later Reading (Dis)abilities: Evidence, Theory, and Practice." In *Handbook of Early Literacy Research*, edited by Susan B. Neuman and David K. Dickinson, 97–110. New York: Guilford.

Soalt, Jennifer. 2005. "Bringing Together Fictional and Informational Texts to Improve Comprehension." *The Reading Teacher* 58 (7): 680–683.

Answer Key

Unit 1

Week 1

Day 1 (page 11)

1. A **2.** B **3.** B **4.** C **5.** D

Day 2 (page 12)

1. B **2.** D **3.** B **4.** B **5.** C

Day 3 (page 13)

1. C **2.** D **3.** B **4.** B

5. Example: Because the ingredients were different in the United States compared to Italy, Italian American pizzamakers used paprika in their sausage instead of chilies. This created pepperoni.

Day 4 (page 15)

1. D **2.** B **3.** D **4.** B **5.** A

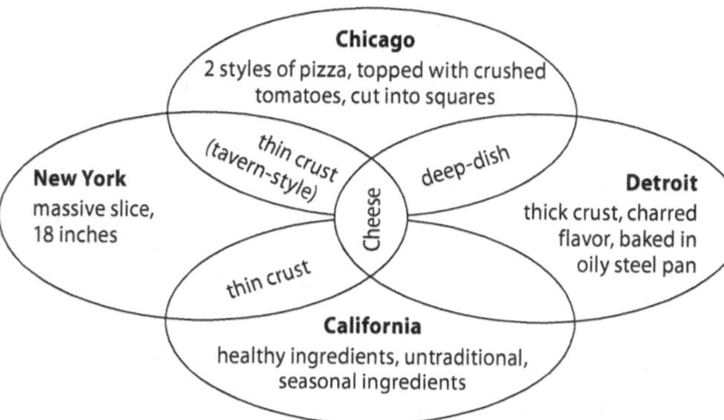

Day 5 (page 16)

Letters should explain which pizza is the best and why.

Week 2

Day 1 (page 17)

1. C **2.** D **3.** A **4.** A **5.** A

Day 2 (page 18)

1. C **2.** A **3.** D **4.** C

Day 3 (page 19)

1. D **2.** B

3. Example: It is important to spend time and learn from family members while you can.

4. Example: Guilia is now interested in learning to cook from her grandmother.

Day 4 (page 21)

1. A **2.** C **3.** D **4.** B **5.** D

6. Example: At first, Giulia does not feel as confident making pizzas as she does playing basketball. However, she does allow her grandmother to coach her through the process.

Day 5 (page 22)

Essays should describe times students tried and succeeded at things.

Week 3

Day 1 (page 24)

1. A **2.** C **3.** D **4.** B

5. Example: Ingredient substitutions could be added to the recipe.

Day 2 (page 25)

	Arrival in America	Pepperoni Power	Iconic Pizza Crust Recipe
Text Structure	chronological	description	sequence
Evidence	• Turn of the 20th century • After WWII • During the war	lists details about pepperoni	step-by-step instructions

Day 3 (page 26)

The History of Pizza: Many had little money to spend on food, so they needed to eat cheap meals that were quick to eat. These first pizzas had toppings including tomatoes, oil, and cheese.

Legends say that from that point on, it was called the *pizza margherita*. This type of pizza remains popular today.

Cooking with Nonna: I smile back, and I am grateful she picked the margherita pizza as our first pizza to cook together. The pizza the narrator makes uses few toppings and simple ingredients.

Day 4 (page 27)

Answers may include facts about pizza being an American food because it was created by Italian Americans, pizza evolving during World War II to suit American soldiers' and civilians' eating habits, and that major American cities have their own unique pizza styles.

Day 5 (page 28)

Recipes should include descriptions, ingredients, and steps.

Unit 2

Week 1

Day 1 (page 29)

1. B **2.** D **3.** A **4.** D **5.** C

Day 2 (page 30)

1. A **2.** D **3.** D **4.** B **5.** C **6.** C

Day 3 (page 31)

1. B **2.** D

3. Lewis and Tolkien both wrote series of books. They both grew up in England and taught at Oxford. Answers should explain why or why not that is enough to form a friendship.

4. Answers may include that the author uses a question to engage the reader or to show what the passage will attempt to answer.

Answer Key (cont.)

Day 4 (page 33)

1. C 2. A 3. C 4. B 5. B 6. D
7. Answers may include that they bonded over similar interests and experiences, they created their own book club, they began writing books and sharing their ideas, and they grew apart later in life.

Day 5 (page 34)

Answers may include questions about why the authors were jealous of each other and if they regret losing their friendship.

Week 2

Day 1 (page 35)

1. C 2. B 3. D 4. D 5. B

Day 2 (page 36)

1. D 2. C 3. D 4. A

Day 3 (page 37)

1. B 2. A
3. Answers may include that Bethany walks away from Kendall because she is upset and is going to cry.
4. Answers may include that Bethany is hiding something from Kendall because she does not trust her not to gossip.

Day 4 (page 39)

1. D 2. C 3. A 4. A 5. B 6. C
7. Answers should explain how one would apologize to a friend if they were Kendall.

Day 5 (page 40)

Stories should be about a friend asking Kendall about Bethany and the events that follow.

Week 3

Day 1 (page 42)

1. B 2. B 3. A 4. A 5. C
6. Answers may include more conflicts or details about the girls' high school experience.

Day 2 (page 43)

Lewis and Tolkien: Bonded over writing
Kendall and Bethany: Worked out their fight by talking
Both: Encouraged each other, had a fight, regretted their fight

Day 3 (page 44)

Central Idea: A strong friendship is baseed on support and time.
Swift and Gomez: They have made time for each other, they stay in contact, they publicly support each other and promote each other's work.
Bethany and Kendall: Video calls to stay in contact, learn how to navigate conflict, Kendall checks on Bethany daily during her parents' divorce.

Day 4 (page 45)

Time lines should include the who, what, when, where, why, and how.

Day 5 (page 46)

Answers may include communication, making time for each other, being supportive, having common interests, and talking through difficulties.

Unit 3

Week 1

Day 1 (page 47)

1. A 2. C 3. B 4. A 5. B

Day 2 (page 48)

1. A 2. D 3. D 4. C 5. A

Day 3 (page 49)

1. A 2. C 3. D 4. B
5. Example: The difference between public profiles and private profiles is who can see the posts. Public profiles have no restrictions on who can view posts, while private profiles have more control over who sees posts.

Day 4 (page 51)

1. C 2. A 3. B 4. C 5. A
6. **Problem:** Social media can take up too much of a user's time. **Solutions:** Make a plan for social media use, have a "screen-free" day, create and consume content, follow accounts that encourage you.

Day 5 (page 52)

Answers should be written in the form of a persuasive speech.

Week 2

Day 1 (page 53)

1. B 2. A 3. A 4. C 5. A

Day 2 (page 54)

1. D 2. D 3. C 4. A 5. D

Day 3 (page 55)

1. D 2. C 3. B 4. A
5. Example: Social media is making Aisha feel unsure of herself. For example, she cannot decide what to use for her first post.
6. Answers may include advice on being yourself, or posting her art and pictures of herself that make her feel good.

Day 4 (page 57)

1. D 2. B 3. A 4. C 5. B 6. D
7. Examples: **Social Media Posts:** People are just showing you a highlight reel of all the cool stuff in their life. Janet might have had a cool meal at a cool restaurant.
   Real Life: People don't often post about the tough day they had or the things they're actually struggling with, she might have also had a tough day at home.

Answer Key (cont.)

Day 5 (page 58)

Answers should include an image and a description of it.

Week 3

Day 1 (page 60)

1. C 2. D 3. A 4. D 5. B
6. Answers may include how comments can affect other users.

Day 2 (page 61)

Example:
Cause: Seeing fun moments in people's lives.
Effects: We may feel insecure and like our lives are less interesting, become unhappy, or feel like we have to be just as interesting.

Day 3 (page 62)

Example:
Common Idea or Theme: Social media can be a great way to share your creativity.
What Matters Most: I think your idea to share photographs is a neat idea, and I think people will really like them.
Using Social Media with Intention: Creating on social media may also look like posting creative photos or filming your own quick videos.
A benefit of social media is that they give us a chance to stretch our creative skills.
It might make social media more mindful and engaging for you to use!

Day 4 (page 63)

Replies should include details about how to be a kind consumer and creator online.

Day 5 (page 64)

Details about the app may include ways to promote positive comments, the importance of creativity, and being yourself.

Unit 4

Week 1

Day 1 (page 65)

1. C 2. A 3. D 4. B 5. B 6. A

Day 2 (page 66)

1. C 2. D 3. C 4. A 5. A 6. B

Day 3 (page 67)

1. C 2. D
3. Answers should explain which tips from the text they found most helpful.
4. Answers may include that people want to help a cause they are passionate about, to help their communities, to learn new skills, try something new, or to meet people with similar interests.

Day 4 (page 69)

1. C 2. A 3. D 4. A 5. C
6. **Central Idea:** There are ways to volunteer for everyone.
Example Details: Help clean up the environment; Help in your neighborhood; Help students in need.

Day 5 (page 70)

Letters should include a specific volunteer opportunity, interest in the opportunity, and the benefits of the opportunity for both the cause and the volunteers.

Week 2

Day 1 (page 71)

1. D 2. B 3. B 4. A 5. C

Day 2 (page 72)

1. D 2. C 3. B 4. A 5. B 6. B

Day 3 (page 73)

1. B 2. B 3. A 4. C
5. Answers should describe connections students made to the story.

Day 4 (page 75)

1. A 2. D 3. D 4. A
5. Ella encourages people to donate money to the polio cause.
6. Answers should describe how they would volunteer and how that compares to Ella Fitzgerald's work.

Day 5 (page 76)

Answers may include information about how Ella brought people together, helped support troops, and raised money for polio patients.

Week 3

Day 1 (page 78)

1. A 2. D 3. B 4. C
5. Answers should include suggestions to add to the flyer.
6. Answers may include to build friendships and gain experience.

Day 2 (page 79)

Volunteers during COVID-19: worked as nurses, delivered groceries, sent cards
Both: comforted people in need
Ella Fitzgerald during WWII: sang for soldiers

Day 3 (page 80)

Who Are Volunteers?: during, while, in times of crisis
A Heart Full of Happiness: with more time, until, when, while, when

Day 4 (page 81)

Answers might include the following:

- Ella Fitzgerald felt nervous and not good enough, but then she was strengthened by her music.
- She appreciated making money doing what she loved.
- She was passionate about how to help and to leave a positive legacy.

Answer Key *(cont.)*

Day 5 (82)
Storyboards may include Ella's performance at the Apollo, Ella receiving a phone call to audition with Chick, and Ella performing on live television to ask for donations for polio patients.

Unit 5

Week 1

Day 1 (page 83)
1. B **2.** D **3.** A **4.** C **5.** B

Day 2 (page 84)
1. C **2.** A **3.** D **4.** C **5.** D

Day 3 (page 85)
1. A **2.** D **3.** A **4.** B
5. Example: A person may choose to wear electronic textiles to better their health. For example, some electronic textiles can help a user learn about their sleep patterns.
6. Answers may include assessing exercise, health, and habits.

Day 4 (page 87)
1. C **2.** C **3.** C **4.** A **5.** D **6.** B
7. Causes may include: she focused on the users, she interviewed people, people thought traditional hearing aids were unattractive, people with arthritis had a hard time changing the batteries.
Effects may include: Dr. Heiss's design looks like a crystal, her design includes a rechargable battery

Day 5 (page 88)
Pitches should give a detailed description of a new type of smart clothing.

Week 2

Day 1 (page 89)
1. B **2.** D **3.** B **4.** C **5.** A **6.** D

Day 2 (page 90)
1. C **2.** D **3.** D **4.** A

Day 3 (page 91)
1. D **2.** A **3.** B
4. Jaden responds to his conflict by trying to use his smart clothing with purpose.
5. Jaden will improve his running speed by using the data from his smart socks and his human coach.

Day 4 (page 93)
1. B **2.** A **3.** B **4.** C **5.** C **6.** B
Example: Somebody: Jaden; Wanted: He wants to get a bunch of smart clothes; But: His dad asks him to think about the "why" behind it; So: Jaden tries out some new smart socks his dad gave him; Then: Jaden decides to keep the smart socks but get rid of some other smart clothes.

Day 5 (page 94)
Answers should be in the form of persuasive speeches and include details from the text.

Week 3

Day 1 (page 96)
1. D **2.** C **3.** A **4.** D
5. Answers should include wearable technology that have come out since 2010.

Day 2 (page 97)

	Smart Watches, Smart Rings	Medical Wearables
Adjectives	smart, deeper, discrete, powerful, more	attractive, tiny, shiny, confident, regular
Adverbs	deeply	discreetly

Answers may include that the language is positive and optimistic.

Day 3 (page 98)
Smart Socks: pressure applied to feet while running, pace, distance
Smartwatches: steps, calories burned, blood oxygen levels, sleep routine
Smart Rings: sleep patterns, heart rate, body temperature

Day 4 (page 99)
Essays should include an opinion and reasons and evidence to support it.

Day 5 (page 100)
The award should include the hearing aid and necklace designed by Dr. Heiss.

Unit6

Week 1

Day 1 (page 101)
1. B **2.** C **3.** B **4.** D **5.** A **6** B

Day 2 (page 102)
1. D **2.** C **3.** A **4.** C

Day 3 (page 103)
1. A **2.** B **3.** C **4.** C
5. Answers may include that music creates emotional connections and can affect memories.

Day 4 (page 105)
1. B **2.** A **3.** C **4.** C
5. Answers may include that music helps people trust one another, singing and listening to music releases oxytocin, music can connect people across generations, and music can increase empathy.
6 Answers should describe times when music helped students connect with others.

Answer Key (cont.)

Day 5 (page 106)

Answers should include the title of a song, the artist/singer, a description of the memory it recalls, and a description of the way it makes the student feel.

Week 2

Day 1 (page 107)

1. D **2.** A **3.** C **4.** B **5.** B **6.** A

Day 2 (page 108)

1. C **2.** B **3.** C **4.** C **5.** D

Day 3 (page 109)

1. B **2.** D **3.** C **4.** A

5. Answers may include that Melinda is beginning to miss music.

6. Answers may include that the mood is regretful.

Day 4 (page 111)

1. C **2.** A **3.** B **4.** C **5.** B

7. Answers may vary, and examples are given.

Theme: Be careful what you wish for.
Detail 1: '"Are you ready to cry 'uncle' yet, my musically devoid friend?' a chipper voice asked behind me."
Detail 2: "She said, 'I figure this experiment has probably gone on long enough, so there's no need to drag this out.' She snapped her fingers, and my whole world went *poof* in a cloud of dark gray smoke."
Detail 3: "It didn't matter whether it was real or not because the sound was music to my ears, and either way I would be more careful about telling my complaints to Eun-Ji!"

Day 5 (page 112)

Answers should include Eun-Ji teaching her friend a lesson about complaining.

Week 3

Day 1 (page 114)

1. B **2.** B **3.** D **4.** D **5.** C

6. Example: The author's opinion of the three American songs is that they are simple, and that helps make them catchy.

Day 2 (page 115)

Examples:

The Soundrack of Our Lives: endless, integral part of our lives, compelling reasons, lights up different parts of the human brain, deeply connected

Our Musical Bonds: trust hormone, lift our levels of this trust hormone, both trust and generosity strengthen connections between people, great meaning

Day 3 (page 116)

Example:

	This Is a Sad, Sad World	**A World of Music**
Mood	regretful	grateful
Words and Phrases that Reveal the Mood	sauntered instead shuffled by me with his gloomy head down blaring but there was no one fallen hopelessly out of rhythm—and with it, had lost some of its soul, too	brand-new morning *"Was it all a dream?"* most beautiful sound in the world—the melodic *chirp-chirp-chirp* of my blue jay the sound was music to my ears
How do the moods compare? The mood shifts from regretful to grateful. The narrator is regretting her wish, and then she is very grateful to hear music again.		

Day 4 (page 117)

Answers should describe why the song is a classic and what students think or feel when they hear it.

Day 5 (page 118)

Flyers may include muted colors, images that reflect participants at the dance feeling gloomy, and no mention of music.

Unit 7

Week 1

Day 1 (page 119)

1. D **2.** B **3.** C **4.** D **5.** D

Day 2 (page 120)

1. A **2.** B **3.** A **4.** B **5.** C **6.** A

Day 3 (page 121)

1. C **2.** A **3.** D **4.** B

5. Answers should be supported by reasons and details from the text.

Day 4 (page 123)

1. C **2.** D **3.** D **4.** A **5.** B **6.** B

7. Example:

Author's Perspective: Kabaddi, chess boxing, and octopush are unique and interesting games.

Detail 1: The player must keep repeating "kabaddi, kabaddi" or they're out!

Detail 2: Chess boxing is a hybrid sport that pairs two (seemingly incongruous) activities together.

Detail 3: Most people have seen ice or field hockey in action, but octopush takes the pucks down to the floor of a swimming pool.

Day 5 (page 124)

Flyers should include details from the text and explanations for why the sports should be played at school.

Answer Key *(cont.)*

Week 2

Day 1 (page 125)

1. D **2.** B **3.** C **4.** A **5.** D

Day 2 (page 126)

1. A **2.** B **3.** D **4.** D **5.** B

Day 3 (page 127)

1. C **2.** C **3.** A

4. Example: A "remix" means to combine different parts of something to make something new. In this case, a new sport.

5. Example: Eloise and Ravi plan their sport by researching different sports around the world and choosing rules they like.

Day 4 (page 129)

1. B **2.** A **3.** C **4.** D

5. **Eloise:** focused, supportive
Both: creative, determined
Ravi: overly excited

Day 5 (page 130)

Responses should include details about playing the game.

Week 3

Day 1 (page 132)

1. D **2.** A **3.** A **4.** B **5.** C **6.** D

7. Answers should include details from the text to support student thinking.

Day 2 (page 133)

Example:
Mood: humorous
A Postcard from England: What a city! So big! So much tea!; Sandie, every year for this event, people chase a double Gloucester cheese down this unbelievably steep hill; which seems completely absurd, don't you think?
Ravi and Eloise Create a New Sport: Then, we move to the pasta-eating station, where you must first wear a papier-mâché mask—and then try to eat as much pasta as you humanly can in three minutes.; The team who has won the most rounds will be our ultimate Tag with Pasta champion!; This might be the most ridiculous game I've ever heard of.

Day 3 (page 134)

Chess Boxing: Rounds last three minutes; combines two different activities.
Kabaddi: Players must tag other players.

Day 4 (page 135)

Postcards should include details about the game, such as wearing a papier-mâché mask while eating pasta, playing tag, the players being very competitive, and that the game was so fun that it lasted twenty rounds instead of seven.

Day 5 (page 136)

Flyers should include details about how the sports are unique.

Unit 8

Week 1

Day 1 (page 137)

1. B **2.** A **3.** A **4.** C **5.** B

Day 2 (page 138)

1. B **2.** D **3.** C **4.** C **5.** A

Day 3 (page 139)

1. D **2.** D

3. Example: Different species live in different parts of the rainforest because each layer has different features. For example, some birds will live in the emergent layer so they can fly.

4. Example: Because the rainforest layers have different features, different animals live there.

5. Answers should include one of the following layers: emergent layer, canopy, understory, or the forest floor.

Day 4 (page 141)

1. B **2.** B **3.** B **4.** C

5. Examples: produce medicine, store large amounts of carbon dioxide, produce oxygen, generate a large amount of moisture that supports the water cycle, provide food, provide shelter for indigenous communities.

Day 5 (page 142)

Reports may include details about the layers of the rainforest, the ways rainforests support human life, and the problem with deforestation.

Week 2

Day 1 (page 143)

1. D **2.** C **3.** A **4.** A **5.** D **6.** B

Day 2 (page 144)

1. A **2.** A **3.** D **4.** B **5.** B

Day 3 (page 145)

1. C **2.** B

3. Example: The author builds suspense by having the birds sing a song that the narrator's father sang to her before he passed away.

4. Example: The narrator is frightened by the birds' communication. However, the birds want to welcome her because they were connected to her father.

Day 4 (page 147)

1. D **2.** C **3.** A **4.** C **5.** C **6.** D

7. Example: The backstory helps readers feel empathy for the characters and understand the purpose of the trip to the Amazon.

Day 5 (page 148)

Diary entries should include details about the narrator's grandmother and the relationship between the grandmother and the mother.

Answer Key *(cont.)*

Week 3

Day 1 (page 150)

1. B 2. D 3. A 4. C 5. A 6. D
7. Deforestation is happening because humans are cutting down rainforests. People cut down trees to for logging and make room to livestock grazing.

Day 2 (page 151)

Rainforest Layers: lush, dense, home to many animals, abundant food
Many Talking Birds: colorful birds
Both: Many birds live there, lots of fruit

Day 3 (page 152)

Examples: extinction of rainforest species, deforestation, climate change.

Day 4 (page 153)

Itineraries may include: exploring the layers of the Amazon Rainforest, touring the Amazon River, and bird watching.

Day 5 (page 154)

Letters should include reasons why both temperate and tropical rainforests are important.

Unit 9

Week 1

Day 1 (page 155)

1. B 2. A 3. D 4. A 5. B 6. C

Day 2 (page 156)

1. B 2. C 3. D 4. D 5. C

Day 3 (page 157)

1. A 2. B 3. B 4. C
5. Example: The ofrendas are significant because they represent the person who has passed away.
6. Example: It is an important holiday because it helps people remember loved ones they have lost.

Day 4 (page 159)

1. A 2. D 3. D 4. C 5. B
6. **Diwali:** called the "Festival of Lights," five day festival, celebrated by Hindus, Jains, and Sikhs, signifies the triumph of light over darkness, people light lanterns
   Both: festivals in India bring people together
   Holi: celebrates end of winter, called the "Festival of Color", people throw colored powders at each other

Day 5 (page 160)

Letters should include details about a holiday and compare the holiday to Diwali or Holi.

Week 2

Day 1 (page 161)

1. B 2. A 3. D 4. C 5. B

Day 2 (page 162)

1. A 2. C 3. B 4. B 5. A 6. C

Day 3 (page 163)

1. D 2. B
3. Li Jie and his mother want different career paths for Li Jie.
4. Both Li Jie and Benjamin struggle at times with their new languages, but they both support each other.

Day 4 (page 165)

1. A 2. D 3. D 4. B 5. C 6. A
7. Example: The ending of the story helps develop the theme because the boys are becoming good friends through the goal of practicing a new language. In the end, they have decided to continue to be friends and practice speaking in English and Mandarin.

Day 5 (page 166)

Answers should be written from the point of view of either Li Jie or Benjamin.

Week 3

Day 1 (page 168)

1. C 2. A 3. B 4. D
5. They are festivals that take place around the world.
6. Answers should be supported by reasons.

Day 2 (page 169)

Example:

Loy Krathong Festival	Similarities	Diwali and Holi
Loy Krathong is a day to give thanks to the goddess of water, Pra Mae Khongkha.	Share food and have large feasts	Celebrates light overcoming darkness
Celebrated in Thailand	Light candles/ lamps	Celebrated in India
Celebrate with floating krathongs down the water.	Named "Festival of Lights"	Light oil lamps called diyas.

Day 3 (page 170)

Example:
Common Central Idea: Some holidays are celebrated with costumes.
Details: I love to get creative and craft a costume no one's seen or done yet; It is an annual and colorful celebration with costumes, dancing, and lots of food; Parades of people, dressed in elegant finery, glide through the canals of the city by gondola

Day 4 (page 171)

Summaries should include details from one of the holidays in the graphic on page 167.

Day 5 (page 172)

Invitations should include the names of the holidays, the purposes of the holidays, and the activities planned for celebrating.

Answer Key *(cont.)*

Unit 10

Week 1

Day 1 (page 173)

1. D 2. A 3. C 4. B 5. B 6. D

Day 2 (page 174)

1. D 2. A 3. A 4. B 5. C 6. D

Day 3 (page 175)

1. B 2. D 3. A 4. A
5. Example: Rendville is an important small town because it has a legacy of Black leadership.
6. Example: The central idea of the text is that a small town can have a large historical impact.

Day 4 (page 177)

1. C 2. D 3. D 4. B
5. Example: People visit daily, so she does not feel lonely.
6. Examples:
   Gilbert: coolest town
   Monowi: population of one
   International Dark Sky Park: far from city lights
   Elsie Eiler: mayor and treasurer

Day 5 (page 178)

Questions may be focused on her many jobs, paying her bills, community, and loneliness. Answers may be focused on her being the sole resident, interest in the town, love of the tavern, and missing her husband.

Week 2

Day 1 (page 179)

1. D 2. A 3. D 4. A

Day 2 (page 180)

1. C 2. C 3. C 4. B 5. D

Day 3 (page 181)

1. B 2. D
3. Example: Shira's advice is important to the narrator because the narrator wants to make friends. Shira's advice is helpful in making new friends, so the narrator reflects on her advice.
4. Answers may focus on how to fit in at a new school or in a new town.

Day 4 (page 183)

1. B 2. C 3. A 4. B 5. B 6. B

Event	Change
Shira advises the narrator to be "interested" instead of "interesting."	The narrator reflects on how he talks to others.
The narrator spends time with his cousin, Shira.	The narrator makes two new friends, Cyrus and Sebastian.
The narrator has his first day of school.	The narrator realizes he already knows his math teacher and feels more comfortable.

Day 5 (page 184)

Narratives should include Shira's advice (be interested, not interesting), a conversation between the narrator and Shira in dialogue format, and the narrator reflecting on her advice.

Week 3

Day 1 (page 186)

1. D 2. B 3. A 4. A 5. D
6. Example: This resource could help people better understand the different types of places people live.

Day 2 (page 187)

1. Elier is the town's mayor, treasurer, clerk, secretary, and librarian. Elier files paperwork every year, and there is a local government.
2. Answers should include information comparing the texts' structures, language, purposes, and any other things related to the author's craft.

Day 3 (page 188)

Examples: the narrator shares a common interest in basketball with his cousin and new friends; Cyrus and the narrator have a shared interest in beating Shira and basketball; Shira, Cyrus and the narrator all live in Wellspring.

Day 4 (page 189)

Essays should be focused on how the character is complicated. Internal struggles may focus on missing Boston, feeling strange about people knowing his name when he goes out, starting a new school, but also liking the gelato, learning to be "interested" instead of "interesting," and making new friends.

Day 5 (page 190)

Advertisements should include key information about the town and encourage tourists to visit it.

Unit 11

Week 1

Day 1 (page 191)

1. A 2. A 3. C 4. D 5. D

Day 2 (page 192)

1. C 2. A 3. D 4. C 5. B 6. C

Day 3 (page 193)

1. C 2. D
3. Example: Sharing money is a good way to support causes that are important to you.
4. Example: The three categories are connected because the more money you put in one category, the less you will have to put into the other categories.

Answer Key (cont.)

Day 4 (page 195)

1. B 2. B 3. D 4. A 5. B
6. Answers should list items and dollar amounts. They should add up to $100. Example:

Spend		Save	Share
Needs Notebook: $5 Pencils: $2	**Wants** Comic book: $13 Latte: $8 Flip flops: $22	**Future Investment** Trip to Disney World: $35	**Person/ Group Close to Your Heart** Animal Shelter: $15

Day 5 (page 196)

Answers may include how to budget for things that are a priority first, such as needs and significant wants.

Week 2

Day 1 (page 197)

1. A 2. A 3. B 4. A 5. D

Day 2 (page 198)

1. D 2. D 3. A 4. B 5. C 6. D

Day 3 (page 199)

1. A 2. A 3. C
4. Example: Deja sees her aunt as a mentor. Deja listens to her advice and reflects on what she says about budgeting.

Day 4 (page 201)

1. A 2. A 3. D 4. C
5. Answers may include that she trusts her niece will turn her spending around or that she and Deja are very close.
6. Example:

Theme: It can be difficult to set a budget, but it is worth it.
Detail 1: I think you have touched on one of the most difficult parts of saving money, because, yes, it does involve changing some of our habits.
Detail 2: In many ways, it was empowering for me to choose new financial goals.
Detail 3: I liked to have fun with my friends, and it was sometimes tough for me to tell them I could not afford to do all the activities they wanted to do.

Day 5 (page 202)

Time line events for Aunt Merritt may include her separation, starting her own budget, setting new goals, and going on the Colorado trip. Time line events for Deja may include starting a budget, needing help with her budget, and going on the Colorado trip.

Week 3

Day 1 (page 204)

1. D 2. B 3. D 4. C 5. B 6. A
7. Example: If too much is spent in one category, a budgeter can spend less money in another category.

Day 2 (page 205)

Flexibilities of a Budget	
Creating a Budget: Part 2	deciding how much to allocate in different categories
Getting Flexible	letting go of take-out tacos to meet a target goal
Samir's Monthly Budget	spending less on paint supplies and more on coffee

Day 3 (page 206)

Answers should include logical reasons for the rankings.

Day 4 (page 207)

Essays should include a claim about money management and evidence to prove the claim.

Day 5 (page 208)

Budget templates should include categories for spending, saving, and sharing.

Unit 12

Week 1

Day 1 (page 209)

1. C 2. B 3. D 4. B 5. D

Day 2 (page 210)

1. B 2. C 3. C 4. C 5. A 6. D

Day 3 (page 211)

1. A 2. B 3. A
4. Example: It may be beneficial to reflect on our own weak points because it helps us see ourselves clearly. It can also help us see that we are not alone, and others may have experienced similar difficulties.
5. Example: Self-pity is focused on problems, while self-compassion is focused on reflection and connection to ourselves. When we pity ourselves, we focus on the negative. When we are compassionate, we consider we are not alone and can move forward with our goals.

Day 4 (page 213)

1. D 2. A 3. B
4. Answers may include that it is easier to forgive your own shortcomings when remembering that other people struggle in the same way or that it helps to give you more perspective on a situation.

Key Element	Situation	What You Might Say
Self-kindness	when I make a mistake	"May I be kind to myself."
Common Humanity	when I am going through a difficult time	"Other people have experienced this, too." "I am not alone."
Mindfulness	when I have negative feelings and thoughts	"This hurts." "This is a moment of suffering."

Answer Key *(cont.)*

Day 5 (page 214)

Letters should give personal examples of times when they have or could use at least one of the key elements of self-compassion.

Week 2

Day 1 (page 215)

1. A **2.** C **3.** A **4.** A **5.** D

Day 2 (page 216)

1. B **2.** C **3.** C **4.** D **5.** A

Day 3 (page 217)

1. C **2.** B **3.** D **4.** C

5. Example: Ms. Iona helps Chantelle by giving her a space to let her feelings out.

Day 4 (page 219)

1. D **2.** A **3.** B **4.** D

5. Example: Chantelle thinks it is helpful to be tough on herself. I do not agree with her thinking because it's harder to recover from your mistakes if you're too hard on yourself.

Somebody	Chantelle
Wanted	She wanted to deal with all of her problems by herself.
But	Ms. Iona, the school counselor, invited Chantelle to into her office to talk.
So	Chantelle began disclosing, or revealing, her problems.
Then	Ms. Iona taught Chantelle how to use self-compassion when dealing with difficult issues, and she challenged her to write herself a letter.

Day 5 (page 220)

Letters should be and in first-person point of view. Answers should include ideas from "Being Kind to Herself," such as speaking to yourself with encouragement, warmth, and kindness the way you would your little sister.

Week 3

Day 1 (page 222)

1. A **2.** A **3.** D **4.** D

5. Answers may include that the tone of the letter is compassionate, understanding, informal, or friendly.

6. Example: Aubrey shows herself self-compassion acknowledging the struggles she is facing, reminding herself that she is not alone, and reminding herself that she is a good friend.

Day 2 (page 223)

Tips for Self-Compassion	Aubrey's Application
Talk to yourself with kindness. Say, "May I be kind to myself." Put your hand over your heart. Acknowledge pain without judgement.	Reminds herself she is a good friend to Julie. Tells herself she'll use her calendar for deadlines. Reminds herself it is ok to make mistakes, everyone does. Directs herself to put her hand over her heart for comfort.

Day 3 (page 224)

	When Everything Falls Apart	Asking for Help
Powerful Adverbs	accidentally, silently, already	simply
Powerful Verbs	dropped, forgot, screamed, ignore, scolded	paced, collect, chantelle, invited, disclosing, listened, felt, beating herself up

Day 4 (page 225)

Letters should include details about the three key elements: self-kindness, common humanity, and mindfulness.

Day 5 (page 226)

Flyers should offer tips and suggestions and include images to support them.

Digital Resources

Accessing the Digital Resources

The digital resources can be downloaded by following these steps:

1. Go to **www.tcmpub.com/digital**
2. Use the 13-digit ISBN number to redeem the digital resources.
3. Respond to the question using the book.
4. Follow the prompts on the Content Cloud website to sign in or create a new account.
5. The content redeemed will appear on your My Content screen. Click on the product to look through the digital resources. All file resources are available for download. Select files can be previewed, opened, and shared.

For questions and assistance with your ISBN redemption, please contact Shell Education.

email: customerservice@tcmpub.com

phone: 800-858-7339

Contents of the Digital Resources

- Standards Correlations
- Writing Rubric
- Fluency Rubric
- Class and Individual Analysis Sheets